This book may be kept

FOURTEEN DAYS

A fine will be charged for each day the book is kept overtime.

NOV. 6 1991		
MAY 1 4 1992 MAY 2 0 1992		
APR. 6 1993 APR. 2 0 1993		
MAY 1 9 1993		
JAN 1 9 1994		
8/16/95		

GAYLORD 142   PRINTED   3.A.

MINNESOTA

D1167057

DISCIPLES IN

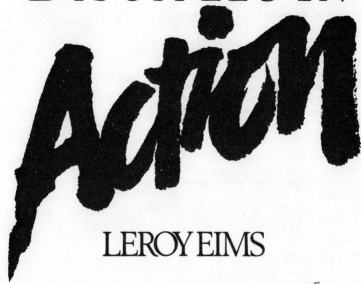

LEROY EIMS

226.607
E 3487
31939

NAVPRESS
A MINISTRY OF THE NAVIGATORS
P.O. Box 6000, Colorado Springs, CO 80934

VICTOR BOOKS

a division of SP Publications, Inc.
WHEATON, ILLINOIS 60187
Offices also in Fullerton, California ● Whitby, Ontario, Canada ● Amersham-on-the-Hill, Bucks, England

While this book is designed for your personal profit and enjoyment, it is also intended for group study. A Leader's Guide with Multiuse Transparency Masters is available from your local bookstore or from Victor Books, P.O. Box 1825, Wheaton, IL 60187.

The Navigators is an international, evangelical
Christian organization. Jesus Christ gave his
followers the Great Commission to go and make
disciples (Matthew 28:19). The aim of The
Navigators is to help fulfill that commission by
multiplying laborers for Christ in every nation.

NavPress is the publishing ministry of The
Navigators. NavPress publications are tools to
help Christians grow. Although publications
alone cannot make disciples or change lives,
they can help believers learn biblical discipleship, and apply what they learn to their lives
and ministries.

© 1981 by LeRoy Eims
All rights reserved, including translation
Library of Congress Catalog Card Number:
81-80284
NavPress ISBN: 8-89109-477-6
14779/595

Scripture Press
ISBN: 0-88207-343-56-2343

Unless otherwise identified, Scripture quotations
are from *The Holy Bible, New International
Version,* © 1978 by the New York International
Bible Society. Other versions used are the *New
American Standard Bible* (NASB), © 1960,
1962, 1963, 1968, 1971, 1972, 1973, 1975 by
the Lockman Foundation; *The New Testament in
Modern English, Revised Edition* by J. B. Phillips
(PH), © 1958, 1960, 1972 by J. B. Phillips,
published by The Macmillan Company, New
York and Collins Publishers, London; and the
King James Version (KJV).

Printed in the United States of America

Dedication

To Miss A. Wetherell Johnson,
founder of Bible Study Fellowship,
whose love for and study of the Scriptures
has led to hundreds of thousands of God's people
being grounded in the word of God.

Contents

Foreword

As I was leading a home Bible study through the Acts of the Apostles, LeRoy Eims kindly invited me to write a foreword to this book. As I perused the manuscript, my mind was stirred and my heart warmed. Here was the outworking in the early church of the revolutionary principles the Lord Jesus taught his twelve co-workers.

In the four gospels, Jesus disclosed God's strategy for reaching people throughout the world. His strategy is so different from our churches' preoccupation with programs that it seems unnoticed in the rush and bustle of modern church life, cluttered with crash programs. If only each church today would follow God's strategy! The consequences would be nothing short of revolutionary. The principles brought out with stark clarity in this book reveal the essentials for establishing each church as an equipping center where each Christian can be developed and trained to his or her full potential for ministry.

Any advance for the kingdom of God has a price tag. The cost for the local church is being willing to move the accent away from programs to the principles of discipleship.

May our sovereign Lord use this book to reorient many, many churches by causing them to adopt this lost art of disciplemaking, and to thrust out a great number of disciplemakers among the nations to win them for Christ.

Dr. Dudley Foord
Christ Church St. Ives
Sydney, Australia

Preface

In the early spring of 1956, Dawson Trotman (founder of The Navigators) asked my wife and me to go to Omaha, Nebraska, and begin the Navigator ministry in the Midwest. As I thought about that assignment, I was burdened to pray that God would begin a mighty work in the lives of thousands of people. I began asking him to make a strong impact on that part of the world through the knowledge of Christ and by helping us to raise up men and women who would be true disciples of Christ. From those prayers came the idea of doing a thorough personal study of the Book of Acts. I wanted to discover the secrets which enabled the first-century Christians to fill Jerusalem with their teaching, to minister so effectively that all the Jews and Greeks in the province of Asia heard the Lord's word, and to turn the world upside down. So I began my first real study of the Book of Acts.

Since then I have restudied Acts half a dozen times. Each study netted a fresh catch of new insights. I completed my last study in the summer of 1978. I was speaking at various Navigator conferences and training programs throughout Europe and had some time on my hands. I was free during the hours when I was not speaking because all the meetings were conducted in Norwegian, Swedish, French, Finnish, or Dutch. So to make use of my free time, I plunged into another study of Acts and spent five to eight hours a day sifting through its pages and jotting down the fresh truths the Lord revealed. In the providence of God, I had all of my previous study notes with me. During those conference days, I combined all my notes and this book emerged.

If one wants to study leadership training, one would do well to study the four Gospels—Matthew, Mark, Luke, and John. In those four books we observe how Jesus trained the Twelve. His redemptive ministry was accomplished by his death on the cross and by his resurrection from the tomb. But his day-to-day ministry of the word focused on the training of the apostles whom he had chosen.

Toward the end of his days on earth, Jesus gave the Twelve *their* commission. They were to go out into the world to preach the gospel to every creature and to make disciples of all nations. Just as we must study the Gospels to learn the art of training leaders, so we must study the Book of Acts to learn disciplemaking. The Book of Acts is the Holy Spirit's record of how the apostles went about accomplishing the mission on which Christ had sent them.

This book approaches Acts from the standpoint of discipleship. It is not a verse-by-verse exposition of Acts. It is not a study of the history and environment in which the apostles functioned. It is a study of how they went about their evangelism, how they followed up new believers and helped them to become established in the faith, how they equipped future workers for the kingdom of God, and how the apostles trained the leaders who would eventually replace them. These are the principles we need to focus on in our ministry for Christ today.

As the story unfolds, applications are freely made to other aspects of the life of discipleship. An effort is made to focus our attention back to the beginnings—back to our spiritual roots—back to the foundations that were laid by the apostles of Christ as they labored under the blessing, power, and guidance of the Holy Spirit. We need the same blessing, power, and guidance to be effective for Christ.

I'm sending this book out with the prayer that God will use it to deepen our devotion to Christ, sharpen our effectiveness for Christ, focus our lives to the glory of Christ, and impart a clearer vision of what each of us might do to reach the world of people for whom he died.

LeRoy Eims

1
Men of Action

ACTS POINTS US back to men of action, doers, men on the march. Acts does not record the meditations of the apostles, but their acts. The book's title suggests movement, progress, and initiative. It sets a tone. This title points to our first principle of discipleship: we need to be disciples in action.

Today, when we hear of temporary agreements among church and mission leaders to stop sending missionaries into the world with the only message of hope, peace, and salvation—the gospel of Jesus Christ—it is refreshing to reread a book that pictures men consumed with the idea. The apostles were forever lifting up their eyes and looking over the fence into the next fields which were overripe and ready to harvest. We do not find our ancestors in the faith sitting cross-legged in the clover of Palestine. They were not indolent and dreamy men. Nor do we find them sitting in classrooms speculating and theorizing. They had their orders. They were up and doing.

Today, much is being taught about the witness who waits to be prompted by an unregenerate sinner. Some teachers refer us to Peter, who gave us the sensible command to "in your hearts set apart Christ as Lord. Always be prepared to give an answer to everyone who asks you to give the reason for the hope that you have" (1 Peter 3:15). Of course! But that's the beauty of the Bible. It is so finely tuned, so delicately balanced, that to remove one verse, or to exaggerate or minimize another, distorts the Bible's overall teaching. We must balance an emphasis on waiting to answer with Paul's charge to "preach the Word; be prepared in season and out of season" (2 Timothy 4:2).

We also hear much about "friendship evangelism" today. This promotes the notion that our job is to be a friendly, passive person who waits to be asked a leading question before speaking about the Lord. True, another person sometimes asks a question that opens the way for a presentation of the gospel. It has happened to me. But if we buy that concept and build a witnessing lifestyle on it, we will find ourselves sitting idly by like loungers in the park. When we open our Bibles we find a book that tells us about the apostles' actions, not their reactions. They were constantly going, doing, praying, preaching, and working.

What did God use to develop that mentality? What made them men of action? For three years they walked with one who was a "doer/teacher." Luke wrote about "all that Jesus began to do and to teach" (Acts 1:1).

Jesus is the greatest teacher the world has ever seen. He had a way with words that shattered false beliefs, turned men around and set them on a new course that was completely foreign to human values—a course of sacrifice, suffering, and hardship. His followers marched gladly into the face of persecution. His words raised the dead, calmed the seas, and sent demons scurrying. No man ever spoke like him.

Jesus was also a doer. His witness was straightforward and positive. Ask yourself, humanly speaking, *How long had he known the woman at the well?* (see John 4:1-42), or Zacchaeus? (see Luke 19:1-10). Had he established a long-standing friendship? No. If we look at the life of our Lord and the apostles he chose, led, and trained, we find the Holy Spirit painting a different picture than the "reaction" philosophy of some of our contemporaries. Jesus was a man of action.

The Worth of the Individual

The first verses of Acts reveal another important principle of discipleship: the worth of the individual. In the first verse of Acts we meet Theophilus. Luke also wrote the Gospel of Luke to Theophilus so that he might "know the certainty of the things" he had been taught (Luke 1:4). Imagine that! Two complete books of the Bible—one of the four Gospels, and Acts, the only historical book in the New Testament—were written to the same man. Luke had a proper perspective on the worth of the individual. How refreshing! Yet today the individual is hardly noticed. Crowds are admired, sought after, and craved. How often have you heard the question, "How did the meeting go last night?" followed by, "Oh, it was wonderful! We had a great meeting. The place was packed. We had to bring in extra chairs!"

Why should that make it a great meeting? A large attendance doesn't really mean anything, does it? Apparently it does to some people.

Or, how often have you heard someone ask, "How did it go last night?" only to be told, "It was terrible. Hardly anyone showed up. The place was half empty. It was a disaster."

Was it really a disaster? Does a big crowd alone make a good meeting? Notice that good equals lots of people, and bad equals few people. Let's examine that for a minute.

Was anyone converted? Did anyone go away with a determination to pray more, and with some ideas on how to go about it? Did anyone leave with a desire to memorize the word and with a simple plan to follow? Was anyone left with a greater burden for his neighbor? Did anything more than merely the gathering of a large crowd take place?

Thank God for Luke! Thank God forever! Thank God for this man of God who had the needs of the world burning in his heart, and yet was consumed with the importance of the individual and his needs!

Purity of Life

In Acts 1:4, Luke invites us to listen to one of the intimate, quiet conversations between the risen Lord and his closest followers. This conversation provides the motivation for another principle of discipleship: purity of life. "On one occasion, while he was eating with them, he gave them this command: 'Do not leave Jerusalem, but wait for the gift my Father promised, which you have heard me speak about. For John baptized with water, but in a few days you will be baptized with the Holy Spirit'" (Acts 1:4-5).

Notice that Jesus did not tell them exactly how many days they were to wait. He simply said, "in a few days." Suppose he had said, "ten days from now." For nine days they could have been occupied with other things. Then on the tenth day, they could have shaped up and prepared for the coming of the Holy Spirit.

Notice, too, the words spoken on the Mount of Olives by the two men dressed in white. They said, "Why do you stand here looking into the sky? This same Jesus, who has been taken from you into heaven, will come back in the same way you have seen him go into heaven" (Acts 1:11). The hope that he would come again motivated his disciples to be ready for his return.

I remember when that blessed hope first possessed me during the early days of my Christian life. As a non-Christian, my life was filled with drinking, gambling, cursing, and many other bad habits. Then I became a Christian. Cursing was easy to overcome—I became ashamed of my speech and hated myself when I took the Lord's name in vain. There were occasional slips, but they became few and far between. Soon they vanished. Gambling was no longer a problem because my new friends didn't gamble.

But drinking was another matter. My dad came from Germany, and we always had his home-brewed beer around the house. Early in life I had been taught how to drink, and I had acquired a taste for beer. While serving in the First Division of the Marine Corps during World War II, I found I could drink most of the big bruisers in my company under the table. They liked to have me go along on their drinking bouts because I could keep up with them at their parties and in the bars, and still be able to round them up and get them back to the base. Consequently, after I became a Christian I still had a craving for beer and whiskey.

Nothing had such a cleansing jolt on my life as the realization that Jesus was coming again—possibly today. As I began to live my life in the light of the second coming of Jesus Christ, things really changed. Realizing he would return gave me a desire to stop drinking, and motivated me to witness, to live a pure life, and to deepen my devotion to Jesus Christ. John wrote, "Dear friends, now we are children of God, and what we will be has not yet been made known. But we know that when he appears, we shall be like him, for we shall see him as he is. Everyone who has this hope in him purifies himself, just as he is pure" (1 John 3:2-3). The reality of Jesus' return motivates us to live a pure life.

It has always interested me that the apostles wanted to have a prophecy conference during their last conversation with the risen Lord. They were taken up with the future. What's around the corner? What do tomorrow, next month, and next year hold?

A Witnessing Strategy
Along with the command to witness, Jesus promised power. His Spirit enables, empowers, and enlightens us along the way. This same portion of Acts reveals a possible diversion from witnessing, one of the primary objectives Jesus gave his disciples. Jesus did not rebuke the apostles for their interest in the future. He simply turned their attention to the urgent needs of today. He left them with an all-consuming vocation—witnessing. They were to turn their attention to the most important activity in life: bearing the name of Jesus to those next door, and then to those in the uttermost parts of the world. They were to be like pebbles dropped into a pond which would generate ripples in ever-widening circles—from

Jerusalem, to Judea, to Samaria, and to the ends of the earth.
They followed their instructions to the letter. They filled
Jerusalem with their doctrine. They moved out into Judea.
Then Samaria heard the message from Philip. Peter was used
to bring Cornelius, the first Gentile convert, to Christ. Until
finally, primarily under the generalship of the apostle Paul, the
soldiers of Christ carried the message to the ends of the earth.
For the apostles, Jesus' invitation to follow him resulted in the
command to go and preach. The apostles whom he had
chosen to follow him, learn of him, to walk, and talk with him
became the vanguard of a vision that encompassed the world.
"He appointed twelve—designating them apostles—that they
might be with him and that he might send them out to preach"
(Mark 3:14).

Our response to the "Come unto me" of Jesus (Matthew
11:28) should also become the responsibility to obey the "Go
ye" of Jesus (Matthew 28:19). We are saved to serve. We do
not witness because we are redeemed. We are redeemed to
witness. But we are not left to flounder in our own strength.
Jesus goes with us.

The Holy Spirit's Power
This was driven home to me in an experience I had while in
Kota Kinabalu, a city in Sabah, East Malaysia. I was to speak at
a conference at 7:30 P.M. It was 7:25 P.M., and I was lying in a
crumpled heap on the bathroom floor, throwing up
everything I had eaten. I was a soggy, perspiring mess—so
weak I could hardly move. I called out to Virginia, my wife,
and asked her to contact the emcee and say I couldn't make it
to the meeting. Then I remembered that people had been
planning and praying for this conference for over a year.

The Lord brought to mind some verses that I had
memorized such as, "You will receive power" (Acts 1:8), and,
"Trust in the Lord with all your heart" (Proverbs 3:5). I began
to reconsider. Would God enable me to fulfill the task he had
given me? I took courage and asked my wife not to contact the
emcee. I staggered to my feet, washed up as best I could, put

on a clean shirt, and got my Bible. In minutes we were on our way to the meeting.

When I arrived it was as though I had not had a sick day in my life. I have never experienced a greater sense of God's presence and strength. By all accounts God mightily blessed the meeting. But five minutes after I returned to my hotel room, I was back on the bathroom floor, perspiring and vomiting. If I had not gone to the meeting, the people would have excused me and understood. But God was waiting for me to take a step of faith so he could provide the power I needed.

An Urgent Task
There are some things that require immediate action. They have a sense of urgency about them. That's the message that comes through to us as we listen to the Lord Jesus describe his strategy for world conquest. He told the apostles to start in Jerusalem, and then move out into Judea, Samaria, and finally into the uttermost parts of the earth.

One winter my wife and I were in Hong Kong, staying in a hotel on Nathan Road, in Kowloon. About 3:00 A.M. one morning the sound of sirens woke my wife. She got up and looked out the window. Fire trucks were arriving in front of the hotel. She opened the door and looked out into the hallway, but she couldn't see much because it was filled with smoke. She then began the difficult task of waking me out of a sound sleep. After a few minutes I realized what she was saying. The hotel was on fire! Within minutes we were on our way down the emergency stairs with scores of others. Fortunately, all that burned was the disco. In an hour we were all back in our rooms trying to get back to sleep.

The fire trucks and the smoke had awakened our instincts for survival and communicated a sense of urgency to us. We knew we had to leave immediately. Everyone responded with an urgency I have seldom seen.

Christian, that's the message communicated by the Holy Spirit in the book of Acts. There is no time to lose. The task of world evangelization cannot be carried out at our leisure. The gates of hell are open wide. The welcome mat is out. The devil eagerly waits to capture for eternity all who enter a Christless grave. The command of Christ is clear: "You will be my witnesses" (Acts 1:8).

Seeking God's Will

The first chapter of Acts ends with an incident that has always been a challenge to me. Christ's followers were gathered in an upper room to pray. Peter called their attention to the Scriptures which spoke of a replacement for Judas. Peter said, "It is written in the book of Psalms, 'May his place be deserted; let there be no one to dwell in it,' and, 'May another take his place of leadership'" (Acts 1:20). Peter quoted Psalm 69:25 and Psalm 109:8. After praying about the matter and asking the Lord to show them his will, they followed an Old Testament pattern to help them discover God's will.

We can learn a great lesson from this story. In the midst of prayer, the apostles searched the word, tried to discern the will of God, and then acted on what the Lord showed them. They were his men; it was his work; let him decide. So the apostles offered two men to the Lord from whom he could choose one to watch over the ever-growing flock of God and to colabor with them in the ministry.

Tending God's Flock

Here again we see the marvelous wisdom, grace, and love of God manifested to his people. The good Lord, in his desire to help his people be their best and do their best, has provided overseers—spiritual leaders—men whose experience in the ministry and years of devotion to Christ can be drawn upon by younger workers in the harvest. Such overseers are free to visit the younger men, pray with them, counsel them, and share ideas. The elder's experience will set the ministry ahead, and help the younger workers avoid some mistakes.

Another concept, or principle, that emerges regarding the role of these older leaders among God's people is found later in Acts 20:28: "Guard yourselves and all the flock of which the Holy Spirit has made you overseers. Be shepherds of the church of God, which he bought with his own blood." Leaders oversee the flock of God as his undershepherds. Leaders are required to be diligent in the attention they give to those they are leading. They are taught, "Be sure you know the condition of your flocks, give careful attention to your herds" (Proverbs 27:23). Leaving a flock unattended, unprotected, unloved, and uncared for is seen by God as gross negligence, a sin of the worst kind.

It amazes me that occasionally some Christian workers resent the ministry of a God-ordained overseer. I have heard of men who have told their supervisors, "You have no right to check up on me." Often pride, self, and ignorance prevent us from receiving God's best for our lives, especially when it comes through someone in authority.

Three essentials in the life of an overseer are love, patience, and the ability to encourage and inspire those he leads. When a leader visits younger workers and comes across as a cold, mechanical, and demanding person, he will naturally meet with resistance from those he wants to help. The overseer must not be overbearing. He should imitate the one who was meek and lowly of heart. His ministry and relationship to those in it should be patterned after the life of the Chief Shepherd. As Peter wrote,

> To the elders among you, I appeal as a fellow elder, a witness of Christ's sufferings and one who also will share in the glory to be revealed: Be shepherds of God's flock that is under your care, serving as overseers—not because you must, but because you are willing, as God wants you to be; not greedy for money, but eager to serve; not lording it over those entrusted to you, but being examples to the flock. And when the Chief Shepherd appears, you will receive the crown of glory that will never fade away (1 Peter 5:1-4).

So the first chapter of Acts ends with the eleven apostles

letting the Lord choose the right man to take up the ministry of an overseer.

SUMMARY:

Luke begins his portrait of discipleship by describing the disciples as—
- holy men and women of God;
- involved in the urgent task of taking the gospel to the world in the power of the Holy Spirit;
- following the leaders chosen by God.

2
The Disciples Multiply

ACTS 2 CELEBRATES the birthday of the church. It took place during the feast of Pentecost, a harvest festival, fifty days after the Passover. During this particular festival, a new kind of harvest was reaped. Three thousand souls were gathered into the kingdom of God. That harvest day began a reaping process that is still going on worldwide. The Spirit of God continues the work he began in Acts 2. He will never cease working until the Lord comes to ring down the final curtain of time.

The curious events that confront us in this passage must be looked upon in the light of the Great Commission of Christ. In fact, everything in life, everything in history, everything in the church must be looked upon in that light. We must govern our lives in light of Christ's Great Commission. That must be a major factor in any decision we make.

But God's people usually fail at this point. During "missions week" we are reminded of world needs. We hear about the work of Christ in some remote country, and we are challenged to pray and to give. Most of us do, but the thought of planning our lives and making our decisions in light of the Great Commission never crosses our minds. It should. It would add a zest and flavor to life that nothing else can. We would be involved in something that is worth our time, worth our financial investment, and worth our very lives. Few things are worthy of our best. Most people are caught up in temporal pursuits. We try to make life satisfying by feeding it with material things, but it doesn't work. We are spiritual beings. Trying to satisfy ourselves with earthly activities when we were made for heaven is foolishness. But with Christ at the center of our lives, and his Commission burning in our hearts, life becomes what it was meant to be—filled with adventure, excitement, meaning, and purpose. As Acts 2 reveals, the apostles made that discovery.

The Great Commission
The apostles were human. They had the normal limitations, doubts, fears, and hang-ups that we all have. What do you suppose filtered into their minds as they tarried together in Jerusalem for those few days following the ascension of Christ? Do you think they discussed the Commission Christ had given them? Do you think Peter or John might have begun to wonder how they were to set about carrying that out? Let's review the Great Commission and consider how it might have influenced the apostles' thinking.

Matthew recorded the command of Christ to make disciples.

> Then Jesus came to them and said, "All authority in heaven and on earth has been given to me. Therefore go and make disciples of all nations, baptizing them in the name of the Father and of the Son and of the Holy Spirit, and teaching them to obey everything I have commanded you. And surely I will be with you always, to the very end of the age" (Matthew 28:18-20).

Mark gave us the scope of Christ's command. "He said to them, 'Go into all the world and preach the good news to all creation'" (Mark 16:15).

Luke gave us some clues as to how to help fulfill it.

Then he opened their minds so they could understand the Scriptures. He told them, "This is what is written: The Christ will suffer and rise from the dead on the third day, and repentance and forgiveness of sins will be preached in his name to all nations, beginning at Jerusalem. You are witnesses of these things" (Luke 24:45-48).

John wrote, "On the evening of that first day of the week, when the disciples were together, with the doors locked for fear of the Jews, Jesus came and stood among them and said, 'Peace be with you!' After he said this, he showed them his hands and side. The disciples were overjoyed when they saw the Lord. Again Jesus said, 'Peace be with you. As the Father has sent me, I am sending you'" (John 20:19-21).

John's account gives us a picture of the cost of being involved in Christ's Great Commission. Jesus showed his disciples his hands and his side before he said to them, "As the Father has sent me, I am sending you." Why do you think he showed them his hands and side? To show them the nail prints and the wound from the sword. He communicated a vivid picture of the cost of discipleship. He did not promise them a rose garden. It would be no outing in the park. He communciated suffering, difficulty, even death.

Then in Jerusalem Jesus gave them the specifics for the strategy of the Commission. "But you will receive power when the Holy Spirit comes on you; and you will be my witnesses in Jerusalem, and in all Judea and Samaria, and to the ends of the earth" (Acts 1:8).

As Peter and John reflected on this, I'm sure the magnitude of the mission Christ had given them overwhelmed them. How could they share the gospel in a meaningful way with a Parthian, a Mede, an Elamite, or someone from Mesopotamia? They had probably never even met anyone from Mesopotamia, Cappadocia, Egypt, or Libya. But if they worried about that, they were concerned about the wrong thing, because Jesus had it all planned.

The beginning of his strategy was spectacular.

When the day of Pentecost came, they were all together in one place. Suddenly a sound like the blowing of a violent wind came from heaven and filled the whole house where they were sitting. They saw what seemed to be tongues of fire that separated and came to rest on each of them. All of them were filled with the Holy Spirit and began to speak in other tongues as the Spirit enabled them (Acts 2:1-4).

Why were these tongues given? Remember that Christ's Great Commission was central to it all. Notice what followed.

Now there were staying in Jerusalem God-fearing Jews from every nation under heaven. When they heard this sound, a crowd came together in bewilderment, because each one heard them speaking in his own language. Utterly amazed, they asked: "Are not all these men who are speaking Galileans? Then how is it that each of us hears them in his own native language? Parthians, Medes and Elamites; residents of Mesopotamia, Judea and Cappadocia, Pontus and Asia, Phrygia and Pamphylia, Egypt and the parts of Libya near Cyrene; visitors from Rome (both Jews and converts to Judaism); Cretans and Arabs—we hear them declaring the wonders of God in our own tongues!" (Acts 2:5-11).

The Lord Jesus simply gave the apostles a headstart. He brought the Parthians, Cappadocians, Egyptians, and others *to them.* He also gave the apostles the ability to communicate the gospel clearly in the foreigners' languages. Naturally there were some scoffers in the crowd. There usually are. "Amazed and perplexed, they asked one another, 'What does this mean?' Some, however, made fun of them and said, 'They have had too much wine'" (Acts 2:12-13).

The Word in the Heart
At this point Peter did an amazing thing. Rather than be offended by this accusation, or get into an argument, he simply quoted a passage of Scripture.

Then Peter stood up with the Eleven, raised his voice and addressed the crowd: "Fellow Jews and all of you who are in Jerusalem, let me explain this to you; listen carefully to what I say. These men are not drunk, as you suppose. It's only nine in the morning! No, this is what was spoken by the prophet Joel: 'In the last days, God says, I will pour out my Spirit on all people. Your sons and daughters will prophesy, your young men will see visions, your old men will dream dreams. Even on my servants, both men and women, I will pour out my Spirit in those days, and they will prophesy. I will show wonders in the heaven above and signs on the earth below, blood and fire and billows of smoke. The sun will be turned to darkness and the moon to blood before the coming of the great and glorious day of the Lord. And everyone who calls on the name of the Lord will be saved'" (Acts 2:14-21).

I would be hard pressed just to stand up and quote Joel 2:28-32 as Peter did. Remember he hadn't just come from his study with a sheaf of notes in his hands. He was in the street. He had no prepared sermon. He simply stood up and quoted the Bible.

Where did he get that idea? The answer is simple. He had walked for three years with one who, when he was accused or challenged, would often say, "Haven't you read in the Law?" or "Have you never read in the Scriptures?" or "Have you not read in the book of Moses?" and then Jesus would quote the Bible (Matthew 12:5, 21:42, and Mark 12:26).

On many occasions Jesus answered his critics by quoting Scripture and left a marvelous example for his men. They heard him constantly referring to the Scriptures, and the lesson took. In Peter's first sermon after his Lord returned to glory, he began by quoting God's word. As a matter of fact, the apostles often quoted the Scriptures in their times of fellowship.

In Acts 1:16 Peter referred to Psalm 41:9. In Acts 1:20 he quoted Psalm 69:25 and Psalm 109:8. In Acts 2:25-28 he quoted Psalm 16:8-11. In Acts 3:22-23 he quoted Deuteronomy 18:15 and 19. The Scriptures were central in the apostles' fellowship and during times of decision making, prayer, and preaching. The apostles were men of the word, and they lived under its authority. Christ set them a clear example. Peter could have sent a boy to the temple to fetch the Joel scroll and then read the passage aloud, but he didn't; he quoted it from memory.

It was an amazing scene. Here was Peter, recently arrived from the fishing boats of Galilee, a plain, roughly hewn man now facing a city filled with richly robed priests, brilliant scribes, meticulous Pharisees, doctors of the Law, and zealous Sadducees. As he spoke, the streets of Jerusalem rang with the truth of the gospel. No one had ever seen or heard anything like it.

It surprises me that Peter spoke so powerfully. Most of us are timid when we start out. Do you remember your reaction when you were first called upon to give a word of testimony, or to pray out loud? I surely do! I was in a Sunday school class, and afterwards, as we stood for prayer, the teacher said, "Perhaps LeRoy would close in prayer." I almost fainted. My knees buckled, and if I hadn't been holding onto the pew in front of me, I would have fallen down. I'm sure I turned green, white, and red. Seeing my difficulty the teacher said, "Perhaps brother Hansen would close in prayer." I stood there thanking God for Cliff Hansen!

Peter was mightily fortified by the word of God in his heart. As we reflect on this simple truth, it becomes obvious that our lives and witness would improve if we would engage in the diligent practice of Scripture memory. But there's a problem.

Were you ever in a fight? I mean the kind where you square off with another man and go at it. I remember quite clearly the last fight I ever had before I became a Christian. The fellow knocked me flat. As I lay on the ground I could see stars. I received a black eye and a wounded ego. No one likes to take a beating, and when we experience one, we remember it.

Now the devil also has a long memory. He remembers as if it were yesterday the day he and Jesus had it out on the mount of temptation. Three times he tried, and three times

Jesus completely devastated him with the word of God. Satan remembers. When we become motivated to saturate our hearts and lives with the Scriptures, he will do everything in his power and pull every deceitful lie out of his bag of tricks to stop us. He cannot face the word of God head on and win. And he knows it.

The Gospel

There were some other aspects of Peter's sermon which gave it power. He preached the gospel, which is the power of God.

> Men of Israel listen to this: Jesus of Nazareth was a man accredited by God to you by miracles, wonders and signs, which God did among you through him, as you yourselves know. This man was handed over to you by God's set purpose and foreknowledge; and you, with the help of wicked men, put him to death by nailing him to the cross. But God raised him from the dead, freeing him from the agony of death, because it was impossible for death to keep its hold on him (Acts 2:22-24).

Paul summarized the gospel by saying, "For what I received I passed on to you as of first importance: that Christ died for our sins according to the Scriptures, that he was buried, that he was raised on the third day according to the Scriptures, and that he appeared to Peter, and then to the Twelve" (1 Corinthians 15:3-5). Christ died—that's history. He died for our sins—that's good news. Peter went on: "God has raised this Jesus to life, and we are all witnesses of the fact. Exalted to the right hand of God, he has received from the Father the promised Holy Spirit and has poured out what you now see and hear" (Acts 2:32-33). But Peter didn't stop there. He preached the lordship of Jesus Christ: "Therefore let all Israel be assured of this: God has made this Jesus, whom you crucified, both Lord and Christ" (Acts 2:36).

What happened as a result of his preaching? "Those who accepted his message were baptized, and about three thousand were added to their number that day" (Acts 2:41). Three thousand were reaped into the kingdom of God on this great harvest festival.

As we observe Peter we exclaim, "What a man! What a great servant of Christ!" Yes, that's true. But to keep things in perspective, look at the last verse of the chapter. The believers were "praising God and enjoying the favor of all the people. And the Lord added to their number daily those who were being saved" (Acts 2:47). It wasn't Peter; it was the Lord who was doing it all. This is the first great principle of witnessing for Christ: God does it. The second principle is that he uses people. When those two great principles gripped my soul, it was such a release. I was no longer under a burden. It was not my work, it was God's! And, praise his name, he wanted to use me!

Let's return to Acts 2:42: "They devoted themselves to the apostles' teaching and to the fellowship, to the breaking of bread and to prayer." Here is an inside look at the genesis of Christian fellowship. Here is the foundation of Christian discipleship. Here's the original design. What a resource for those who want to follow the New Testament pattern of discipleship. What characteristics do we see?

Teachable

For one thing, these believers were teachable. They were eager and ready to learn. They devoted themselves to the apostles' teaching. They were not doubters, they were believers. They were responsive individuals, not critical spirits. An eagerness to learn, a teachable spirit, is one of the master keys to usefulness in the cause of Christ.

Available

Second, they were available. Availability is another master key to growth and usefulness in the kingdom of God. To illustrate, let's say a young man shows up at the football field and tries out for the team. He is a remarkably well-coordinated athlete, fast, and muscular. The coach immediately recognizes he has the makings of a superstar. But a problem develops; he does not show up for practice. No matter how much potential he has, if he is not on the field to be trained and coached, he will never reach his potential.

On the other hand, here is another young man with equal potential who practices diligently. He becomes a fine player, but he has another problem; he does not show up for the games. He may be the best player on the team, but if he does not show up to play, he is worthless. If you would be used of God—be available to him.

Worshipful

Third, they were worshipful. The fellowship of the Lord's Supper, prayers, and praise were an integral part of their lives. Churches today often wish that some of the early Christians' spirit of worship would catch fire in our assemblies. The elements of worship may be present, but it is all in vain if our minds are wandering, our hearts set on other things, and our spirits are cold. We have a great heritage, a great foundation. We need the touch of God on our souls to restore us to the kind of heartfelt worship our ancestors in the faith practiced.

Joyful

The rest of Acts 2 gives further insight into the lives of the early believers. They displayed another characteristic that is badly needed today; they were a glad people. Gladness is a powerful force for good in the world. There is healing and strength in a glad spirit. When you are with a glad person, you are helped and strengthened in many ways. In fact, Nehemiah said, "the joy of the Lord is your strength" (Nehemiah 8:10). Paul exhorted us, "Rejoice in the Lord always. I will say it again: Rejoice!" (Philippians 4:4). Jesus said, "I have told you this so that my joy may be in you and that your joy may be complete" (John 15:11). In his teaching on prayer he said, "Until now you have not asked for anything in my name. Ask and you will receive, and your joy will be complete" (John 16:24). Joy is second in Paul's listing of the fruit of the Spirit (Galatians 5:22). The early Christians were a joyful, rejoicing, glad people who enjoyed each other and their walk with the Lord.

Joyfulness is often a matter of choice. We can choose to be glad and thankful, or we can choose to be grumpy. I was speaking at a conference at Mount Hermon in northern California. After a busy day, I was tired and went to bed quite early. Shortly after I retired, a group of three couples gathered outside my bedroom window. They were laughing and joking and having a great time together. I had a choice. I could have thought, *Why don't they keep quiet. Don't they know I'm tired?* Or, I could have thought, *Isn't that great! These couples are enjoying Christian fellowship—praise the Lord.* As it turned out, that is what I did and I was asleep in minutes in spite of the noise. We can choose our attitude.

Sacrificial
The early Christians were also sacrificial. "All the believers were together and had everything in common. Selling their possessions and goods, they gave to anyone as he had need" (Acts 2:44-45). Many have speculated as to why they entered into this expression of communal living. It seems to me that the answer is in the commission that Jesus had given. The commission was not just to get converts, but to *make disciples.*

Marks of a Disciple
Jesus Christ gave us a clear picture of a disciple.

He continues in the word of Christ. "To the Jews who had believed him, Jesus said, 'If you hold to my teaching, you are really my disciples'" (John 8:31).

He manifests the love of Christ. "A new commandment I give you: Love one another. As I have loved you, so you must love one another. All men will know that you are my disciples if you love one another" (John 13:34-35).

He is fruitful in his walk with Christ. "This is to my Father's glory, that you bear much fruit, showing yourselves to be my disciples" (John 15:8).

He is single-minded in his service for Christ. "No one can serve two masters. Either he will hate the one and love the other, or he will be devoted to the one and despise the other. You cannot serve both God and Money" (Matthew 6:24).

There is no rival for his devotion to Christ. "If anyone comes to me and does not hate his father and mother, his wife and children, his brothers and sisters—yes, even his own life—he cannot be my disciple" (Luke 14:26).

He follows Christ through thick and thin. "Anyone who does not bear his cross and follow me cannot be my disciple" (Luke 14:27).

He is not in love with the things of the world. "In the same way, any of you who does not give up everything he has cannot be my disciple" (Luke 14:33).

Over the years the apostles had heard Jesus explain discipleship. It was clear to them that their work was more than just bringing people to faith in Christ. Three times Jesus told Peter to feed his lambs and sheep (John 21:15-17). The last words of Peter's epistle are, "But grow in the grace and knowledge of our Lord and Savior Jesus Christ. To him be glory both now and forever! Amen" (2 Peter 3:18).

Why had such a large crowd gathered in Jerusalem on the day when Peter gave his first sermon? They were there to celebrate the feast of Pentecost. They only planned to stay until the end of the celebration. Then they would return home. But a strange and unexpected thing had happened. Three thousand of them were converted to Christ and baptized into the fellowship of believers. The apostles had no choice but to invite them to stay in Jerusalem. It would have been criminal to have allowed them to return home. They would have been lost to the Great Commission. They needed to be discipled, trained, and equipped to take their place in the ranks as soldiers of Christ.

But you know how it is on a trip. If you stay longer than you planned, you can run out of money. So everyone began to share whatever they needed—clothing, food, and shelter. Here was a teachable, available, faithful, consistent, worshipful, joyful, committed, and sacrificial band of people looking to the apostles to help them in their lives and service. Did the apostles do their part diligently? Yes, both in their personal example and by systematic teaching. "Day after day, in the temple courts and from house to house, they never stopped teaching and proclaiming the good news that Jesus is the Christ" (Acts 5:42).

SUMMARY:

Now we have seen the apostles in action—
- with the Great Commission burning in their hearts;
- under the authority of the word;
- with the gospel ever on their lips;
- with Christ as the Lord of their lives.

3
A Gentle,
Flexible Attitude

THE APOSTLES HAD their priorities straight. Luke tells us, "One day Peter and John were going up to the temple at the time of prayer—at three in the afternoon" (Acts 3:1). Peter and John were committed to prayer and the ministry of the word (See Acts 6:4). They had set times and places for prayer.

It is good to have set times for prayer, both private and public. This has been the practice of men of God from of old. Daniel had set times of prayer which he kept even at the risk of his own life: "Now when Daniel learned that the decree had been published, he went home to his upstairs room where the windows opened toward Jerusalem. Three times a day he got down on his knees and prayed, giving thanks to his God, just as he had done before" (Daniel 6:10). David said, "Evening, morning and noon I cry out in distress, and he hears my voice" (Psalm 55:17). Choosing a fixed time for prayer should not bind you into a legalistic straightjacket, but become a simple reminder. We need all the help we can get to remain faithful in prayer.

David Steele came to America from England some years ago to work at Glen Eyrie, The Navigators' headquarters in

Colorado Springs, Colorado. David did not eat lunch. Instead, every day from noon until 1:00 P.M., he spent time with the Lord in prayer. If you were to ask David, he would tell you it was not a burden but a joy.

We should ask ourselves, "When would be the best time for me to invest some time in prayer? Where would be the best place?" Then make a plan and proceed. That is what Peter and John did. They decided to go to the place of prayer at the hour of prayer. But God had something else in mind for them of which they were totally unaware, which would radically affect their lives, bring thousands into the kingdom, and eventually place them in jail.

Be Flexible

It all began with a simple incident. "Now a man crippled from birth was being carried to the temple gate called Beautiful, where he was put every day to beg from those going into the temple courts. When he saw Peter and John about to enter, he asked them for money" (Acts 3:2-3).

What was Peter's response? He could have said, "Old man, don't bother me. Can't you see we are on our way to a prayer meeting? After all, this is the hour of prayer, this is the place of prayer, and we are men of prayer. Some other time, perhaps, but not now. We have a fixed schedule, a regimented pattern of life, and an inflexible determination to hold to it." But he didn't. He had an entirely different reaction, as we'll see later.

Flexibility was one of the hallmarks of these men. I'm sure that three years with Jesus contributed significantly to that lifestyle. If it wasn't a woman with an issue of blood, or a hungry multitude that needed to be fed, it was a blind beggar calling out to the Son of David for mercy. Interruptions and changed plans were nothing new to Christ's companions.

In the summer of 1978 I took a tour of the great Derdap Dam that spans the beautiful Danube river between Yugoslavia and Romania. It was exciting to go inside that marvel of engineering. It is the fifth largest dam in the world.

Our guide took us down into the center of that structure where the mighty turbines whirled at an amazing speed, and the deafening roar of millions of tons of water combined to send vibrations throughout the entire structure.

I was walking through the dam with my son, Randy, and a gentleman from the Smithsonian Institute. This man saw the apprehensive looks on our faces as we felt the very floor under our feet shaking from the strain and power of the machinery. He had visited similar dams all over the world, and so he gave us a reassuring smile. "Remember," he said, "that which doesn't vibrate shatters."

Since then I've thought a lot about those words. There is a great lesson for us all as we walk with the Lord. Stay flexible. Learn to roll with the punches. Yes, we must set goals and maintain some order in our lives. Yes, we must establish some spiritual habits that require a fixed time and place. But don't become rigid, uptight, or inflexible. Maintain clear objectives in the framework of an orderly life, but surround them with a gentle, flexible attitude.

People-Oriented

Here's another lesson. There are two kinds of people in the world: goal-oriented and people-oriented. The westerner, the individual from Europe or North America, tends to be goal-oriented; while the person from Latin America, Asia, Africa, or the Middle East, tends to be more people-oriented. If a person in the Philippines is on his way to a meeting that begins at 7:00 P.M. and sees that his sick grandmother is lonely and wants to talk, he will try to cheer her up before arriving at the meeting at 8:30 P.M. This approach to life drives the average westerner crazy, but I think it is commendable.

Peter and John had clear objectives. The Great Commission of Christ was fresh on their minds and burned in their hearts: "Preach the gospel—make disciples." The world must hear the good news. People should be won and discipled in every corner of the earth. Peter and John were men on the move with a clear vision and purpose.

They could have looked at the old, lame man as an obstacle. Peter could have said, "What possible good would it do to stop and deal with this man's difficulties? How could this helpless old man be of any value to the cause of Christ?" Peter could have "passed by on the other side," as the priest and the Levite had done in the story Jesus told of the man who fell among thieves (see Luke 10:30-37).

I have watched men catch the vision of reaching the world for Christ. I have caught this vision, and have dedicated my life to this grand and glorious aim. But I have seen some men become so goal-oriented that to achieve their goals they roughly shoulder their way past people who need help and encouragement.

But what is our objective? What are our goals? When we all get to heaven it will be vividly and pointedly clear. We will find only people in heaven. There will be no committee notes, no scholarly papers on intriguing themes, no lengthy studies, memos, or surveys. People are the raw material of heaven. If we become enamored with projects, goals, and achievements, and never lend a hand to people along the way; and if we say, "Doing this will not help me accomplish my objective," what are we really thinking about? Self! Exactly opposite to the lifestyle of Jesus Christ.

So even though it was not immediately evident that the old man would be of any use in fulfilling the Great Commission, Peter did not rebuke the man for shouting to get their attention. Instead, Peter stopped, looked straight at him, and spoke to him. He began by telling the man he had no money. Not a penny. But wait, was that really true? Didn't we just read that the people were "selling their possessions and goods"? Don't the Scriptures say, "There were no needy persons among them. For from time to time those who owned lands or houses sold them, brought the money from the sales and put it at the apostles' feet, and it was distributed to anyone as he had need" (Acts 4:34-35)? How could Peter say he didn't have any money? Because the money was not given for the apostles' personal use, but for the advancement of the ministry. They had all the money they needed to carry on the work of Christ, but they were not becoming rich men through it all. It was God's money to be used in his name, in his work. The apostles laid no claim to it. It wasn't theirs and they did not use it for personal gain.

This is a great temptation. Worldly gain and self-glory are two of the devil's prime means of leading us to destruction. Paul's testimony rings true and clear: "I have not coveted anyone's silver or gold or clothing" (Acts 20:33). To the Thessalonians he gave a firm reminder: "Surely you remember, brothers, our toil and hardship; we worked night and day in order not to be a burden to anyone while we preached the gospel of God to you" (1 Thessalonians 2:9). He did not covet their wealth or want personal glory. So Peter spoke the truth when he made his dramatic statement. Peter was a poor man, but what he gave was far greater than money. In the name of Jesus Christ he gave back to the man his ability to walk.

Humility

This created quite a stir among the people. Their comments made Peter realize the crowd mistakenly believed the apostles' power had healed the man. He was quick to deny it. "When Peter saw this, he said to them: 'Men of Israel, why does this surprise you? Why do you stare at us as if by our own power or godliness we had made this man walk?'" (Acts 3:12).

If Peter had fallen for that subtle temptation, it would have ended his ministry right then and there. To claim the glory that rightfully belongs to God is deadly. To grab and claw after even a small fraction of his honor is the way to a fruitless life. Even to sit passively and let others drape it around your shoulders is the sure way to ruin. I'm sure Peter knew well the truth taught by Isaiah, "I am the Lord; that is my name! I will not give my glory to another or my praise to idols" (Isaiah 42:8). Why is this true?

The Bible warns us, "Pride goes before destruction, a

haughty spirit before a fall" (Proverbs 16:18-19). "A man's pride brings him low, but a man of lowly spirit gains honor" (Proverbs 29:23). "The fear of the Lord teaches a man wisdom, and humility comes before honor" (Proverbs 15:33). "Before his downfall a man's heart is proud, but humility comes before honor" (Proverbs 18:12). "Let us not become conceited, provoking and envying each other" (Galatians 5:26). "Do nothing out of selfish ambition or vain conceit, but in humility consider others better than yourselves" (Philippians 2:3). I have listed these Scriptures to provide some passages for you to memorize. You will discover great value in writing these passages on the tables of your heart, praying over them, and meditating on their warnings and promises.

Peter was well aware of the dangers that lurked in the incident with the crippled man, so he immediately turned everyone's attention toward God:

> The God of Abraham, Isaac and Jacob, the God of our fathers, has glorified his servant Jesus. You handed him over to be killed, and you disowned him before Pilate, though he had decided to let him go. You disowned the Holy and Righteous One and asked that a murderer be released to you. You killed the author of life, but God raised him from the dead. We are witnesses of this. By faith in the name of Jesus, this man whom you see and know was made strong. It is Jesus' name and the faith that comes through him that has given this complete healing to him, as you can all see. Now, brothers, I know that you acted in ignorance, as did your leaders (Acts 3:13-17).

As a great crowd gathered, what was Peter's first impulse? I'm sure that both he and John were caught up in the excitement of the occasion. Did he lead the crowd in the singing of psalms of praise? There would have been nothing wrong with that. Did he lead the people in prayers of thanksgiving? There certainly would have been nothing wrong with that. Did he try to explain the scriptural teaching on the gift of healing? No, his first impulse was to preach the gospel. He spoke about

Christ's death and resurrection. He knew there is one message that people must hear. Unless a person hears the gospel and responds, he is eternally lost. The apostles knew beyond a shadow of a doubt that their first and foremost mission in life was to bear clear witness to the death and resurrection of Jesus Christ. His last words to them, "be my witnesses," never faded in importance as the years passed and other needs and urgent matters pressed upon them. They were his witnesses, so Peter used this occasion as an opportunity to witness.

A Witnessing Opportunity

A common question around the world is: "What is a witnessing opportunity?" While in Auckland, New Zealand, I was to speak at 6:00 one evening to some students. The fellow who came to pick me up at the motel arrived an hour early so we could spend some time together. When he came he said he wanted to watch me witness to someone. He felt he could learn more by watching me witness than by talking about witnessing. He suggested that we could stop on our way to the meeting, knock on someone's door, and witness. I glanced at my watch. It was about 5:00 P.M. I thought about the state of the average home at that time of day. The lady of the house is getting the evening meal ready. Her husband will soon arrive, want to clean up, and relax before dinner. Their children will be tired and hungry, and probably not on their best behavior. Hardly an ideal situation for witnessing, I thought.

"Let me stop in the office on our way out, to see if my laundry is ready, " I said. So we went in and inquired about my clothes.

"Oh, I'm so sorry Mr. Eims," said the lady at the desk. "I promised you they would be ready and they should have arrived by now, but apparently there has been a delay."

"No problem," I replied. "I'm just going out and thought I'd check. I really don't need them until tomorrow. I'm on my way to a Bible study now. This fellow is a university student and he meets regularly with other students to study the Bible."

"My," she said, "isn't that wonderful!"

"Yes," I agreed, "it is wonderful to see young men studying the Bible. I certainly wasn't doing that at their age."

"Neither was I," she replied.

"In fact," I said, "the first time I ever thought seriously about God was while I was serving as a machine gunner with the First Marine Division in the South Pacific during the Second World War." With that I began to share my testimony and explained how I had become a Christian.

By then a man had come out of the office and was also listening. They both seemed quite interested in the story of my conversion to Christ. I was about to ask them if they had ever received Christ when the phone rang. At that moment three people entered the lobby and came over to the desk to inquire about accommodations for the night. I was unable to continue our conversation, so I said goodbye and went to the car with my student friend. As we drove off I said, "Well, there it was."

"There was what?" he asked.

"Well, you expressed an interest in watching me witness, and that's what I just did," I said.

He stopped the car, looked at me in surprise and said, "You did, didn't you!"

It was so natural, so effortless, so simple, that he had completely missed it. He had wanted us to make a special effort to witness by going somewhere and doing something. It seemed more natural to me to take advantage of the situation right where we were. The Holy Spirit opened the way, and the witness was given.

After dinner at the apartment, I stepped outside for a breath of fresh air. I went along the street and saw a young man standing beside a large motorcycle. He was dressed in the garb of a "bikee," Auckland's equivalent of a Hell's Angel. He was a rough looking individual—big, muscular, hairy, wearing dark glasses, black leather jacket, and boots. I walked over and said, "That's quite a motorcyle you have."

"Yes," he said with pride, "I built it myself."

"You did? That must have been quite a job!"

"Yes, I found a frame, these wheels, this engine, and put it all together. But," he said, "yesterday I took it into the garage and I'm afraid they damaged the engine. Here, listen." He started the engine and revved it up. The roar was deafening. You could have heard it sixteen blocks away. He listened intently, looked at me, and shouted, "Do you hear that?"

"Yes," I shouted back, "I can hear that." I was sure half the neighborhood could hear it. Then he turned it off and expressed his low opinion of the garage mechanic.

Then one of the students called me in for our meeting. I told the bikee I had to go, and explained we were meeting to discuss the Bible. That comment led to a brief witness to him before I had to run. One of the students asked, "What were you doing with the bikee?"

"Witnessing," I said.

"To him!" he exclaimed.

"He actually seemed quite interested," I replied. "Haven't you ever witnessed to him? He lives in the green house you pass every day." The student admitted that the thought of witnessing to the bikee had never entered his mind.

How different from Peter. In spite of the excitement at the temple, the first thought that popped into his mind was to witness to the death and resurrection of his Lord. We marvel at men like these and are amazed at the impact they had on the world in a few short years. Yet I'm sure we could have the same kind of impact if we thought like Peter.

Repentance

Peter called for action. He called for repentance. "Repent, then, and turn to God, so that your sins may be wiped out, that times of refreshing may come from the Lord" (Acts 3:19). He followed the example he had seen in the life and ministry of Jesus Christ. Jesus said, "Unless you repent, you too will all perish" (Luke 13:3). Jesus taught his disciples, "This is what is written: The Christ will suffer and rise from the dead on the third day, and repentance and forgiveness of sins will be preached in his name to all nations, beginning at Jerusalem" (Luke 24:46-47). Peter never tired of this theme. Later he wrote, "The Lord is not slow in keeping his promise, as some understand slowness. He is patient with you, not wanting anyone to perish, but everyone to come to repentance" (2 Peter 3:9).

What is repentance? Suppose you are driving along the road of life and you see Christ at a crossroads ahead, indicating that he would like to travel the road of life with you. So you stop, open the back door of your car, and wait for him. He hesitates and immediately you see your mistake. You reach back, close the door, and quickly open the front door on the passenger side. Again he hesitates, and you are puzzled for a moment. Then you understand. You close the door on the passenger's side, open the door on the driver's side, slide into the passenger's seat, and invite him to take the wheel. That's repentance. You are no longer going your way, but God's way. You are not leading, but following. You travel the road of life going Christ's way, with him in control. He controls the accelerator, the steering wheel, and the brakes.

Rogers McCrae, a friend of mine, called me from Kansas City. He told me about a man who was moving to Colorado Springs. The man had a drinking problem and was hoping that in a new city with a new job, and a new set of friends, he might be able to lick it. Rogers had given the man my name in case he needed someone to talk to about his problem. Eventually the man called me and we arranged to meet. After a relaxed conversation I presented the gospel to him and shared with him his need for Christ. I showed him some passages of Scripture, explained faith and repentance, and used the story of the man driving along the road of life. I then asked if he wanted to give Christ control of his life and let him take the wheel. His answer was classic: "LeRoy, "he said, "when you've been traveling as long as me and have had about one wreck a day, it is time to get a new driver." With that he went to his knees, prayed, and invited Christ into his life.

Peter's message was forceful. "Repent ye therefore, and

be converted" (Acts 3:19 KJV). *Repent* is active. God calls on us to repent. *Be converted* is passive. God will do his part. This is the work of the Holy Spirit in response to faith. Often the clearest way to explain this truth is simply to explain how it happened in your own life. Explain how the Holy Spirit has given you new goals, a new joy, peace, love, and a new life.

Repentance, the supernatural act of God, is expressed in a number of ways in the Bible. David said, "As far as the east is from the west so far has he removed our transgressions from us" (Psalm 103:12). Micah wrote, "You will again have compassion on us; you will tread our sins underfoot and hurl all our iniquities into the depths of the sea" (Micah 7:19). Jeremiah cited the word of the Lord which said, "'No longer will a man teach his neighbor, or a man his brother, saying, "Know the Lord," because they will all know me, from the least of them to the greatest,' declares the Lord. 'For I will forgive their wickedness and will remember their sins no more'" (Jeremiah 31:34). What a picture of the grace of God!

Justification

The Old Testament Scriptures I've cited all illustrate the great doctrine of justification—which was the basis of Peter's message. When Paul used the term *justified* in Romans 5:1, he used a legal term: "Therefore, since we have been justified through faith, we have peace with God through our Lord Jesus Christ." It means the legal act whereby God simply declares us righteous and justified in his sight, based solely on the perfect righteousness of Jesus Christ.

Let me illustrate that I was married over thirty years ago. The ceremony took place in a small Presbyterian church in Neola, Iowa. There were two ministers. The church was full. My buddies were lined up on one side as best man and groomsmen, and Virginia's girlfriends stood beside her as bridesmaids. As Virginia started down the aisle, I was legally single. When she was halfway along the aisle I was still legally single. Then the climactic moment came when the minister said, "I now pronounce you man and wife." My legal standing changed in a split second. The minister simply declared us married; he pronounced us man and wife. At that moment my legal status was changed for all time. The minister declared it so. That's what happens when we are converted and our sins are blotted out. We stand perfectly free and clean in God's sight—not based on our works or righteousness, but on the work of Christ on the cross, his resurrection, and his perfect righteousness.

As Peter continued his sermon, he was interrupted by the priests, the rulers of the temple, and the Sadducees. His last words before being interrupted were, "Unto you first God, having raised up his Son Jesus, sent him to bless you, in turning away every one of you from his iniquities" (Acts 3:26 KJV). It is intriguing that he did not talk to them about their being turned from their infirmities, but from their iniquities. After all, wasn't the main event in this scene the healing of the lame man? And don't you suppose that in a crowd that large there were others who needed a healing touch from God to cure their various sicknesses and ailments? Quite possibly. But Peter used the occasion to talk about the work of God.

In his message Peter led the crowd step by step toward faith. He had commanded the man to rise up and walk in the name of Jesus Christ. He assured the people he had done this in the name and power of Christ. He showed them the awfulness of their sin by pointing out that they had freed Barabbas, a killer, and killed the author of life.

Peter quoted Moses and Abraham—both great heroes of the faith whom the people highly revered. He told them that these great men of God spoke about Jesus Christ.

Patiently, persistently, and earnestly Peter pursued his one great goal: bringing them to faith in Jesus Christ. Peter may have been surrounded by physical needs, but his mind and heart were on the spiritual needs of the people. He longed for them to come into the joy of salvation and eternal life. Through his faith in Jesus Christ, Peter became the channel through whom the power of God could flow. It is on God's heart for us to see the needs of the world about us, and to use us to meet those needs. But we need to share Peter's compassion and conviction that Jesus Christ is truly the answer. When we are gripped by these beliefs, we are prepared and equipped to be a blessing to the world.

SUMMARY:

Peter and John modeled four primary qualities of discipleship.
- They were committed to prayer.
- They were flexible.
- They demonstrated humility.
- They were alert, compassionate, and loving witnesses.

4
The Apostles Under Attack

OPPOSITION TO THE apostles' message soon began to build. "The priests and the captain of the temple guard and the Sadducees came up to Peter and John while they were speaking to the people. They were greatly disturbed because the apostles were teaching the people and proclaiming in Jesus the resurrection of the dead" (Acts 4:1-2).

The Sadducees proclaimed far and wide that there was no resurrection from the dead. Obviously, if the apostles were right, then the Sadducees were out of business. So "they seized Peter and John, and because it was evening, they put them in jail until the next day" (Acts 4:3).

Notice the very next verse. "But many who heard the message believed, and the number of men grew to about five thousand" (Acts 4:4). The number of believers had now risen to over five thousand men! What had prompted this great increase? The healing of an old, lame beggar was the catalyst to faith for thousands. An old man, who seemed irrelevant to Christ's Great Commission, was instrumental in the salvation of many.

I'm sure that as Peter and John looked back on it all, they

were delighted they had canceled their original plans to pray and stopped to help the crippled man. Like them, we too might never know the outcome of a deed done in the name of Christ. God can take the most unlikely situation and use it for his glory.

Remember God's word in Isaiah: "'For my thoughts are not your thoughts, neither are your ways my ways,' declares the Lord. 'As the heavens are higher than the earth, so are my ways higher than your ways and my thoughts than your thoughts'" (Isaiah 55:8-9). God does not always follow patterns that make sense to our mortal minds. Yes, many were brought into the kingdom, but the healing of the old man also landed Peter and John in jail. Eventually the incident led to violence, widespread persecution, and suffering. These events were also used by God to spread the faith, but suffering is suffering. Beatings are not pleasant. Going to jail is not a picnic. Such experiences are hard. So now we find the apostles in jail for the first time.

The next morning the two apostles were brought before a powerful and deadly group of men—the rulers, elders, and the teachers of the law. The memory of the sight of the Son of God hanging in agony on the cross was still fixed clearly in the apostles' minds. They knew this group of men had crucified Jesus. They knew the dangers they faced. They had seen the power of these men in full sway. By all rights the apostles should have cowered in craven fear before this august body. Surely, such an educated group could silence the apostles by refuting their simple message. After all, the apostles were plain men from Galilee, fishermen who had followed the Carpenter.

The officials' first question showed their deadly subtlety. "By what power or what name did you do this?" (Acts 4:7). Power is force, name is authority. The officials were asking, "By what magical power did you do this, and by what right did you use this power?" They were trying to bring Peter and John under the death sentence prescribed by the Old Testament law (see Exodus 22:18 and Deuteronomy 13:1-5).

I am sure Peter and John knew that. Their lives were

hanging by a very slender thread. What was Peter's reaction to all of this—this man who shortly before had succumbed to fear and denied his Lord?

> Then Peter, filled with the Holy Spirit, said to them: "Rulers and elders of the people! If we are being called to account today for an act of kindness shown to a cripple and are asked how he was healed, then know this, you and everyone else in Israel: It is by the name of Jesus Christ of Nazareth, whom you crucified but whom God raised from the dead, that this man stands before you completely healed. He is 'the stone you builders rejected, which has become the capstone.' Salvation is found in no one else, for there is no other name under heaven given to men by which we must be saved" (Acts 4:8-12).

The Holy Spirit had changed Peter from one who denied his Lord to one filled with the power to bear witness boldly to the resurrection of Jesus Christ. What was different? The first seven words of Acts 4:8 explain it all: "Then Peter, filled with the Holy Spirit." The Holy Spirit is our source of strength, boldness, courage, and faith. A holy life is a powerful weapon in the hands of the Holy Spirit. He had taken up residence in Peter's life. Peter was controlled by God from within.

Jesus had forewarned his followers,

> But be on your guard against men; they will hand you over to the local councils and flog you in their synagogues. On my account you will be brought before governors and kings as witnesses to them and to the Gentiles. But when they arrest you, do not worry about what to say or how to say it. At that time you will be given what to say, for it will not be you speaking, but the Spirit of your Father speaking through you (Matthew 10:17-20).

What was Peter's defense? He made none. Peter knew that the best defense is a good offense, so he went on the attack. He said his accusers were the criminals. He became the prosecuting attorney, and they the defendants. They were now on trial for murdering the Messiah.

When we study this in light of the ministry of the Holy Spirit, it all makes sense. What is the Spirit's ministry in the life of the believer?

Jesus clearly explained the Holy Spirit's ministry to his disciples. He will be our helper, teacher, and guide.

But what about his ministry in the life of the unbeliever? The Holy Spirit will be the counsel for the prosecution who will convince the world of its sin (see John 16:8-11).

So Peter, led by the Spirit, showed his accusers the magnitude of their sin in murdering the Messiah. Now notice something astounding.

When Jesus walked the earth, he was asked a question similar to the one the Sanhedrin asked Peter. "Jesus entered the temple courts, and, while he was teaching, the chief priests and the elders of the people came to him. 'By what authority are you doing these things?' they asked. 'And who gave you this authority?'" (Matthew 21:23). Jesus countered with another question. He asked the elders whether John's baptism came from heaven or from men. Since they would not answer his question directly, Jesus said he would not tell them by what authority he was teaching. After telling them two parables, Jesus concluded that conversation by saying, "Have you never read in the Scriptures: 'The stone the builders rejected has become the capstone; the Lord has done this, and it is marvelous in our eyes'?" (Matthew 21:42). Now notice Peter's response to his questioners: "He is 'the stone you builders rejected, which has become the capstone'" (Acts 4:11).

This incident shows us the awesome power of example. Peter did just what Jesus had done. Jesus had cited Psalm 118:22 and so Peter did the same. This is a good lesson for us. Someone is watching us, someone is listening to us, just as Peter observed Jesus. That knowledge alone should keep us on the straight and narrow path. You are the finest Christian that some person in the world knows. When he talks about a real Christian, he will be thinking of you. Therefore, what you do—the way you behave, the amusements you enjoy, how you spend your time, your activities—will be copied by someone. You are his example. In the situation recorded in Acts 4, Peter did exactly as Jesus had done.

A Consistent Message

There is a consistency to Peter's messages throughout Acts. On the day of Pentecost he spoke about the death and resurrection of Jesus (Acts 2:23-24). He gave the same message to the crowd that gathered in Jerusalem (Acts 3:14-15). Now he gave the same message to the Sadducees: "Then know this, you and everyone else in Israel: It is by the name of Jesus Christ of Nazareth, whom you crucified but whom God raised from the dead, that this man stands before you completely healed" (Acts 4:10). Peter repeated this message before the Sanhedrin: "The God of our fathers raised Jesus from the dead—whom you had killed by hanging him on a tree" (Acts 5:30). Still later we find him repeating the same message to Cornelius: "We are witnesses of everything he did in the country of the Jews and in Jerusalem. They killed him by hanging him on a tree, but God raised him from the dead on the third day and caused him to be seen" (Acts 10:39-40).

When the apostle Paul was before Agrippa, he cited this same message as the crux of his witness: "But I have had God's help to this very day, and so I stand here and testify to small and great alike. I am saying nothing beyond what the prophets and Moses said would happen—that the Christ would suffer and, as the first to rise from the dead, would proclaim light to his own people and to the Gentiles" (Acts 26:22-23).

The question arises, Why did they always give this particular message? The answer is found in Paul's letter to the Corinthians: "Now, brothers, I want to remind you of the gospel I preached to you, which you received and on which you have taken your stand. By this gospel you are saved, if you hold firmly to the word I preached to you. Otherwise, you have believed in vain. For what I received I passed on to you as of first importance: that Christ died for our sins according to the Scriptures, and that he was buried, that he was raised on the third day according to the Scriptures" (1 Corinthians 15:1-4). This is the gospel. This is the good news. Jesus explicitly told his followers to "preach the good news to all creation" (Mark 16:15). Peter, and all the other apostles, obeyed his command.

Peter gave a firm, clear, ringing witness to the uniqueness of our Lord Jesus Christ. "Salvation is found in no one else, for there is no other name under heaven given to men by which we must be saved" (Acts 4:12). Other religions can tell us what we ought to be. Christ *transforms* us into what we ought to be. Other religions make us *aware* of our needs. Christ *meets* our needs.

This is evident when one visits countries which are dominated by other religions. I could take you to a certain temple in one of the most exotic cities in the world. As we entered you would see a lovely young woman wearing a beautiful gown. Her hair would be done attractively. She would be poised, and gracious. But you would soon notice something strange. Her right index finger would be missing. If you asked her how she lost her finger, she would quietly tell you that she burned it off. It took about two hours. If you asked her why she did it, she would say she was trying to find forgiveness for her sins and trying to show God her sincerity.

My wife and my son Randy were traveling through the jungles of Asia. Suddenly Randy cried out, "What is that?" A man wearing a long brown robe, stooping under the heavy weight of a cross he was carrying, walked down the road. He was trudging along with the heavy wooden cross on his back. A few days later the mystery of why he was doing that was solved. His picture was on the front page of the local newspaper. In the photo he was not carrying the cross. Instead, it was lying on the ground, and some men were nailing him to it. A reporter held a microphone out and asked him why he was doing this. His reply was simple: "I am trying to find forgiveness for my sins."

Once I was in another beautiful Asian city and got caught in a traffic jam. But it wasn't a jam caused by cars, trucks, motor bikes, ox carts, and bicycles. It was a "people jam." Thousands filled the streets. The men walked along together in groups of twenty. The central figure in each group was a man carrying a large metal structure on his shoulders. A metal bar lay across his shoulders and stuck out about two and a half feet on each side. Another curved steel bar, shaped like a half moon, extended up over his head and was connected to the ends of the bar lying across his shoulders. The complete structure weighed about sixty pounds. Scores of thin wires like bicycle wheel spokes extended down from the curved bar over his head and were fastened to his flesh with steel hooks. In addition, a metal skewer pierced his right cheek, his tongue, and protruded from the left side of his face. Each of these men swayed through the streets, twisting and turning, followed by scores of others who were all carrying similar burdens through the dusk. A light rain was falling, and a demon-possessed priest walked in front of each man. Finally I got out of our stalled car. "Why are these men doing this?" I asked a bystander. "To seek forgiveness for their sins," I was told.

Other religions can point out man's need for forgiveness. But only Jesus can forgive sins.

The Fullness of the Holy Spirit

Acts 4 reveals that Peter preached his remarkable message to the rulers and elders under the influence of the Holy Spirit. He was experiencing the Spirit's fullness. What does it mean that Peter was "filled with the Holy Spirit" (Acts 4:8)?

The apostle Paul gave a clear command: "Do not get drunk on wine, which leads to debauchery. Instead, be filled with the Spirit" (Ephesians 5:18). The Greek word for filled is *pleroo,* which means "to control." When we look carefully at the tense of the verbs, the sentence reads "Be continually controlled by the Spirit." Paul cites that as an alternative to being drunk with wine. When a person has had too much liquor, we say he is "under the influence." The liquor is in control. When he makes a fool of himself with some outlandish comment, we say the wine is speaking. We give the man the benefit of the doubt—if he was sober he would not talk like that. So Paul said we should continually be under the controlling influence of the Holy Spirit. And how does that take place? If you read and compare Ephesians 5:18 to 6:7 with Colossians 3:16-3:23, you will discover many parallel truths. In Ephesians Paul exhorts the believers to be filled with the Spirit. He urges the Colossians to be filled with the word.

Is there a difference? The answer is found in the teaching of Christ. Jesus said, "The Spirit gives life; the flesh counts for nothing. The words I have spoken to you are spirit and they are life" (John 6:63). Did you catch that? His words *are* Spirit. If we want to be under the constant control of the Holy Spirit, we must live in daily obedience to the word of God. That was Peter's experience, and the Spirit used him mightily to proclaim the gospel of Christ.

The authorities who heard Peter came to one conclusion. These uneducated, simple, plain-spoken men had been with Jesus. They sensed that the apostles were influenced by the same Spirit, the same truth, the same power, that characterized Jesus' life. They did not know what to do about the miraculous healing of the crippled man. So they conferred among themselves and decided on a plan. "Then they called them in again and commanded them not to speak or teach at all in the name of Jesus" (Acts 4:18). "Never, never mention the name of Jesus—not once, not at all,'" they ordered the apostles. They thought the issue was settled and the case closed. But it was not quite that simple.

Obedience
The apostles were already under different orders (Acts 1:8), so they had to decide whom they would obey. They decided to obey their Lord. "But Peter and John replied, 'Judge for yourselves whether it is right in God's sight to obey you rather than God. For we cannot help speaking about what we have seen and heard'" (Acts 4:19-20). After further threatenings they were set free.

The Sovereignty of God

What happened next? First, they went to the brethren, and gave a report on what had transpired. Then they prayed.

> "Sovereign Lord," they said, "you made the heaven and the earth and the sea, and everything in them. You spoke by the Holy Spirit through the mouth of your servant, our father David: 'Why do the nations rage and the peoples plot in vain? The kings of the earth take their stand and the rulers gather together against the Lord and against his Anointed One.' Indeed Herod and Pontius Pilate met together with the Gentiles and the people of Israel in this city to conspire against your holy servant Jesus, whom you anointed. They did what your power and will decided beforehand should happen. Now, Lord, consider their threats and enable your servants to speak your word with great boldness. Stretch out your hand to heal and perform miraculous signs and wonders through the name of your holy servant Jesus" (Acts 4:24-30).

Their prayer was dynamite. First they admitted they faced formidable opposition. But even their opponents were under God's divine authority and power. The authorities, the Gentiles, and the people of Israel were not doing what *they* determined, but what *God* determined. If there was ever a clear statement of faith in the sovereignty of God, this was it. God controls everything, everywhere, all the time. It may not always seem so, but it is so.

The apostles' faith was unshaken by these threats of punishment. They were in God's hands. He would not fail; he cannot fail. He is God! After prayerfully acknowledging God's sovereignty over their opponents, the second thing they did was to pray for boldness to speak the word. And God answered in no uncertain terms. "After they prayed, the place where they were meeting was shaken. And they were all filled with the Holy Spirit and spoke the word of God boldly" (Acts 4:31).

After asking for boldness they prayed, "Stretch out your hand to heal and perform miraculous signs and wonders through the name of your holy servant Jesus" (Acts 4:30). Visualize the scene. They were being harassed, hassled, and threatened. The rulers were gathered together against the Lord and against his Christ. The apostles were under attack by powerful, clever people. Their lives were in danger.

Let us say that we were threatened by someone who could do us great bodily harm. What would be our natural response? It would be to respond in kind, to retaliate. But what did these people ask God to do? Did they ask him to perform great miracles of vengeance upon their enemies? Did they ask him to step in and with one sweep of his mighty hand overpower them? No! They asked God to continue to do miracles of mercy such as he had done in the healing of the lame man at the temple. Amazing! Not miracles to hurt their enemies, but miracles to heal them. They were not concerned about their own fate, but consumed with a desire to communicate the gospel of the love of God.

Church Growth

Luke now refers to "the multitude of them that believed" (Acts 4:32 KJV). It is interesting to trace the growth of this body of believers. Luke's reporting gives a vivid description of first-century church growth. At first there were 120 believers (Acts 1:15), then 3,000 more (Acts 2:41). Soon there was an increase of another 5,000 (Acts 4:4). God worked in their midst in response to their faithful preaching of the gospel.

The leadership was never off track. The apostles had one prime mission in life: to bear witness to Christ. And they stuck with it. "With great power the apostles continued to testify to the resurrection of the Lord Jesus, and much grace was with them all" (Acts 4:33).

In the work of Christ today it often seems that the further along one goes in the ministry, the less time there is for the real work of the kingdom. A chaplain shared about his frustrations with his administrative load. His desk was covered with reports, reports, reports (all of which had to be filled out in triplicate), emergency leave requests, sick leaves, hardship cases—a mountain of paperwork. Although all of it was necessary, it was consuming most of his time. On top of that he had to give morality lectures, and attend staff meetings and social gatherings. This chaplain told me he had entered the service for one reason—to preach the gospel. But he was frustrated. It seemed that there was time for everything else but that.

Leaders of mission organizations have told me the same thing. They must wrestle with personnel decisions, budgets, governmental red tape, public relations, and problems among their staff. Often men and women in such positions find that an endless variety of such things keeps them from proclaiming the word of God. But that was not the case with the apostles. They stayed on track.

Two more reasons for the success of these early believers are recorded in Acts 4:32: "All the believers were one in heart and mind. No one claimed that any of his possessions was his own, but they shared everything they had." Two lessons can be drawn from this verse. The first is unity. The early Christians put forth a united witness. They were one in heart, soul, spirit, and mind. The second is sacrifice. They were willing to give whatever it took to get the job done. They gave their lives, their money, their time, their all. They did not hold back. Sacrifice was part of their lifestyle. Jesus had shown the way and they followed him gladly.

The teamwork of the two who were the main actors in the drama of Acts 4—Peter and John—is another evidence of the power of God to blend men's hearts together and to unite them as a team. Here was Peter—impulsive, straightforward, a decisive man of action. And here was John—the disciple of love. But under the control of the Holy Spirit there was no conflict. So the apostles were united and the people were united. Their teamwork contributed to a great and powerful witness for Christ that changed their world, and which continues to change our world to this very day.

Evidence of their sacrifical spirit is found in Acts 4:34-37: "There was no needy person among them. For from time to time those who owned lands or houses sold them, brought the money from the sales and put it at the apostles' feet and it was distributed to anyone as he had need. Joseph, a Levite from Cyprus, whom the apostles called Barnabas (which means Son of Encouragement), sold a field he owned and brought the money and put it at the apostles' feet.''

SUMMARY:

The apostles were advancing in the face of opposition through the power of the Holy Spirit and under the protection of their sovereign God. The life and ministry of the disciples demonstrates—
- the power of example;
- the power of the gospel;
- the power of a united witness;
- the power of sacrifice.

5
A Witnessing Lifestyle

ACTS 4 ENDS with Barnabas bringing a gift to the apostles. Acts 5 opens with the story of Ananias and Sapphira bringing their gift. But what a contrast there is between the two incidents!

Does the gospel say, "Believe on the Lord Jesus Christ, give your possessions to the church and you will be saved"? No! Salvation is the free gift of God. The only thing we give to God is our sinful lives. He does not demand that we give money, deeds to property, possessions, or anything else. We cannot purchase salvation. Did the apostles require new believers to give their lands and possessions before they were accepted into the fellowship? No! The apostles accepted one and all unconditionally. They were eager to help them, train them, pray for them, and include them in their fellowship. So we look at Ananias and Sapphira and ask, What was this all about?

There were among the believers a band of people who were somewhat more involved than the others. This is still true in any church today. There are those who are totally committed to following Christ, and some who are not. There may be those to whom Jesus Christ means practically *nothing*. There are others to whom Jesus Christ means *something,* just as there are always those—usually a small band—to whom Jesus Christ is *everything*. Their lives, their possessions, all that they are and have—are dedicated to him. Barnabas was one of those committed individuals. Throughout the history of the church God has always accomplished his purposes through a small band of dedicated men and women.

One day Ananias and Sapphira decided they wanted to be known for their commitment to Christ. They wanted a reputation as dedicated disciples, but were not willing to pay the price required for a life of discipleship. They said one thing but did another. Together, they came up with a scheme and put it into action. But God was not deceived. God knew what would happen to his small band of consecrated followers if it was infiltrated by hypocrites. So he took drastic action to protect the spiritual health and vigor of this group of committed disciples.

There are two key lessons here. One is the danger of hypocrisy. Jesus dealt very tenderly with open sinners, but bluntly condemned all hypocrites. I must not brag about things I haven't actually done. Nor must I promise to do something and then fail to do it. "When you make a vow to God, do not delay in fulfilling it. He has no pleasure in fools; fulfill your vow. It is better not to vow than to make a vow and not fulfill it" (Ecclesiastes 5:4-5).

The Holy Spirit is also known as the Spirit of truth, so a person who is led by the Spirit will tell the truth. Often when I travel overseas, I will send a souvenir home to my wife or children. A gift can be delivered free of customs charges if it costs less than ten dollars. The sender must declare the cost of the gift on the package. Frequently, a storekeeper will offer to mark such a gift's value as less than ten dollars even though it actually costs more. When I refuse to allow him to do that, he will assure me that no one will find out. "There's no problem," he says, "We do this all the time." He tries to assure me that this is standard practice all over the world. I know that, but I must still refuse to let him do it. Occasionally, a storekeeper will even become angry with me. "What's the matter with you? Are you crazy? Why don't you do what everybody else does?" Then I will try to explain my convictions to him. As a follower of Christ, I must tell the truth.

The second key lesson is one of encouragement for us. Notice Acts 5:3-4:

> Then Peter said, "Ananias, how is it that Satan has so filled your heart that you have lied to the Holy Spirit and have kept for yourself some of the money you received for the land? Didn't it belong to you before it was sold? And after it was sold, wasn't the money at your disposal? What made you think of doing such a thing? You have not lied to men but to God."

Satan can tempt me to sin, but not *force* me into it. It is always *my* decision. In the process God always provides an alternative. When a temptation comes slinking up, a way of escape comes marching alongside. I then evaluate the two and make my decision. "No temptation has seized you except what is common to man. And God is faithful; he will not let you be tempted beyond what you can bear. But when you are tempted, he will also provide a way out so that you can stand up under it" (1 Corinthians 10:13). So we cannot place the blame on the devil. He can tempt us, but that is all he can do. God has placed him within some limits. We can never truthfully say, "the devil made me do it."

In spite of Satan's attacks, the ministry kept growing. "More and more men and women believed in the Lord and were added to their number" (Acts 5:14). God was blessing and the people were rejoicing, but not the authorities. "Then the high priest and all his associates, who were members of the party of the Sadducees, were filled with jealousy. They arrested the apostles and put them in the public jail" (Acts 5:17-18).

The Sadducees had their choice. They could either do greater works than the apostles or they could try to halt the apostles' ministry. So they chose to attempt to disrupt the ministry of the apostles. It was a bad choice because when one picks a fight with God, he is in trouble. No matter who he is, regardless of his position or title, his background, education, or status in the community, his nation, or the world—if anyone tries to oppose the Lord, he has taken on more than he can handle. God is a formidable foe. It is far better to work with him than against him.

Why did the Sadducees make that choice? Because they were filled with jealousy. Can you imagine that? The high priest and his associates were the most powerful men in the nation. They were accustomed to receiving honor. But in spite of their dignified roles, their hearts were filled with jealousy. They envied these common, honest, plain-spoken men, so they put them in prison. But God sent an angel who released them and sent them to the temple to teach the word of life.

"At daybreak they entered the temple courts, as they had been told, and began to teach the people. When the high priest and his associates arrived, they called together the Sanhedrin—the full assembly of the elders of Israel—and sent to the jail for the apostles" (Acts 5:21). The Sanhedrin was the most dignified and august assembly that Jersualem could produce. This body of men had awesome power. There they sat, robed in splendid garments. They waited for the apostles. They were ready to fix their stern, disapproving gazes on the helpless prisoners. But there was one minor flaw. The prisoners were in the temple teaching the people.

> But on arriving at the jail, the officers did not find them there. So they went back and reported, "We found the jail securely locked, with the guards standing at the doors; but when we opened them, we found no one inside." On hearing this report, the captain of the temple guard and the chief priests were puzzled, wondering what would come of this. Then someone came and said, "Look! The men you put in jail are standing in the temple courts teaching the people" (Acts 5:22-25).

The apostles knew they were in danger. Why didn't they flee or hide? Why didn't they take precautions against being captured again? For one simple reason: they had been told to witness. So they witnessed. We have been given the same command. Peter wrote, "But you are a chosen people, a royal priesthood, a holy nation, a people belonging to God, that you may declare the praises of him who called you out of darkness into his wonderful light" (1 Peter 2:9). Peter was qualified to write those words because he lived them. At the risk of his own life he bore testimony to Jesus Christ. He was everlastingly at it. Witnessing was his lifestyle. What does it take to have a witnessing lifestyle? I believe five elements are involved.

See Things as Jesus Does

To make witnessing a regular, normal, and vital part of our lives, we need to *see things as Jesus saw them*. "When he saw the crowds, he had compassion on them, because they were harassed and helpless, like sheep without a shepherd. Then he said to his disciples, 'The harvest is plentiful but the workers are few. Ask the Lord of the harvest, therefore, to send out workers into his harvest field'" (Matthew 9:36-38).

Jesus saw the harvest as plentiful. He also spoke about the harvest on another occasion. "Do you not say, 'Four months more and then the harvest'? I tell you, open your eyes and look at the fields! They are ripe for harvest" (John 4:35). He said the harvest is ready to be gathered in.

Is that the way you see things? When you look at the world about you, do you see a vast, overripe harvest? Most people don't. As Deputy President for The Navigators, my job gives me an opportunity to travel. Wherever I go, there is a universal conviction that something has gone wrong with the harvest. I visit people in a student ministry, and they tell me all about their problems. I visit pastors and missionaries who tell me about their problems. But there have always been problems. Problems are not a new discovery. Problems were not born in the last quarter of the twentieth century.

Have you noticed what Jesus said when he sent his men

out? "I am sending you out as sheep among wolves. . . . But be on your guard against men; they will hand you over to the local councils and flog you . . . But when they arrest you, do not worry . . . All men will hate you because of me . . . When you are persecuted in one place, flee to another" (Matthew 10:16-23).

After providing his disciples with all the resources they needed to do the job, a brief job description, and some guidelines for the ministry, Jesus prepared them for rejection. He forewarned them of trouble, persecution, and difficulty along the way.

A Battle Mentality

We must adopt a battle mentality to develop a witnessing lifestyle. We must see ourselves as soldiers in the eternal war between good and evil, righteousness and unrighteousness, Satan and God. We must recognize the fact that we are soldiers in the army of Christ. Paul wrote, "Endure hardship with us like a good soldier of Christ Jesus. No one serving as a soldier gets involved in civilian affairs—he wants to please his commanding officer" (2 Timothy 2:3-4).

How does a battle mentality relate to a witnessing lifestyle? The apostle Paul said, "I press on toward the goal to win the prize for which God has called me heavenward in Christ Jesus" (Philippians 3:14). Paul did not say, "I glide toward the goal," "I drift toward the goal," or "I float toward the goal." No. He said, "I *press* toward the goal."

The word *press* always implies resistance. We live in a day when comfort is king. The good life is the soft life. The best way is the easy way. If it is smooth and pleasant with no problems, it must be right. But if it is hard, difficult, and rough, it must be wrong. If we face opposition, we must not be doing things the way they "should" be done—there must be a flaw in our thinking.

A Laborer's Mentality

The third thing we need for a witnessing lifestyle is to *see ourselves as laborers,* which, Jesus said, "are few." Being a laborer is not easy. It is hard work. But unless the harvest is reaped while it is ripe, there will be no harvest.

I was born on a farm in Iowa. When the harvest season rolled around, everyone was prepared to work long hours. It was hot and dusty out in the fields. We became thirsty. We grew tired. Our muscles ached. Our feet were sore. Sometimes we developed blisters. Our backs hurt. But we kept on harvesting.

Spiritual harvesting is even more difficult. The apostle Paul was not complaining when he gave a brief history of his harvesting experiences. He was simply stating the facts. He wrote,

> Five times I received from the Jews the forty lashes minus one. Three times I was beaten with rods, once I was stoned, three times I was shipwrecked, I spent a night and a day in the open sea, I have been constantly on the move. I have been in danger from rivers, in danger from bandits, in danger from my own countrymen, in danger from Gentiles; in danger in the city, in danger in the country, in danger at sea; and in danger from false brothers. I have labored and toiled and have often gone without sleep; I have known hunger and thirst and have often gone without food; I have been cold and naked. Besides everything else, I face daily the pressure of my concern for all the churches (2 Corinthians 11:24-28).

We Christians have not chosen the life of a perpetual vacationer. We have not chosen to be among those who spend their lives lying on tropical beaches. We have chosen the life of a laborer. Let us roll up our sleeves and go out into the hot, dusty fields to labor.

Using Your Resources

The fourth thing we need to become a lifetime witness is to *learn to use our resources.* When Jesus sent the apostles into the field he equipped them with the resources they needed to do the job. He still does. Now, what are our resources?

The indwelling Holy Spirit. While he was with his disciples, Jesus gave them clear instruction about the work of the Holy Spirit. He said, "And I will ask the Father, and he will give you another Counselor to be with you forever—the Spirit of truth. . . . You know him, for he lives with you and will be in you" (John 14:16-17). He would come to help the disciples in the same ways Jesus had helped them. He would abide with them forever and become part of their lives. His Spirit would infuse them with his life, his mind, himself! The fullness or control of the Holy Spirit may vary, but the *presence* of the Holy Spirit is an established fact in the life of every Christian.

When describing the ministry of the Holy Spirit, Jesus said, "When the Counselor comes . . . he will testify about me but you also must testify, for you have been with me from the beginning" (John 15:26-27). Jesus referred to two witnesses—the Holy Spirit and the Christian. Both are powerful witnesses. The Holy Spirit's witness conveys the ring of truth. When God speaks, the unbeliever knows he is hearing the truth. He may mock and scoff, but deep in his soul, he knows that what he is hearing is the truth. The Holy Spirit can reveal Christ to the unbeliever in a way we can't. He has a supernatural power to help people see the reality, love, grace, and mercy of the Lord Jesus Christ. But remember, your witness is powerful, too, because it has behind it the reality of a transformed life.

I was attending a conference in Norway at which a young lady gave her testimony. She had been a Marxist-Leninist for many years and had devoted her life to spreading communism. One day her dream came true—she was going to visit Czechoslovakia. She could hardly wait to visit a country which she thought of as a communist paradise. But she couldn't believe what she saw. Her dream was shattered. She was left with the stark realization that all she had believed and propagated was a lie. She went home to Norway disillusioned and empty. At that point in her life, someone witnessed to her about new life in Jesus Christ. She responded by accepting Christ, and today she shares her story freely. Her witness is a powerful witness to other young communists because it is backed by the glorious reality of the love and peace of Christ—and her own transformed life.

Jesus also explained the purpose of the Holy Spirit's ministry by saying, "But when he, the Spirit of truth, comes, he will guide you into all truth. He will not speak on his own; he will speak only what he hears, and he will tell you what is yet to come. He will bring glory to me by taking from what is mine and making it known to you" (John 16:13-14). The Holy Spirit will guide the Christian in his walk with Christ.

Think of a railroad. The engine is the believer. The power that drives the engine is the Holy Spirit. The track upon which he guides the believer is the word of God. The Holy Spirit never guides us·contrary to the Bible. Therefore, never judge the Bible by your experience. Instead, you must always judge your experience by the Bible.

Another facet in the ministry of the Holy Spirit is that he will glorify Christ. To glorify means to exalt, to magnify, to give him the preeminence in everything. I was explaining this to some university students some time ago and likened the Holy Spirit's ministry to a stage play in a theater. The one who is the main person in the drama of life—who always occupies center stage—is Jesus Christ. Far behind the upper balcony— in the shadows—is a person who operates the spotlight and keeps it focused on the person at center stage. The one operating the spotlight is the Holy Spirit, and the light is the word of God. To call upon the Holy Spirit to come down from his God-given place— the place of his own choosing—to leave the shadows and come to the front and occupy the spotlight with Jesus is doing the Holy Spirit a disservice and putting him in an awkward position. He has no desire for it. His ministry is in the background doing all within his mighty power to reveal and exalt the Lord Jesus Christ.

The word of God. Our second resource for becoming a lifetime witness is the word of God. "For you have been born again, not of perishable seed, but of imperishable, through the living and enduring word of God" (1 Peter 1:23). Since people are born again by the word of God, our prime responsibility as a witness is to share that word which is "living and active" (Hebrews 4:12).

At a Christian leadership conference near Wellington, New Zealand, a young man from Samoa gave his testimony. Because of financial difficulties in his family, as a young boy he was sent to live with an uncle and aunt. His uncle was a drunken, foul-mouthed, mean brute of a man. He frequently beat his wife unmercifully. During his years in their home this young man wondered time and time again how his aunt could bear to live with such a person. Eventually he went to New Zealand for his university training.

After some months, his aunt and uncle came to visit him. He couldn't believe what he heard and saw. His uncle was a new man. He was filled with love, joy, and peace. He was a kind, gracious gentleman. The Samoan student couldn't figure out how it had happened. He knew of no power on earth that could bring about such a transformation. His uncle told him the changes were the result of reading the Bible.

A few weeks after his uncle and aunt had visited him, this student was invited to join some other students who were studying the Bible together. He was eager to learn about the book that had so completely changed his uncle's life. As he studied the Bible for himself, he too responded to the gospel.

The gospel. Our third resource is the gospel. "I am not ashamed of the gospel," wrote Paul, "because it is the power of God for the salvation of everyone who believes: first for the Jew, then for the Gentile" (Romans 1:16). We must remember two things about the gospel. First, it must be audible. When the angel released the apostles from prison he said, "Go, stand in the temple courts . . . and tell the people the full message of this new life" (Acts 5:20). He did not say they were to go and let the people *see* their transformed lives. Faith does not come by seeing but by hearing.

Second, the gospel must be clear. I must know how to make it understandable to someone else. If I don't know how to do that, I'm helpless.

While visiting Norway I stayed in a large, wooden guest house. It was a beautiful, splendid old building. As I entered I thought to myself, *This place would be a fire trap if it caught on fire. It would burn quickly.* But when I entered my room my mind was set at ease. There, next to my door, was a new, bright red fire extinguisher. I relaxed and fell asleep. The next morning I looked more closely at the fire extinguisher to familiarize myself with the instructions—they were in Norwegian! Upon closer examination I discovered the instructions were also provided in English. Had those instructions only been in Norwegian, I thought to myself, their message would be like the gospel is to many people. The gospel is perfectly capable of accomplishing the purpose God intends, but the message itself is useless unless it is explained in a way that people can understand.

Prayer. Fourth, we have the resource of prayer. "Do not be anxious about anything, but in everything, by prayer and petitition, with thanksgiving, present your requests to God. And the peace of God, which transcends all understanding, will guard your hearts and your minds in Christ Jesus" (Philippians 4:6-7). Pray about everything! But how should we pray for a non-Christian? I make it a practice to pray about three things: that he will see his need; that he will see that Christ is the only one who can meet that need; and that he will make the only intelligent decision possible on the basis of those two facts. I don't believe it is possbile for anyone who understands the gospel message to decide *intelligently* to reject the Lord Jesus. To decide to live without God under the control of Satan and spend eternity in hell is not an intelligent decision.

As you pray remember the promise, "Let us not become weary in doing good, for at the proper time we will reap a harvest if we do not give up" (Galatians 6:9). Psalm 126:5-6 adds further light: "Those who sow in tears will reap with songs of joy. He who goes out weeping, carrying seed to sow, will return with songs of joy, carrying sheaves with him"

The transformed life. I attended a dinner in Sydney, Australia, with two non-Christians. The one on my right agreed with everything I said. He knew it was true. The one on my left, however, a university student, had all kinds of intellectual arguments and didn't believe anything I said. Finally, my companion on the right spoke to the student. "Oh, it's all true all right. I saw what happened to my friend. The Lord has completely changed his life." Soon I found that the two of us, the non-Christian on my right and myself, were witnessing together! Frankly, I have never before been teamed up in a witnessing stiuation with a non-Christian. But he was absolutely convinced of the truth of the gospel. He had seen its results in his friend's life. No one can argue with a transformed life (see Acts 4:14).

A consistent Christian life. The first Christians I met, who were primarily responsible for introducing me to Christ, had not themselves experienced a radical or dramatic conversion. They had been Christians from their youth. Most of them came from Christian homes and were led to Christ either by their parents or by their Sunday school teachers. But that did not handicap their witness. They simply lived the Christian life day by day and their example had a powerful effect on my life. For years I have been trying to explain what I saw in their lives but have been unable to do so. Recently I realized exactly what it was that I saw in their lives. I had seen love, joy, peace, longsuffering, gentleness, goodness, faith, meekness, and temperance. Their lives demonstrated Galatians 5:22-23 in action. I was attracted to their lives and wanted to discover the source of those qualities.

Christian fellowship. Our seventh resource is the fellowship of the church. A gathering of believers who are united in Christian fellowship can have a powerful effect on the non-Christian. I remember my reaction when I walked into a church and heard the gospel. The singing, the lives of the people, and the message all combined to attract me to Christ. Paul wrote, "But if an unbeliever or someone who does not understand comes in while everybody is prophesying, he will be convinced by all that he is a sinner and will be judged by all, and the secrets of his heart will be laid bare. So he will fall down and worship God, exclaiming, 'God is really among you!'" (1 Corinthians 14:24-25). To expose a non-Christian to a dynamic Christian fellowship is dynamite. But what is true Christian fellowship? I think one of the clearest passages on this is Ephesians 4:16. "From him the whole body, joined and held together by every supporting ligament, grows and builds itself up in love, as each part does its work."

Now what does that mean? What is the apostle Paul getting at? His teaching reminds me of a situation I was involved in at Northwestern College in Minneapolis while I was a student. Waldron Scott and I were classmates and drove home together on our school breaks. Scotty lived in Omaha and my parents lived close by. One day we left Minneapolis for Omaha. We hadn't gone very far when our car's engine threw a rod. It began to bang and clatter. Neither of us were mechanically inclined so, not knowing any better, we simply kept driving. Whenever we stopped for gas we were told we couldn't keep driving a car in that condition. But since we could not afford to have it repaired, there was no alternative but to keep driving. We completed the trip.

The next day Scotty decided to fix the engine. Since he couldn't even identify the parts, he took them out one by one and numbered them as he laid them out in rows on the front porch. After disassembling the entire engine, numbering and laying out every part, he took those that needed to be replaced to a junkyard and bought some good used parts. Then he put the new parts into the numbered sequence and reassembled the engine. Miracle of miracles, the engine ran!

Now think with me for a moment. When the engine was dismantled and lying on the front porch, was it "together"? Yes, in a sense. But it had to be reassembled before the engine would run and drive the car. That's what Paul is getting at in Ephesians 4:16. He is saying we must be held together. Every member of the body must work properly. That's fellowship.

A Missionary Mentality

If we are to have a witnessing lifestyle, *we also need a mis-*

sionary mentality. Every heart without Christ is a mission field. Every heart with Christ is a missionary. One of the great sources of power in the New Testament church was that they did not rely on a few "superstars" to do the ministry. In fact, when persecution came and they fled for their lives, even that did not quench their bold witness for Christ. "Those who had been scattered preached the word wherever they went" (Acts 8:4). Those who were scattered were ordinary believers. Philip, the table waiter, had a missionary mentality. When the Lord brought Philip in touch with "an Ethiopian eunuch, an important official in charge of all the treasury of Candace, queen of the Ethiopians" (Acts 8:27), Philip responded naturally, since the Ethiopian was reading a passage from Isaiah: "Philip began with that very passage of Scripture and told him the good news about Jesus" (Acts 8:35).

We must view ourselves as the means for God to shed abroad his love in the world by the Holy Spirit. Sharing the gospel is not optional for missionaries. Far too often we think of the missionary as someone who is "way out there." Admittedly, we must continue to have missionaries "out there," but we must also have them "back here"—in the bank, garage, supermarket, office, and neighborhood. We're elected—we're to be those missionaries! God has appointed us to this task.

After the Sanhedrin learned the apostles were preaching in the temple courts, they sent the captain of the temple guard with his officers to bring the apostles before the council. Then the high priest said, "We gave you strict orders not to teach in this name . . . Yet you have filled Jerusalem with your teaching and are determined to make us guilty of this man's blood" (Acts 5:28).

Peter replied, "We must obey God rather than men! The God of our fathers raised Jesus from the dead—whom you had killed by hanging him on a tree. God exalted him to his own right hand as Prince and Savior that he might give repentance and forgiveness of sins to Israel. We are witnesses of these things, and so is the Holy Spirit, whom God has given to those who obey him" (Acts 5:29-32). The high priest was infuriated by these men. His authority was being challenged. He was losing face. But as you read Peter's reply, you are struck by his poise, assurance, and dignity. Peter was under the control of the Holy Spirit, and demonstrated peace and gentleness—two of the fruits of the Holy Spirit.

However, the Sanhedrin flew into a rage, and were cut to the heart because their plans were frustrated by these bold, truthful men. They decided to murder the apostles. Fortunately, there was one man present, a respected leader, who counselled restraint. He said, "Leave these men alone! Let them go! For if their purpose or activity is of human origin, it will fail. But if it is from God, you will not be able to stop these men; you will only find yourselves fighting against God" (Acts 5:38-39). When the Sanhedrin heard his argument, they calmed down and agreed not to kill the apostles. So they beat them and commanded them never to mention the name of Jesus again.

However the apostles did not take their orders from mortal men, but from the eternal God. "The apostles left the Sanhedrin, rejoicing because they had been counted worthy of suffering disgrace for the Name. Day after day, in the temple courts and from house to house, they never stopped teaching and proclaiming the good news that Jesus is the Christ" (Acts 5:41-42).

SUMMARY:

A witnessing lifestyle requires—
- seeing things as Jesus does;
- a battle mentality;
- a laborer's mentality;
- using your resources;
- a missionary mentality.

6
Serving Tables
and Serving
the Word

IN CHAPTER 6 the devil attacks the disciples who were involved with the apostles in the ministry. We have seen the apostles ashamed, threatened, beaten, and jailed. But since the apostles could not be stopped, the devil tried a new tactic: division. He set the Christians arguing among themselves. Divisiveness has often plagued the church over the years. But did it work during this initial attack?

> In those days when the number of disciples was increasing, the Grecian Jews among them complained against those of the Aramaic-speaking community because their widows were being overlooked in the daily distribution of food. So the Twelve gathered all the disciples together and said, "It would not be right for us to neglect the ministry of the word of God in order to wait on tables. Brothers, choose seven men from among you who are known to be full of the Spirit and wisdom. We will turn this responsibility over to them and will give our attention to prayer and the ministry of the word" (Acts 6:1-4).

The apostles continued to demonstrate that they were

controlled by the Holy Spirit. They did not fly into a rage or reprimand those individuals for their bickering. We must remember their example if we would help people to deal with problems. Admit that a problem exists when someone brings one to your attention. It may not appear to be serious to you, but if the other person thinks it is, it should be treated seriously.

The apostles could have dismissed this complaint as incidental nonsense and returned to their work. After all, they were involved in a world mission. They were following the world's greatest leader, doing the greatest work ever done in the world. They were involved in issues of life and death. So to give thought to a few complaining people who were concerned about such a mundane issue, might not have appeared to them to be worth their time and effort. But that was not how the apostles responded. They stopped to deal with the complaint.

Leadership

This is a great lesson in leadership. If you nip a problem in the bud you may save yourself many hours, weeks, and possibly years down the road. Remember Solomon's advice: "When the sentence for a crime is not quickly carried out, the hearts of the people are filled with schemes to do wrong" (Ecclesiastes 8:11). The apostles acted wisely—mighty evidence that the Lord was guiding them. If they had relied upon the flesh and human wisdom, it might not have happened that way.

What is the difference between self-control and being under the control of the Holy Spirit? I don't believe there is any difference when we understand these concepts properly. Self-control is the fruit of the Spirit (see Galatians 5:22-23). So when I respond to the whispers of God's Spirit by following him in obedience, I am demonstrating self-control—the fruit of the Spirit in my life. Paul gave us a clear admonition when he wrote, "Those who belong to Christ Jesus have crucified the sinful nature with its passions and desires. Since we live by the Spirit, let us keep in step with the Spirit. Let us not become conceited, provoking and envying each other" (Galatians 5:24-26). If I am led or controlled by the Spirit, I will not give vent to my natural passions and desires. If I have crucified the flesh, I will not go about boasting of my achievements, arguing, or envying others.

Spirit-led self-control was evident in the apostles' actions. They looked calmly at the problem and resolved it with God-given wisdom. They called the people together and reminded them of the service God had called them to. Significantly, the words *serve,* or *wait,* in Acts 6:2 and *ministry* in Acts 6:4 come from the same root word. Admittedly, it should be someone's job to serve food, but it was the apostles' job to serve or minister the word. Some of the disciples were to serve that which fed the body, while the apostles served that which fed the soul.

Four Calls

What did this ministry of the word involve? The apostles did the same things they had observed in Jesus' ministry. Jesus structured his ministry within the framework of four calls. The first was *the call to repent and believe.* "After John was put in prison, Jesus went into Galilee, proclaiming the good news of God. 'The time has come,' he said. 'The kingdom of God is near. Repent and believe the good news!'" (Mark 1:14-15). The second was *the call to follow him in discipleship.* "If anyone would come after me, he must deny himself and take up his cross daily and follow me" (Luke 9:23). The third was *the call to go forth as a laborer.* "After this the Lord appointed seventy-two others and sent them two by two ahead of him to every town and place where he was about to go. He told them, 'The harvest is plentiful, but the laborers are few. Ask the Lord of the harvest, therefore, to send out workers into his harvest field'" (Luke 10:1-2). The fourth was *the call to serve as a leader* in the mission of reaching the world. "He appointed twelve—designating them apostles—that they might be with him and that he might send them out to preach and to have authority to drive out demons" (Mark 3:14-15). Jesus was the only model the apostles had for their ministry. They did what he did and as a result the number of disciples multiplied.

Satan launched his attack when all was going well. If your ministry seems to be going well, with no problems in sight, brace yourself. Trouble could be lurking just around the corner.

Satan's Counterattack

I was leading The Navigators' work at the University of Nebraska, and things were going well. After our first year we had two students on campus who were really with us in heart and vision. They were dedicated to Christ and sold on the vision of giving their lives that others might come to know Christ. We spent much time with these two men, and by the end of the second year there were nine such men involved. By the end of the third year, there were forty-two. We planned to place these men strategically throughout the dormitory complex so that by the end of the fourth year we could have shared Christ with every dormitory resident.

At that time we received a visit from Paul Lilienberg, an outstanding pastor from Sweden. When he observed our ministry Paul said, "LeRoy, the devil is hopping mad at what he sees here. Right now he is walking back and forth on the roof of those dormitories plotting his counterattack." I wrote off his warning as an overstatement by a concerned visitor who really didn't understand our situation. But I was wrong. The devil launched an all-out surprise attack that no one would have predicted. It happened so swiftly that it took us completely by surprise. We lost many of the men and our plan to evangelize the dormitories was crushed. So when all seems to be going well, be much in prayer for God's protection in the lives of the people involved.

Prayer

The apostles had made two commitments. The first was a commitment to prayer. They had seen this in the life of Jesus and they followed his example. I'm sure they knew they had been chosen as apostles after Jesus had spent a night in prayer (see Luke 6:12-13). The apostles had seen Jesus retire to pray in the midst of a busy schedule (see Luke 5:15-16). They watched him pray in the early morning (see Mark 1:35).

Prayer was an integral part of the Lord's life, and the apostles followed his example. Prayer, therefore, is a crucial habit for the person who wants God to use his life. Prayer is also vital to the four basic areas of Jesus' ministry.

Prayer opens the door for a witness to others. "Devote yourselves to prayer, being watchful and thankful. And pray for us, too, that God may open a door for our message, so that we may proclaim the mystery of Christ, for which I am in chains. Pray that I may proclaim it clearly as I should" (Colossians 4:2-4).

Prayer is the key to establishing believers in discipleship. "For this reason, since the day we heard about you, we have not stopped praying for you and asking God to fill you with the knowledge of his will through all spiritual wisdom and understanding. And we pray this in order that you may live a life worthy of the Lord and may please him in every way: bearing fruit in every good work, growing in the knowledge of God" (Colossians 1:9-10).

Prayer is the key to seeing laborers raised up and thrust out into the harvest. "The harvest is plentiful but the workers are few. Ask the Lord of the harvest, therefore, to send out workers into his harvest field" (Matthew 9:37-38).

Prayer is vital in the selection of leadership, as we have already seen (see Luke 6:12-13).

The Word

The apostles' second commitment was to the ministry of the word of God. Their lives were characterized by the ministry, or serving, of the word. This is precisely what people need. I have attended churches where the word of God was either ignored altogether in the sermon, or merely used as a springboard from which the speaker could plunge into his own ideas, man-made philosophies, or even his political views. I have also been in churches where the ministers taught the word so the people were instructed, but not fed spiritually. We learned facts, figures, history, theology, and doctrine, but our souls were not fed. Our spirit was not strengthened, and our wills were not captured by the Spirit of God for a greater commitment and devotion to Christ. To feed people is to strengthen their spiritual life just as food strengthens their physical life. The word must be understood in our minds, engraved in our hearts, and carried out in our lives. The word of God is the model by which we should fashion all we do in our daily walk.

When we walk through Disneyland we can visit Frontier Land, Adventure Land, Tomorrow Land, and Fantasy Land, but not Wonder Land. If I want to visit Wonder Land, I must open my Bible because all the wonders not yet seen, treasures not yet discovered, promises not yet claimed, food not yet tasted, and directions not yet received are found in it. The psalmist prayed, "Open my eyes that I may see wonderful things in your law" (Psalm 119:18).

As God's people are served the Scriptures, they decide to leave the paths of self-will, self-righteousness, worldliness, hypocrisy, pride, and unbelief. "I gain understanding from your precepts; therefore I hate every wrong path" (Psalm 119:104). Thus the word of God becomes alive and active in our lives through the Spirit of God's quickening work. This should also be our aim as we share God's word with others.

We have studied the framework in which Jesus structured his ministry: evangelizing the lost, establishing the disciples, equipping the laborers, and training leaders. Later these same objectives became the framework for the apostles' lives and ministries. Let us review those four tasks again to see how the word of God has a vital part in helping us to accomplish each objective.

Evangelizing. Jesus spoke of sowers sowing the word. "Listen! A farmer went out to sow his seed. . . . The farmer sows the word" (Mark 4:3,14). Peter noted the power of the seed of the word: "For you have been born again, not of perishable seed, but of imperishable, through the living and enduring word of God" (1 Peter 1:23). Paul constantly used the word when he evangelized. "As his custom was, Paul went into the synagogue, and on three Sabbath days he reasoned with them from the Scriptures" (Acts 17:2).

Establishing believers. "Like newborn babes, long for the pure milk of the word, that by it you may grow in respect to salvation, if you have tasted the kindness of the Lord" (1 Peter 2:2-3, NASB).

Equipping laborers. "All Scripture is God-breathed and is useful for teaching, rebuking, correcting and training in righteousness, so that the man of God may be thoroughly equipped for every good work" (2 Timothy 3:16-17).

Training and launching servant leaders. While the apostles devoted themselves to prayer and the ministry of the word they took action to solve a certain problem. When the Grecian Jews complained that their widows were being overlooked in the distribution of food, the apostles concluded that the answer to their problem was a few good men. The Twelve said, "Brothers, choose seven men from among you who are known to be full of the Spirit and wisdom. We will turn this responsiblity over to them and will give our attention to prayer and the ministry of the word" (Acts 6:3). The apostles refused to allow anything to hinder the ministry of the word.

All too often we think the answer to such a problem is a clever program. If the high school department in the Sunday School is declining in numbers, what do we turn to? If the missions budget is not being met, what do we do? Are films, or famous personalities the answer? No. The answer does not lie in better methods or machinery, but in better men and women. The apostles concluded that the believers should select some well-qualified individuals to wait on tables. Immediately the people saw the wisdom of their advice and chose the seven.

When we look at the qualifications of the seven we are

amazed. Today we would look at such a list and suppose it was for the selection of the president of a Christian organization, the head of a mission board, or the moderator of an assembly of churches. But no—they needed table waiters!

Is there a lesson for us in this? Yes! No job is too small not to require good men. If we keep every job in the church filled with the best man or woman for that job, the church will flourish. That's exactly what happened then: "So the word of God spread. The number of disciples in Jerusalem increased rapidly, and a large number of priests became obedient to the faith" (Acts 6:7). How were the seven selected? Did the apostles choose and appoint them? No. The apostles merely set forth the qualifications for the job. The people chose the seven, and the apostles ratified the decision.

Marks of Maturity

At this point we are introduced to Stephen, an amazing man. Stephen was a mature man of God. His life was characterized by faith, power, wisdom, courage, and love. He was a man of action—he did things. In a war, battles are not won by sitting around giving learned lectures on military strategy and tactics. Battles are not won by wearing fancy uniforms and parading up and down before the loungers in the park. Battles are won by courageous deeds. "Now Stephen, a man full of God's grace and power, did great wonders and miraculous signs among the people" (Acts 6:8).

Today there seems to be a tendency among leaders of Stephen's caliber to organize others to do the work while they sit around discussing issues, writing papers, or studying various problems. Such activities are not bad in themselves, provided they do not detract from our involvement with people and being out in the battle. But most of this paperwork, the interminable reports and studies, just creates a smokescreen to hide behind while staying out of the trenches where the battle rages for the souls of men.

Some years ago, I listened to a television report about furniture breakage. Furniture manufacturers were concerned because much of their furniture was damaged while being shipped. Some of the larger furniture companies consolidated resources and hired two independent groups to analyze this problem and make recommendations to correct it. After several months of intensive study the research groups—working independently of each other—made their reports. Hundreds of man hours were invested. Thousands of dollars were spent. Both groups came to the same conclusion and made identical recommendations. After traveling hundreds of miles, interviewing countless people, and observing the shipping process, they concluded one thing: the movers should be more careful. Like many similar studies, this was a waste of time, money, and effort.

Admittedly, at times we should pull back and evaluate. But after we have done that, let us go forth again—like Stephen—"among the people." And remember, Stephen ran into some opposition. Anyone who is out among the people involved in the work of Christ will encounter difficulties.

When I talked to a man who leads a university ministry in the Netherlands, he told me how a young man put up a poster advertising a gospel meeting. Within an hour it was torn down. He put up another one. It too was taken down. Other posters advertising secular activities remained on the notice board for weeks, and many were outdated. But when a poster went up concerning Jesus Christ, it was taken down.

Why do people oppose God's work? This can be summarized in eight words found in Luke 19:14: "But his subjects hated him and sent a delegation after him to say, *'We don't want this man to be our king.'*" Millions have firmly resolved, "We do not want Jesus to be our king. We will not allow him to reign over us." Such people are set in their sin and determined to live for self.

Why did the members of the Synagogue of the Freedmen oppose what Stephen said? Because they wanted to live according to tradition.

Then they secretly persuaded some men to say, "We have

heard Stephen speak words of blasphemy against Moses and against God." So they stirred up the people and the elders and the teachers of the law. They seized Stephen and brought him before the Sanhedrin. They produced false witnesses, who testified, "This fellow never stops speaking against the holy place and against the law. For we have heard him say that this Jesus of Nazareth will destroy this place and change the customs Moses handed down to us" (Acts 6:11-14).

Stephen's accusers were taken up with three things—the holy place, the law, and the customs of Moses. There was not anything inherently wrong with the temple in Jerusalem, the law of God, or the teachings of Moses. The temple was built with God-given plans. The law was delivered intact, perfect, to Moses the man of God. The lessons he taught the people came through the inspiration of the Holy Spirit. So we know that Stephen, the man of God, did not say or do anything that belittled or condemned any of these. I think his opponents had two problems. They were very proud men, and, as they listened to Stephen, "they could not stand up against his wisdom or the Spirit by which he spoke" (Acts 6:10). Here was a man in the garb of a table waiter sharing the word of God with such power and wisdom that his critics could not cope. These intellectual Jews were offended by Stephen. Their egos were bruised and their pride was hurt. In addition, they completely misunderstood the great purposes of God.

Stephen would never have experienced such trouble if he had been content to wait on tables. But did he take his job lightly? No! Stephen knew his ministry was serving tables. I'm sure he was an excellent worker and his heart was in his work.

All too often people who are involved in some ordinary task lose sight of its importance and chafe under that responsibility, dreaming about the day when they can get into the real ministry. Such an attitude comes from the devil. He always tries to discourage us in our work for Christ no matter what we are doing.

I used to have the privilege of directing summer conferences at Glen Eyrie, The Navigators' conference center. Year after year we watched people come and go. We did our best to provide a program the Lord could use to meet their needs. We invited well-known Bible teachers to come and teach the Scriptures. Our staff would lead discussion and prayer groups. Men like George Sanchez, Skip Gray, Bob Vidano, and Franklyn Elliott, four of the best song leaders I know anywhere in the world, would be on hand to lead singing as well as to preach and lead groups. Toward the end of each conference, I would sit down with a conferee and ask what he or she had learned. More often than not, they made comments like, "I was really amazed at how carefully the grounds staff washed the windows in the castle." Or, "I was greatly challenged by the way those young men mowed the lawn." And, "It was a delight to watch your staff serve food, and clean the floors. Their hearts were really in their work."

Now I'm sure our young men and women thought their work was not noticed in the shadow of the preaching, singing, and discussion groups. But that was not so. Paul's exhortation in Colossians 3:23 applies to everything we do: "Whatever you do, work at it with all your heart, as working for the Lord, not for men."

I'm sure Stephen gave his best. But he also knew that administrative tasks should not crowd out or replace being out "among the people" as a witness for Christ. Stephen had an obvious hunger to share the gospel, and a firm grasp of the word of God. When we read his message we are struck with his command of the Scriptures.

But a person can have a command of the Scriptures and still not be out sharing his faith if he doesn't have a strong desire to do so. How can this spirit be brought to life? For one thing, we can pray over passages such as "I beheld the transgressors, and was grieved; because they kept not thy word. Consider how I love thy precepts: quicken me, O Lord, according to thy loving kindness" (Psalm 119:158-159, KJV). Ask God to bring to life in you a spirit that grieves when people dishonor God, serve the devil, and pollute the world with their selfishness, lust, and pride. Pray for a heart that cannot bear to see people ruin their lives and miss salvation. If I am truly concerned for the glory of God and for the good of my fellow man, I will want to be out there, like Stephen, "among the people."

The Lord Jesus Christ is our greatest example. You recall how he sent forth the apostles as recorded in Matthew 10. Did he then quietly retire to some sandy beach to take it easy, secure in the fact that his men were out there, on the job, proclaiming the gospel? Assuredly not! The record is plain: "After Jesus had finished instructing his twelve disciples, he went on from there to teach and preach in the towns of Galilee" (Matthew 11:1). Jesus Christ was not a "non-working supervisor." He was constantly engaged in spiritual warfare. Let us pattern our lives after his clear example and follow in his steps.

SUMMARY:

The apostles' commitment to the word and prayer led them to give themselves to—
- witnessing for Christ;
- establishing believers;
- training laborers;
- training leaders.

God blessed their commitment and increased the number of disciples and produced men like Stephen who—
- were servants;
- knew the word;
- were involved in the battle.

7
God's Great Plan

SOME FALSE WITNESSES leveled charges of blasphemy against Stephen before the Sanhedrin. The high priest did not waste any words getting down to business. He simply asked Stephen whether the charges were true or false; was he guilty or not? Then Stephen displayed his command of the word of God—his source of strength.

I saw an amazing sight in Istanbul, Turkey. We were sitting in a restaurant when suddenly Randy, our son, turned to us with a surprised look and said, "Don't look out the window. Just guess what kind of animal is on the sidewalk." We guessed everything we could think of, but we never came close.

On the sidewalks of downtown Istanbul was a huge brown bear, muzzled and on a leash. The man walking with the bear carried a long pole and a tambourine. When he came upon a group of people, he stopped and began to shake his tambourine. Immediately the bear stood up on his hind legs and began to dance around. The bear took the pole in his front paws, stood it upright, and hopped round and round the pole. On a command from his keeper, the bear laid down on his back and rolled from side to side. As the crowd applauded, the tambourine became a collection plate. Most people gave something. The man tipped his hat in appreciation and walked off with the bear to look for another audience.

Suddenly a small, mangy, mongrel dog came leaping out from behind some bushes and began barking at the bear. It was a sad sight. This magnificent wild beast, which should have been able to dispatch the dog with one swipe of its powerful paw, was helpless. But more than that, it was terrified. It bounded around trying to dart away and hide. Finally the keeper began swinging his pole and chased the dog away.

Why was this beautiful specimen afraid of a scruffy little dog? As I saw it, there were two reasons. First, the bear was muzzled. Second, it was declawed. Where there should have been five long razor-sharp claws on each paw, five swords that would have been devastating in battle, there was nothing. The bear was muzzled, swordless, and helpless.

As I watched, it reminded me of some Christians I know: muzzled (unable to speak) and weaponless (unable to use the sword of the Spirit against the enemy of their souls).

In contrast, the Bible paints a beautiful picture of a mature man or woman of God. There he stands, his heart filled with the word of God. From the abundance of his heart he shares the unsearchable riches of Christ. He is on a mission of mercy, sent by the Lord. He is trained, equipped, disciplined, and dedicated to God's work with an eye single to his glory. Under the control of the blessed Holy Spirit, he is a formidable force in our needy world.

But all too often, we are confronted by a different picture. The Christian is not trained. He is not equipped. He is not disciplined. He is not single-minded to the things of God. His heart is not saturated with the word of God. He is not familiar with the Scriptures.

How to Develop Spiritual Vigor
What can a Christian do who finds himself in the condition I just described? How can he improve his spiritual health and

vigor? It seems to me there are four steps to take.

First, there must be an inward stirring of the Spirit of God so that he or she has a burning desire to be a man or woman of God. So if today you have such a desire for better things—take heart! The Spirit of God is at work in your life. You are under way.

Second, there must be a mighty resolve to obey what the Lord shows you as you follow him. In the words of the apostles, "We must obey God!" (Acts 5:29).

Third, you must allow the Lord to take you from your attitude of defeated helplessness and stand you upright. Let him put a glint of victory in your eye and a smile of hope on your face.

I saw an example of this while flying from Christchurch to Dunedin in New Zealand. It was a rough flight and the lady across the aisle from us was airsick. Finally, her shoulders drooped and her head slumped forward. She was totally wiped out. The stewardess came by and saw her. "Come, come now," she said. "Buck up and get control of yourself." The lady looked up and slumped forward again. "Come, come, my dear, none of that now!" admonished the stewardess. "Sit up and take courage."

With that she reached down and put her hand under the lady's arm and lifted her upright in her seat. "Here," she said, "chew one of these." The lady declined. "Alright now," she said, "take one." She handed something to the lady and went for some water for her. With the help of the stewardess who was determined to help her get a grip on herself, the lady finished the trip encouraged and strengthened.

This is how the Holy Spirit ministers to us. He comes to help when we are defeated. He admonishes us, encourages us, and puts hope and faith in our lives.

Fourth, apply yourself to the means of grace which the Lord has provided, two of which are the word and prayer.

Pray without ceasing. Pray about everything. Become a thankful Christian. Become a person of praise. Confess your sin and expect God's forgiveness. This is the heritage of the child of God. "If we confess our sins, he is faithful and just and will forgive us our sins and purify us from all unrightousness" (1 John 1:9). Continually confess your need of him. Never think you can go it alone. You can't. But you can do it through Christ. Remember Paul's statement: "I can do everything through him who gives me strength" (Philippians 4:13). That is true for you as well. Isn't that tremendous! Pray for the enlightenment of the Spirit of God upon his word. Ask him to infuse his word with his Spirit, and to breathe life into your soul through that word. As the psalmist wrote, "I am laid low in the dust; renew my life according to your word" (Psalm 119:25).

Get into the word. Take notes on your pastor's sermons and pray over them, asking the Lord to help you apply them to your life. Find a simple reading program that keeps you on a daily schedule throughout the year. Start a good Bible study—one that makes you dig into the word of God for yourself. Find a Christ-centered Bible study discussion group that you can join that has the word of God as the only base and source of discussion.

And don't forget to memorize the Scriptures systematically. This is the key. Through Scripture memory, the blessed Holy Spirit has constant access to your life. He can bring a verse to mind that will encourage you or enable you to help another. Soon, through God's word and prayer, God will transform your life into that of a vibrant, rugged soldier of the cross with an eye single to his glory.

After an early morning Bible study in Elven and Joyce Smith's home in Auckland, New Zealand, I was being driven back to the motel by a couple of men from the study. "Have you ever seen Eden park?" they asked.

"No," I replied.

"Let's go up on a nearby hill so you can see it," one of them said. As we looked down on the beautiful park, Dr. Dave Blaiklock told me that it was once a rubbish heap. Then a certain gentleman decided to reclaim and beautify the area. After much diligent work, the park was opened to the public. Now people come from far and wide to see it. As I listened to the story, I thought, *That reminds me of the Lord. He can take our lives, wrecked and ruined by sin, and transform them into works of beauty.*

God's work in our lives can be likened to that of a good cook. What makes a good cook? Someone who can take a nice cut of steak, some carrots and beans, some bread, a pot of coffee, a chocolate cake, and serve a good meal? Is that the mark of a good cook? Possibly. But in my mind a really good cook is the person who can take some leftovers and blend them together and have everyone smacking their lips. Anyone should be able to take good, fresh ingredients and serve a nice meal.

But God rarely has an opportunity to do something like that. Mostly, he has to work with leftovers. After we have blown a good part of our lives on sin and self, we eventually come to him. Then he takes the broken pieces of our lives, put them all back together, and uses us for his glory. One of the tools he uses is the Bible.

So take a lesson from Stephen. Become a student of the Scriptures. You will never regret one hour spent learning, reading, hearing, memorizing, or meditating on God's word.

Stephen had obviously spent many hours studying the Bible and had memorized many portions. His defense before the Sadducees demonstrates his thorough grasp of the Scriptures. Let's look at Stephen's sermon and take special note of two lessons it contains.

In Stephen's account of Moses' life, he cited an incident from which we learn our first great lesson.

> Moses was educated in all the wisdom of the Egyptians and was powerful in speech and action. When Moses was forty years old, he decided to visit his fellow Israelites. He saw one of them being mistreated by an Egyptian, so he went to his defense and avenged him by killing the Egyptian. Moses thought that his own people would realize that God was using him to rescue them, but they did not (Acts 7:22-25).

What is the lesson here? *Get the facts before you act.*

Moses was a brilliant man, trained in the wisdom of the Egyptians. But he took his brethren's reactions for granted, and his assumptions were wrong. Moses acted angrily, rashly, and hastily. One of the trials of leadership is that we must often make judgments and decisions without complete evidence. But whenever possible, take time to sound out the situation, gather the facts, and talk to the people concerned. Pray over the facts, seeking wisdom from God, and then make your decision relying on his guidance.

We now come to our second lesson in Acts 7. Over the years, the Jews had come to believe that God was their *exclusive possession.* In his sermon, however, Stephen took the Sadducees through the Scriptures to help them understand that the Jews were to be a people who would bring the *whole world* to God. Stephen interpreted the Old Testament in light of the Great Commission.

The Jews thought they were the only nation God was interested in, so they looked upon Jerusalem as the central point of God's concern. In his message, however, Stephen pointed out that most of the great and holy events that make up the history of the Jewish nation took place outside the Holy Land. God appeared to their father Abraham while he was living in Mesopotomia. God spoke to Moses while he was a stranger in Midian—keeping sheep on the backside of the desert. There, in an unlikely place, God spoke to him out of the burning bush. Even the Law was not given in the Holy Land, but out in the desert on Mount Sinai.

The Jews also thought their ornate temple was God's dwelling. They felt as if they could make God stay put. But Stephen gave them a ringing challenge: "However, the Most High does not live in houses made by men. As the prophet says, 'Heaven is my throne, and the earth is my footstool. What kind of house will you build for me? says the Lord. Or where will my resting place be? Has not my hand made all these things?'" (Acts 7:48-50). Solomon himself had acknowledged all of this in his great prayer at the dedication of the temple. "But will God really dwell on earth? The heavens, even the highest heaven, cannot contain you. How much less this temple I have built!" (1 Kings 8:27). As we read Solomon's prayer, we see how he thought the temple was to be primarily a place of prayer.

A God for All People

Although the temple was a place of prayer for God's people, Solomon also referred to the stranger who would hear of the name of God and come and pray. "As for the foreigner who does not belong to your people Israel but has come from a distant land because of your name—for men will hear of your great name and your mighty hand and your outstretched arm—when he comes and prays toward this temple, then hear from heaven, your dwelling place, and do whatever the foreigner asks of you, *so that all the peoples of the earth may know your name and fear you,* as do your own people Israel, and may know that this house I have built bears your Name" (1 Kings 8:41-43).

Stephen made the point that the holy temple was never intended to bring to a standstill God's divine plan for his people. Abraham's descendants had not only completely misunderstood God's purpose for the temple but also his purpose for their lives.

God's Concern for the World

The story of the Bible is the story of God's great plan to make his love and redemption known throughout the whole world. At the fall we see man's rebellion and separation from God. God patiently began to reestablish a universal fellowship with man, but man would have none of it. Man wanted—and still wants—to construct a world without God. The Tower of Babel reflected man's grandest effort. Eventually God gave up dealing with mankind as a whole and started afresh with one man—Abraham.

> The Lord had said to Abram, 'Leave your country, your people and your father's household and go to the land I will

show you. I will make you into a great nation and I will bless you; I will make your name great, and you will be a blessing. I will bless those who bless you, and whoever curses you I will curse; *and all peoples on earth will be blessed through you* (Genesis 12:1-3).

All peoples, all families of the earth, were to find their blessing through Abraham and his descendants. When God called Abraham and Sarah out of Ur of the Chaldees, his eye was not only on the Jews. God had his eye on all the nations of the world!

But as time wore on, these people totally lost sight of that. Somehow they forgot the reason they had been brought into being. They became ingrown, worshiping an exclusively tribal God. But God kept reminding them of the plan he had for them. He spelled it out loud and clear in Exodus 19:5-6: "Now if you obey me fully and keep my covenant, then out of all nations you will be my treasured possession. Although the whole earth is mine, you will be for me a kingdom of priests and a holy nation."

The Jews were to be a kingdom of priests who would bring the whole world to God. But generally speaking, they were blind to this purpose, although there were a few who caught this vision. The psalmist wrote, "May God be gracious to us and bless us and make his face shine upon us; may your ways be known on earth, your salvation among all nations" (Psalm 67:1-2). David realized that God's concern is for men and women of all ages and all social classes. He said, "Kings of the earth and all nations, you princes and rulers on earth, young men and maidens, old men and children. Let them praise the name of the Lord, for his name alone is exalted; his splendor is above the earth and the heavens" (Psalm 148:11-13).

The prophets also repeated the same theme. Through Isaiah God said, "Turn to me and be saved, all you ends of the earth; for I am God, and there is no other" (Isaiah 45:22). Habakkuk proclaimed, "For the earth will be filled with the knowledge of the glory of the Lord, as the waters cover the sea" (Habakkuk 2:14). Malachi described the extent of God's concern. "'My name will be great among the nations, from the rising to the setting of the sun. In every place incense and pure offerings will be brought to my name, because my name will be great among the nations,' says the Lord Almighty" (Malachi 1:11).

We can decry the Israelites' blindness—why didn't they see God's purpose for them? How could they have missed it? Well, look around. What do you see today? Do you see a church that is mobilized to carry the gospel to every creature? There are some who are totally committed to this great task. But all too often we see a contented group of worshipers, giving God an hour or two each week and a dollar or two on Sundays, and that's that.

Has God's purpose for his people changed? No! It is clearer now than ever. He expects us to develop a world vision. This vision can be described in two ways. First, it is getting on your heart what God has on his: *the world.* "For God so loved the world that he gave his one and only son, that whoever believes in him shall not perish but have eternal life" (John 3:16). Second, this vision must be bifocal. We must see the needs in our neighborhood, in our city, right where we live, and we must also lift up our eyes and view the world's desperate plight, and declare that the only answer is Christ.

After interpreting the Old Testament for the Sanhedrin, Stephen then boldly stated that the final revelation of God was the coming of Jesus Christ, "the Righteous One." He referred to Jesus as the *Son of Man*—the Savior of the *whole world*— Jews or Gentiles, slaves or free men. Once more the Jews were blind to God's purpose and plan. Century after century they had resisted the Holy Spirit and persecuted the prophets. Finally, in one great act of defiance, they murdered the Messiah.

Stephen referred to them, as, "stiff-necked people, with uncircumcised hearts and ears! . . . who have received the law that was put into effect through angels but have not obeyed it" (Acts 7:51-53). They had betrayed the greatest trust ever given to a nation, and had demonstrated beyond a shadow of a doubt that they were not worthy of the most glorious honor ever bestowed on a people. Stephen pointed out that they had received a unique revelation from God and had fought for centuries to defeat the purpose for which it was given.

That did it: "When they heard this, they were furious and gnashed their teeth at him. But Stephen, full of the Holy Spirit, looked up to heaven and saw the glory of God, and Jesus standing at the right hand of God. 'Look,' he said, 'I see heaven open and the Son of Man standing at the right hand of God'" (Acts 7:54-56).

The Sanhedrin blew apart in a vengeful, violent, murderous rage.

> At this they covered their ears and, yelling at the top of their voices, they all rushed at him, dragged him out of the city and began to stone him. Meanwhile, the witnesses laid their clothes at the feet of a young man named Saul. While they were stoning him, Stephen prayed, "Lord Jesus, receive my spirit." Then he fell on his knees and cried out, "Lord, do not hold this sin against them." When he had said this, he fell asleep (Acts 7:57-60).

Stephen proclaimed a great message. Perhaps he saw things more clearly than most in his day. It is interesting to note that one of those who stood there taking it all in was Saul of Tarsus. Saul heard every word of Stephen's message. I'm sure the Holy Spirit used Stephen's message to prompt the beginnings of a world vision in his heart. Saul, who was later named Paul, the future great strategist for God—who was always plotting the expansion of the church, never contented, but always pressing onward and outward—received his first glimpse of world vision on the day he stood quietly by listening to Stephen while watching him die.

Yes, a great man was put to death on that day. It was a day which appeared to end in defeat for the small band of soldiers in the army of Christ. But often in the kingdom of God that which appears to be a failure initially, turns out to be a success eventually.

Apparent setbacks often result in ultimate advances for the cause of Christ. I believe that's just what happened on the day of Stephen's martyrdom. On that day something was planted in the heart of Saul of Tarsus that God would eventually use to transform him into the greatest general in the army of Jesus Christ that the world has ever known. Paul the apostle later led the advance of the gospel to the uttermost parts of the earth. From the death of Stephen would come life—eternal life—for millions.

SUMMARY:

Stephen died proclaiming that God is not the exclusive property of the Jews and that Jesus is the Savior of the world. But the Jews completely missed God's grand design. God has the world on his heart, and he plans to reach that world with the gospel.

God will do this through men and women like Stephen—
- armed with the word;
- always praying;
- willing to die for the gospel.

8
Philip
the Evangelist

AFTER SATAN'S FIRST major attack on the disciples in Acts 6, an attack from within, we now come to Satan's second major attack on the people of God in Acts 8, an attack from without. "And Saul was there, giving approval to his death. On that day a great persecution broke out against the church at Jerusalem, and all except the apostles were scattered throughout Judea and Samaria" (Acts 8:1). The strategy Satan devised was to destroy the church through a violent and vicious persecution of the believers. His chief agent for this work was Saul of Tarsus.

Because this is our introduction to a man who played such a key role in the events recorded in Acts, we should note some biographical details. Saul was a freeborn citizen of Rome whose home was Tarsus. He was a Pharisee; by trade, a tentmaker. He was educated at the feet of Gamaliel. Eventually, as we discover in Acts 8, Saul's prime desire was to threaten and slaughter the Christians. Satan had Saul's willing hand, zealous heart, and clever mind at his service.

Destruction is not Satan's only weapon. As we have noted earlier, his first attack was to divide. He also uses the highly effective weapon of discouragement against the man or woman of God. Even great men of God such as David, the man after God's own heart, encounter discouragement. "The sorrows of death compassed me, and the floods of ungodly men made me afraid. The sorrows of hell compassed me about: the snares of death prevented me" (Psalm 18:4-5 KJV).

Deadening our faith is another attack Satan uses. When he experienced an attack the psalmist prayed, "I have suffered much; renew my life, O Lord, according to your word" (Psalm 119:107).

If Satan can't deaden our faith, he tries to dampen it. This happened to the church at Ephesus, and the Lord spoke to them about it. "Yet I hold this against you: You have forsaken your first love" (Revelation 2:4).

During the attack recorded in Acts 8, Satan attempted to destroy and devour the believers. Peter warns us to "be self-controlled and alert. Your enemy the devil prowls around like a roaring lion looking for someone to devour" (1 Peter 5:8). We must be on the alert for these five avenues of danger: Satan's attempts to divide, destroy, discourage, deaden, or dampen our faith. In Acts 8 the Lord was able to turn the situation around to the benefit of the gospel. The attack actually did more good than harm. "Those who had been scattered preached the word wherever they went" (Acts 8:4).

Picture the demons of hell gathered around the devil in a high-level meeting to stop the spread of the message of Christ. Their first attack had come to nothing. God used the willing hands of a few good men to overcome the attempt to divide. So Satan gathered his troops together once again to try to devise a strategy which would defeat the disciples in their work for Christ. What should they do?

"How about telling them that Jesus didn't really rise from the dead," one suggested.

"Don't be stupid. He was seen by more than 500 people after his resurrection."

"How about telling them the gospel really has no power?"

"Are you crazy? They are seeing thousands converted and watching lives being transformed under the power of the gospel!"

So they strategized some more. Finally one suggested, "How about a persecution—a really big one?" That suggestion pleased the devil.

"Now you're talking," he said. "That's a good idea. What's your rank?"

"I'm a second lieutenant, sir."

"Not any more. For such a good idea I'm promoting you. You're now a colonel!"

So the attack was launched, but it backfired completely. Rather than stopping the message, the gospel began spreading like a fire driven by a hot west wind on the prairies of Nebraska. The legions of hell were stunned. They met again.

"Where is the colonel who suggested that persecution?" asked Satan.

The colonel stood and identified himself. "Sit down, private!"

God had once again used the devil-inspired wrath of man to bring praise to himself.

Notice that all were scattered, "except the apostles." They had been granted religious asylum by Gamaliel. But the ordinary, garden-variety Christians fled from Jerusalem. As they went, they preached the word. One of them was Philip—one of the seven table waiters we met earlier.

> Philip went down to a city in Samaria and proclaimed the Christ there. When the crowds heard Philip and saw the miraculous signs he did, they all paid close attention to what he said. With shrieks, evil spirits came out of many, and many paralytics and cripples were healed. So there was great joy in that city (Acts 8:5-8).

The disciples took the gospel into the regions of Judea and Samaria, in direct line with the command of Jesus: first Jerusalem, then Judea, then Samaria (see Acts 1:8). Philip did what came naturally to those early disciples. The apostles had set the example: now it was the disciples' turn. What was the result of their outreach? Great joy in the city. That could have been expected for it was predicted by the angel at Jesus' birth. "Do not be afraid. I bring you good news of great joy that will be for all the people. Today in the town of David a Savior has been born to you; he is Christ the Lord" (Luke 2:10-11).

When I spoke at a university in Adelaide, Australia, the Christians banded together to invite their non-Christian friends to the meeting in the theater. They each agreed to bring at least one non-Christian to the meeting. One young Christian came but saw that the friend he had invited had not come. Quickly he went outside and invited another young student who was just standing around doing nothing. He was happy to come and they sat together in the front row. My topic was "How to be Born Again."

After my talk the Christian asked the fellow he had brought if he would be interested in seeing an illustration about receiving Christ. He said yes, so the Christian presented the gospel to him and asked if he had ever invited Christ into his life. His friend said no. The Christian then asked him if he would like to. His answer was yes, so they read some more Scriptures and prayed together. The new Christian was over-joyed. He had been hungering for God for a long time but didn't have a clue as to how to go about establishing a personal relationship with him. After receiving Christ he left the theater rejoicing in his new found faith.

But the story doesn't end there. This new believer heard that I was going to be speaking at a church the following evening, so he quickly went to his best friend, told him what had happened, and asked if he would like to come to the meeting. His friend came and also received Christ as Savior and Lord.

However, a growing Christian needs something more than joy to sustain his Christian walk. As Philip soon learned, the devil is persistent and does not give up easily. Simon the sorcerer soon came into Philip's life. Notice the difference between these two men. Simon "boasted that he was someone great" (Acts 8:9). Philip, however, turned the Samaritans' attention not to himself but to Christ. Here again the apostles' example (see Acts 3:12-13) bore fruit. Philip did not argue with Simon or debate him. He simply went about and "preached the good news of the kingdom of God and the name of Jesus Christ" (Acts 8:12). Philip knew that you do not dispel darkness by arguing with it, shouting at it, fighting with it, or debating it. You overcome darkness by turning on the light, and he knew that Jesus was the light of the world.

This is also a great lesson for us. How easy it is to fall into the trap of trying to win spiritual battles with carnal weapons—but it never works.

> For though we live in the world, we do not wage war as the world does. The weapons we fight with are not the weapons of the world. On the contrary, they have divine power to demolish strongholds. We demolish arguments and every pretension that sets itself up against the knowledge of God, and we take captive every thought to make it obedient to Christ (2 Corinthians 10:3-5).

The simple strategy used here began in Jerusalem at the harvest festival of Pentecost where 3,000 people met Christ. Those converts, and those who followed later, were carefully trained by the apostles in both word and deed. Many of the disciples displayed a zeal for the gospel, courage under fire, faith in God, a sincere prayer life, obedience to the commands of Christ, a sacrificial spirit, and joy at being counted worthy to suffer for his name.

In Acts 8 we find those who were won to Christ and prepared for service were scattered. *Scattered* is an agricultural term used to describe a farmer sowing his seed. Here was a joyful and sudden expansion of the gospel which at first appeared to be a disaster, but which ultimately was used by God to further his cause. The disciples were scattered like seeds in the wind. Jesus had spoken of this: "The one who sowed the good seed is the Son of Man. The field is the world, and the good seed stands for the sons of the kingdom" (Matthew 13:37-38; see also Matthew 13:24-42).

The sower is Jesus Christ. The good seed are the children of the kingdom—not just seed, but *good* seed. If we are to be good seed in the world, what should characterize our lives? What are the attributes of good seed? We will find answers as we study the lives of Stephen and Philip to see what kind of men they had become under the training of the apostles and the ministry of the Holy Spirit. Let us note seven things that characterized their lives.

Death to self. Jesus spoke of this in John 12:24: "I tell you the truth, unless a kernel of wheat falls to the ground and dies, it remains only a single seed. But if it dies, it produces many seeds." Good seed must die if it is to bear fruit. Men like Stephen and Philip had seen clear examples of this in the life of the Lord Jesus and in the lives of the apostles.

Jesus gave his life. He said, "The reason my Father loves me is that I lay down my life—only to take it up again. No one takes it from me, but I lay it down of my own accord" (John 10:17-18).

The apostles also laid their lives on the line in bold response to the Sanhedrin's threats of murder. Dying requires more than just the courage to face death. It calls for an active commitment of our lives to Jesus Christ as Lord. When we take that step he becomes our life.

Paul wrote, "Since, then, you have been raised with Christ, set your hearts on things above, where Christ is seated at the right hand of God. Set your minds on things above, not on earthly things. For you died, and your life is now hidden with Christ in God. When Christ, who is your life, appears, then you also will appear with him in glory" (Colossians 3:1-4). He also reminded the Romans:

> If the Spirit of him who raised Jesus from the dead is living in you, he who raised Christ from the dead will also give life to your mortal bodies through his Spirit, who lives in you. Therefore, brothers, we have an obligation—but it is not to the sinful nature, to live according to it. For if you live according to the sinful nature, you will die; but if by the Spirit

you put to death the misdeeds of the body, you will live, because those who are led by the Spirit of God are sons of God (Romans 8:11-14).

Death to self is an attribute of good seed. Disciples like Stephen and Philip had given up all rights to themselves. "Then he said to them all: 'If anyone would come after me, he must deny himself and take up his cross daily and follow me'" (Luke 9:23). In obedience to the call of Christ, Stephen and Philip gave themselves as living sacrifices to God. What Paul taught later was already a living reality in their lives. Christ, not sin, now reigned in their mortal bodies.

> In the same way, count yourselves dead to sin but alive to God in Christ Jesus. Therefore do not let sin reign in your mortal body so that you obey its evil desires. Do not offer the parts of your body to sin, as instruments of wickedness, but rather offer yourselves to God, as those who have been brought from death to life; and offer the parts of your body to him as instruments of righteousness. For sin shall not be your master, because you are not under law, but under grace (Romans 6:11-14).

That described Philip's lifestyle. His life was totally separated from sin in surrender to God.

The Word of God. Stephen had an outstanding grasp of the Old Testament. He did not just understand its content; he also had insight into the great purposes of God. He was able to explain the Bible carefully in light of the Great Commission.

When he met the Ethiopian reading Isaiah, "Philip began with that very passage of Scripture and told him the good news about Jesus" (Acts 8:35). The lives and ministry of the apostles set a clear example. Disciples like Philip were converted to Christ as the apostles proclaimed the word—possibly on the day of Pentecost when Peter boldly quoted the Scriptures and the streets of old Jerusalem rang with the truth.

If we would be good seed, we must take steps to saturate

our hearts and lives with the Bible and apply it to our lives with the aid of the Holy Spirit. Jesus taught, "If you hold to my teaching, you are really my disciples" (John 8:31). James reminds us, "Do not merely listen to the word, and so deceive yourselves. Do what it says. Anyone who listens to the word but does not do what it says is like a man who looks at his face in a mirror and, after looking at himself, goes away and immediately forgets what he looks like" (James 1:22-24). The psalmist also spoke about the effect of the Scriptures on his life: "I have considered my ways and have turned my steps to your statutes. I will hasten and not delay to obey your commands" (Psalm 119:59-60).

Prayer. We noticed how Stephen died while praying for his murderers (see Acts 7:60). If we are to be good seed, prayer is not optional. God lists prayer as a compulsory subject in the curriculum for his school of discipleship. Prayer permeated the life and ministry of Jesus (see Mark 1:35). The apostles had committed themselves to prayer (see Acts 6:4). When the authorities commanded them not to speak or teach in Jesus' name, the apostles did not fight or argue; they simply took the matter to the Lord in prayer (see Acts 4:23-31). Cultivate the practice of going to a place where you can be alone to pray earnestly as Jesus did (see Luke 22:40-44).

Fellowship and servanthood. The disciples' lives were characterized by fellowship with one another and service to others. They were a band of men and women who were of one heart, one soul, one spirit, and one mind. They served the Lord in singleness of heart. Stephen and Philip gladly took up the task of serving tables. Sacrificial service and loving fellowship were twin distinctives in their lives.

This was not easily accomplished, for there is a perverse disinclination in most people against working together to achieve a common objective. We do not like to pull together in the harness. We would rather be served than serve—just the opposite of our Lord's example. "For even the Son of Man did not come to be served, but to serve, and to give his life as a ransom for many" (Mark 10:45). Loving service—the badge of discipleship—is often missing in the lives of Christians (see John 13:1-17, and 34-35).

Somehow we are able to shrug off the apostle John's pointed statement. "If anyone says, 'I love God,' yet hates his brother, he is a liar. For anyone who does not love his brother, whom he has seen, cannot love God, whom he has not seen. And he has given us this command: Whoever loves God must also love his brother" (1 John 4:20-21). Paul's command also goes unheeded: "You, my brothers, were called to be free. But do not use your freedom to indulge the sinful nature; rather, serve one another in love" (Galatians 5:13). Yet for the disciple this should be another of the essential foundation stones of life.

Witnessing. Clearly and simply, Stephen and Philip bore witness to Jesus Christ. Philip's first act was to preach Christ in the Samaritan city (Acts 8:5). It is interesting that preaching or proclaiming is mentioned six times in a chapter describing the dispersion of the disciples. This is obviously the chapter's main theme and a lesson the Holy Spirit does not want us to miss. Neither Stephen nor Philip was content to limit his ministry to the administrative functions to which he had also been called. They were both vibrant, joyful, and enthusiastic witnesses for Christ.

Let us say that God has called you to a responsibility in the church. You sing in the choir. You chair a committee. You help with the young people. You teach a class. You usher and pass the collection plate. Good; the church needs those services and could not function properly without them. God has given you one of these tasks, so you must do it well and joyfully for him. But remember the parable of the good seed (see Matthew 13:24-43).

The church does its real work from Monday to Saturday when the church building is empty. Church work is necessary. Do it well; do it heartily as unto the Lord. But imitate Stephen and Philip as well. Be out there like Stephen, "among the people," planting the seed of the gospel. Be out there, like Philip, sharing Christ. Jesus said the field is the world and we are the good seed. Ask him to scatter you abroad in the world where you can die and bring forth fruit unto eternal life.

An eagerness to learn. Remember that the Holy Spirit tells us that the new converts in Acts 2 were learners. They "devoted themselves to the apostles' teaching" (Acts 2:42). Don't you think there were some highly educated, important people among those first 3,000 converts or among the thousands mentioned in Acts 5? In Acts 6 we read that "the word of God spread. The number of disciples in Jerusalem increased rapidly, and a large number of priests became obedient to the faith" (Acts 6:7).

Were there university graduates, nurses, doctors, lawyers, businessmen, and professionals among them? Yes, of course. The apostles, remember, were plain-spoken, ordinary men from Galilee. It would have been easy for some of the more socially prominent, or the highly educated, among the new converts to have resisted the idea of being led and taught by such unrefined men as the apostles. But they didn't. The new converts were learners—eager to be taught.

Stephen, a man full of wisdom, was eager and teachable. Luke commended this characteristic in the Bereans: "Now the Bereans were of more noble character than the Thessalonians, for they received the message with great eagerness and examined the Scriptures every day to see if what Paul said was true" (Acts 17:11). So if you want to become good seed, ask God for a teachable mind and spirit. This is foundational to discipleship.

Consistency. The last thing we will note in the disciples' lives is consistency. They knew their calling from God and they stuck with it. Stephen was faithful even unto death. Twenty years later, when Paul and his traveling companions visited Philip's home, he was still known as Philip the Evangelist, one of the Seven (see Acts 21:8). By then Philip was married, with four grown daughters, but the passing of the years and the pressures of family life had not diverted him from his witness for Christ.

This is a great challenge. Consistency and faithfulness must be built into our lives as permanent foundation stones upon which a life of discipleship can be built. All too often we hear of men of God who started well and ended in spiritual shipwreck. What is the secret of making it over the long haul?

It seems to me the answer is to make it over the short haul. Live for Christ today—today is all you have. Yesterday has gone. We cannot worry about its defeats or glory in its victories. Yesterday has gone and tomorrow never comes. Today is the important word for a consistent walk with Christ.

I must ask myself, "Did I live for Christ *today*? Did I have my morning prayer and Bible reading today? Did I study or memorize some of the Scriptures today? Did I witness for Christ today?" Never mind about yesterday, and don't get all taken up with tomorrow. Be faithful to the Lord today and one day you will hear those blessed words, "Well done, good and faithful servant! You have been faithful with a few things; I will put you in charge of many things. Come and share your master's happiness!" (Matthew 25:21).

Begin with faithfulness in the little things. "Whoever can be trusted with very little can also be trusted with much, and whoever is dishonest with very little will also be dishonest with much" (Luke 16:10). Be faithful in everything. "And if you have not been trustworthy with someone else's property, who will give you property of your own?" (Luke 16:12). Let faithfulness, the royal attribute of Jesus Christ, characterize your discipleship. He is our example. "Therefore, holy brothers, who share in the heavenly calling, fix your thoughts on Jesus, the apostle and high priest whom we confess. He was faithful to the one who appointed him, just as Moses was faithful in all God's house" (Hebrews 3:1-2).

Soon the good news of what God was doing in Samaria reached the ears of the apostles in Jerusalem. Immediately Peter and John went to lend a hand. It wasn't long before they, too, encountered Simon the sorcerer, who wanted to buy the power he saw in their lives. Imagine that! When was the last time anyone approached you or me and offered their hard-earned money to buy the power of God which they had seen in our lives? This was an amazing testimony to the reality of Christ in their lives. But Peter was unimpressed. "Peter answered: 'May your money perish with you, because you thought you could buy the gift of God with money!'" (Acts 8:20). Yes, they would accept gifts for the support of the ministry, but they would not accept bribes.

After Peter and John returned to Jerusalem, God spoke to Philip.

> Now an angel of the Lord said to Philip, "Go south to the road—the desert road—that goes down from Jerusalem to Gaza." So he started out, and on his way he met an Ethiopian eunuch, an important official in charge of all the treasury of Candace, queen of the Ethiopians. This man had gone to Jerusalem to worship, and on his way home was sitting in his chariot reading the book of Isaiah the prophet. The Spirit told Philip, "Go to that chariot and stay near it." Then Philip ran up to the chariot and heard the man reading Isaiah the prophet. "Do you understand what you are reading?" Philip asked (Acts 8:26-30).

Notice how it happened. The Spirit told Philip to go, and Philip ran to the chariot—it was as simple as that. We often read passages like this and marvel at the impact men like Philip made for Christ. If we are not careful, we will attribute their impact to the wrong reasons. Here, in just a few verses, we see one of the great reasons why the first-century disciples were so mightily used by God. They did not hesitate to obey him.

What Philip was told to do did not make much sense from a human point of view. He was in the midst of a great evangelistic opportunity when suddenly he was told to head out into a burning desert. Did he argue? Did he try to point out the unreasonableness of such a command? No, thank God, he was not guided by human reason but by divine authority. He knew who was in charge. So when God spoke, Philip obeyed. He was available to God, he submitted to the will of God, and believed the word of God. His obedience was instant, wholehearted, and unquestioning.

If we would be used of God for his glory, the same foundations of discipleship must grip our spirits and be built into our lives. These qualities can characterize our lives if we are willing. Remember, we are not studying a great prophet like Samuel or a great leader like Moses. Philip was not an apostle. He was a table waiter—one of the workers. But he had learned to obey God and was a bold witness for Christ at every opportunity.

After Philip explained what the eunuch was reading and led him to Christ, the Ethiopian asked him a question: "As they traveled along the road, they came to some water and the eunuch said, 'Look, here is water. Why shouldn't I be baptized?' And he ordered the chariot to stop. Then both Philip and the eunuch went down into the water and Philip baptized him" (Acts 8:36-38).

Philip had not allowed his failure with Simon the sorcerer to discourage him. This was a new day—a new opportunity. Philip might have said, "I'd better go cautiously here, I've already made one big mistake. Maybe I had better not proceed with this man." But he didn't hesitate to seize the opportunity. Philip trusted God and pressed ahead. So don't let a failure or mistake in one situation rob you of victory and success in another.

Incidentally, there is no record of a reprimand from the apostles. They knew that in the early stages of involvement in the ministry it is easy for someone to make mistakes. They had certainly made their share as they walked with Jesus during his earthly ministry. So they did not try to set up guidelines that would confine Philip in a spiritual straightjacket in order to prevent him from repeating his mistake. They knew that the man who makes no mistakes rarely makes anything of his life. If a person is right most of the time, it also means he will be wrong part of the time. This is a great lesson for those in leadership.

Philip's courage and obedience in approaching the eunuch resulted in a thrilling outcome to the story: "When they came up out of the water, the Spirit of the Lord suddenly took Philip away, and the eunuch did not see him again, but went on his way rejoicing" (Acts 8:39).

SUMMARY:

Although a persecution scattered the disciples (Acts 8:1), they went everywhere "preaching the word" (Acts 8:4). Seven things characterized the lives of two of those disciples—Stephen and Philip.
- death to self
- the word of God
- prayer
- fellowship and servanthood
- witnessing
- an eagerness to learn
- consistency

9
On the Road to Damascus

IN ACTS 9, Saul of Tarsus reappears as the archenemy of the church. "Meanwhile, Saul was still breathing out murderous threats against the Lord's disciples. He went to the high priest and asked him for letters to the synagogues in Damascus, so that if he found any there who belonged to the Way, whether men or women, he might take them as prisoners to Jerusalem" (Acts 9:1-2). Saul was continuing his campaign of harassment and murder.

Why was this man obsessed with hatred for the Christians? What had they done? What was their sin? Were they vile, evil people who polluted society by their evil and immoral ways? No! They were known for their love for God and for their brethren. Their lives were filled with joy and peace. What was the problem? It was their message. They were telling everybody that Jesus was alive, that he had risen from the dead and ascended into heaven.

Saul refused to believe that. He thought that Christ's disciples had come to the tomb and stolen his body. This story was common among the Jews. Saul was convinced that the body of Jesus was rotting away in a hidden grave. Those lies about a resurrected Jesus had to be stopped, and Saul was just the man to do it.

But there was another reason for Saul's obsession. Saul knew of Jesus as a leader of an ignorant band of fishermen, publicans, and harlots. Jesus' preaching had not been as severe against open sinners as it was against respectable people like Saul. Jesus called the Pharisees robbers and hypocrites. It was said he actually opposed the laws of Moses. He had dared to predict the destruction of the temple. To add insult to injury, this liar had actually claimed to be the Messiah. To Saul that was impossible. Saul believed that when the Messiah came, he would establish a powerful, splendid kingdom and lead the Jews to victory over their enemies. But Jesus had suffered under the wrath of his persecutors and finally died a horrible, painful death. In Saul's theology, suffering was regarded as a mark of God's displeasure. How could anyone possibly think that this traitor was the Messiah? Jesus was dead and buried. Saul must put an end to all the false hopes and lies that were being spread far and wide by Christ's followers. However, as Saul pursued his campaign, an event occurred that changed the course of Saul's life and ultimately the course of world history.

"As he neared Damascus on his journey, suddenly a light from heaven flashed around him. He fell to the ground and heard a voice say to him, 'Saul, Saul, why do you persecute me?' 'Who are you, Lord?' Saul asked. 'I am Jesus, whom you are persecuting,' he replied. 'Now get up and go into the city, and you will be told what you must do'"(Acts 9:3-6).

Imagine Saul's dilemma. Everything that he formerly believed was wrong. Everything he had done previously was misguided. The one whom he knew to be rotting away in a hidden grave had suddenly appeared to him from heaven, alive and well. Saul had been opposing the Lord of glory in the name of God! As Saul's mind reeled, he fell to the ground. When he got up he was blind, and his friends led him by the hand to Damascus. "For three days he was blind, and did not eat or drink anything" (Acts 9:9). During those days in

Damascus, as he adapted to his blindness, the conflict within Saul began.

In his mind's eye he saw a great balance. In one scale was his encounter with the risen Lord—Jesus Christ. In the other scale was all of Saul's ambition, his family, his friends, his position, his prestige, his power, wealth, honor, comfort, the word of God as he had always understood it, and the only religion God had ever given. So for three days he battled it out. Finally, the issue was settled. Saul made his choice. Later, he explained it to the Philippians.

> But whatever was to my profit I now consider loss for the sake of Christ. What is more, I consider everything a loss compared to the surpassing greatness of knowing Christ Jesus my Lord, for whose sake I have lost all things. I consider them rubbish, that I may gain Christ and be found in him, not having a righteousness of my own that comes from the law, but that which is through faith in Christ—the righteousness that comes from God and is by faith (Philippians 3:7-9).

Commitment

Everything that was once gain to Saul he now considered as loss. What once was precious was now rubbish. Saul weighed everything and the scales tipped in favor of Christ. Now he was on a new road. He knew the dangers. He knew the reality of the whips and jails he would have to face because he was accustomed to persecuting Christians. If he left Damascus as a converted Jew, Saul knew he would become a target for harassment and persecution. But he committed himself to Christ regardless of the consequences.

Peter once faced a similar decision the morning after an unsuccessful fishing trip (see Luke 5:1-11). Jesus was preaching the word and the people were pressing in to hear. Jesus suggested to Peter that he should "put out into deep water, and let down the nets for a catch" (Luke 5:4). Peter reminded the Lord that they had spent the whole night fishing and had caught nothing.

He could also have said, "Besides, I'm a fisherman and you're a carpenter. You don't understand the fish in this lake. During the day the sun warms the water on top so the fish stay on the bottom. We fish at night when they come to the top to feed. Also, my wife has breakfast ready and will be upset if I am late. You can't expect a woman to keep breakfast waiting."

But Peter didn't say that. Whether it made sense to him or not, because Jesus suggested it, he did it. "Because you say so," Peter said, "I will let down the nets" (Luke 5:5). Faith needs no precedent. No matter if it has never been done before—if Jesus gives the word—we must respond.

A Pile of Fish
The results were startling. "They caught such a large number of fish that their nets began to break" (Luke 5:6). Soon they had two boats so full of fish that they both began to sink. They were astonished. They had never had such a catch. "Then Jesus said to Simon, 'Don't be afraid; from now on you will catch men'" (Luke 5:10). Peter understood what Jesus said. He knew the implication of those words. He could easily have said, "Lord, this is not the time to quit the fishing business!" Peter had a decision to make. So when they brought their boat to the shore, Peter looked at the mountain of fish. Then he looked at Jesus. He looked back at the fish and reflected on all they stood for. There was a vast amount of money there. Enough to pay all the bills and buy new clothes for his wife and family. He could even put a little away for a rainy day. There was enough for all sorts of things. So he looked, and looked, and looked again. Then he looked back at Jesus and made his decision. He left everything and followed him.

Great Wealth
Jesus had given the same option to another man: the rich young ruler. When this young man told Jesus he had kept the commandments since his youth, Jesus said, "One thing you lack, . . . Go, sell everything you have and give to the poor,

and you will have treasure in heaven. Then come, follow me" (Mark 10:21). But the young man had a problem. "He went away sad, because he had great wealth" (Mark 10:22). He too understood what Jesus had told him. He also had a decision to make. He thought about his wealth, power, and prestige. He thought for a long time. Then he considered Jesus. After a while he looked back at Jesus and made his decision. Today, we don't even know his name. He decided to live for himself—for security and comfort—and eventually he faded away. His life had no impact on the world.

But think of Peter. His name is known around the world and his life has affected the lives of millions. What was the difference between the two men? It was Peter's commitment to Jesus as the Lord of his life.

What does such a commitment mean in practice? One of the finest statements of that sort of commitment was written in the summer of 1974 in Lausanne, Switzerland. I was one of the delegates to the International Congress on World Evangelization held in Lausanne and had been invited to lead a workshop on "How to Help a New Christian Grow." Before the Congress I wrote to my good friend, the late Paul Little, who was the program director and offered my services to him. I knew he was carrying a heavy load and I wanted to lend a hand. I was thinking about such chores as moving chairs, distributing materials, ushering, and any other practical tasks I could perform to lighten Paul's load. He wrote back and said, "I've got a job for you."

Every day the nations represented met in private sessions to discuss their national strategies for evangelizing their countries. My job was to summarize reports of these discussions and give them to Paul. It was an exciting and informative assignment. I learned a great deal about the work of God around the world while spending many hours poring over these papers. On the last day of the Congress, each nation turned in its final report. I read each of them to look for trends and similarities in the way the Lord was leading his people around the world. Some of the reports were detailed, and reading them took time.

Christ and His Word

Toward late afternoon I came across a report that was just one page long. It immediately caught my attention. As I read it, I was challenged to the depths of my soul. Here is what I read:

Papua, New Guinea
National Strategy Group Report

1) We recognize that our Melanesian and Polynesian culture with its animistic religions has evidenced a general revelation of God within the context of Romans 1:19.

2) From this our people have always known the need for a supernatural authority to control life and destiny.

3) Belief in the gods of our forefathers provided a system of spiritual authority.

4) We feared these gods but found no reason to love or respect them.

5) We know that within ourselves and within our culture the Evil one has been doing his own work of deception and that this has resulted in a great spiritual blindness.

6) The coming of the Holy Spirit of Truth with the preaching of the Gospel of our Lord Jesus Christ has revealed how great was our darkness.

7) We humbly acknowledge that while there is much in our culture that we cherish and want to see continued yet there is very little that has provided any foundation for a meaningful experience of the true God.

8) As those who have now been delivered from idols to serve the living and true God (1 Thessalonians 1:9-10), we are convinced that there is only one meaningful authority for life and that is the redeeming love of our Lord and Savior Jesus Christ.

9) We also affirm that from our own experience we have found there is only one sure guide for life and that this is the revealed will of God as recorded in his Word, the Bible.

10) The new spiritual perception so graciously given to the

believer in Christ enables us to see certain things of our religious beliefs for what they really are, namely, strange gods and idols.

11) Humbly, yet willingly and joyfully, do we place ourselves under the sole authority of Christ and his holy Word. And in so doing we affirm that this allegiance is the only real way to both preserve and enrich the values of our cultural heritage.[1]

Let the concluding words of this report sink into your soul: "Humbly, yet willingly and joyfully, do we place ourselves under the sole authority of Christ and his holy Word." Now there is a national strategy! What if every Christian in the Netherlands did that? What if every Christian in Canada did that? What if every Christian in your country did that? What would be the effect upon your nation? What if every Christian in your city, and every believer in your church made such a commitment? What would be the effect upon your life if *you* did that?

Live for Christ

With those thoughts lingering in my mind, I continued to speak at various meetings throughout Europe that summer and finished the trip in Helsinki, Finland. When I arrived in Finland, I was studying Mark 15:31: "In the same way the chief priests and the teachers of the law mocked him among themselves. 'He saved others,' they said, 'but he can't save himself!'" After reading that I asked myself, *Who else mocked him?*

This is what I discovered: "Those who passed by hurled insults at him, shaking their heads and saying, 'So! You who are going to destroy the temple and build it in three days, come down from the cross and save yourself!'" (Mark 15:29-30).

Matthew wrote, "In the same way the robbers who were crucified with him also heaped insults on him" (Matthew 27:44).

Luke observed that "the soldiers also came up and

mocked him. They offered him wine vinegar and said, 'If you are the king of the Jews, save yourself' " (Luke 23:36-37). The mockers formed a microcosm of the world. There were religious leaders, the military, criminals, and passers-by. What was the basis of their mockery? To answer that question I reviewed Mark 15:31: " 'He saved others,' they said, 'but he cannot save himself!' " Suddenly the full impact of those words hit me. "Right, right!" I shouted. "That's exactly right!" I startled my wife who was reading in the same room I was studying in. In a flash I saw the truth of Mark 15:31.

Even though those who mocked Jesus had spoken jeeringly, they had spoken a deep spiritual truth. If you would save others, you cannot save yourself. A life lived for Christ will not be lived for selfish aims. It cannot be. Jesus taught us, "If anyone would come after me, he must deny himself and take up his cross and follow me. For whoever wants to save his life will lose it, but whoever loses his life for me and for the gospel will save it" (Mark 8:34-35).

Life Is a Vapor

We might ask ourselves, *Why should I make such a commitment?* It seems to me that there are three reasons. The first is found in James 4:14: "For what is your life? It is even a vapour, that appeareth for a little time, and then vanisheth away" (KJV). The next time the temperature is low enough for you to see your breath, step outside the house and blow in the air. In the cold your breath will appear for a moment and then vanish. That's what your life is like! One vapor. But don't blow twice, for that would double your life span. You only have one. Since your life is so short, don't settle for a small life, immersed in self and sin. Live a big life doing the will of God. There are only three things that last for eternity: God, his word, and the eternal souls of people. If your life is immersed in these, you are involved in eternal issues. Let your life be carried along in the grand sweep of God's will in the world. Be caught up with Jesus Christ and his Great Commission. If you do that, even though your life is short, it won't be little.

Lasting Goals

The second reason for making a commitment to Christ is found in 2 Peter 3:10: "But the day of the Lord will come like a thief. The heavens will disappear with a roar; the elements will be destroyed by fire, and the earth and everything in it will be laid bare." Everything is going to burn one day.

We were at the breakfast table at our home in Omaha, Nebraska, in 1957 when Bob Stephens, a young man who lived with us, startled us with an announcement. He was an instructor in the School of Engineering at the University of Nebraska in Omaha, and had a promising career. He had graduated second in his class from the University of Maryland and was a member of the top engineering societies in America.

He said, "I have decided to live my life totally for Jesus Christ." What brought Bob to that commitment? The truth of 2 Peter 3:10. "If I give my life to designing roads, buildings, or bridges," he said, "nothing that I have done will last. It will all burn." Bob had seen a great spiritual truth. An engineer could do all of the things he mentioned and still be blessed by God. But he could not *live* for those things. An engineer can do his job and live for Christ as well. It is not what we do, but what we give our lives to while we are doing those things that really counts. Some of the most productive disciples of Christ that I know are doctors, dentists, builders, military men, politicians, laborers, nurses, and housewives. What is their secret? They live for Christ—their lives are committed to him.

Work That Counts

The third reason for making such a commitment is 1 Corinthians 15:58: "Therefore, my dear brothers, stand firm. Let nothing move you. Always give yourselves fully to the work of the Lord, because you know that your labor in the Lord is not in vain."

In the summer of 1976 I was in Tennessee speaking to the staff of a Christian organization. One of the men I met had a keen interest in studying World War II. When he learned I had served with the Marines in that war, he asked where I had fought. I mentioned the island of Pelelieu and he told me he had some books that described the battles there and offered to send them to me.

I read the books he sent. One of them sent a great wave of depression over my spirit. After giving an account of a horrible battle, where hundreds of lives were lost, the writer concluded that it should never have been fought. He said the place could easily have been bypassed and it would have made little difference.

As I read that, my mind pictured many young Americans and Japanese lying dead on that lonely strip of coral. They had died in vain! After reading that book I thanked God for the truth of 1 Corinthians 15:58. Think of it! Whatever you do for Christ matters. It counts for something. Your work is not in vain. If you commit your life to him and to his cause you will be significant and you will have a significant ministry in the world around you.

Leave Your Old Crowd

How do you go about making such a commitment to Christ? Picture yourself in a large group of people standing on a hillside at dusk. The crowd is looking at a man who stands before them. He says, "If anyone would come after me, he must deny himself and take up his cross daily and follow me" (Luke 9:23). Then he slowly turns and walks away. At that point what do you see yourself doing? Do you step out from the crowd and follow Jesus no matter what the circumstances, no matter what the cost? Or do you see yourself turning and shouldering your way through the crowd and walking off in the opposite direction? Commitment is stepping out from the crowd and following Jesus Christ as Lord. Commitment is deciding to follow Jesus without turning back. That's exactly what Saul of Tarsus decided to do after he met Christ.

A Disciple Named Ananias

As Saul meditated on his decision to follow Christ in Damascus, the Lord was speaking to Ananias:

The Lord called to him in a vision, "Ananias!" "Yes, Lord," he answered. The Lord told him, "Go to the house of Judas on Straight Street and ask for a man from Tarsus named Saul, for he is praying. In a vision he has seen a man named Ananias come and place his hands on him to restore his sight." "Lord," Ananias answered, "I have heard many reports about this man and all the harm he has done to your saints in Jerusalem. And he has come here with authority from the chief priests to arrest all who call on your name." But the Lord said to Ananias, "Go! This man is my chosen instrument to carry my name before the Gentiles and their kings and before the people of Israel. I will show him how much he must suffer for my name" (Acts 9:10-16).

"A disciple named Ananias." Who was Ananias? What was his background? All we know is that he was a disciple. If we heard that the biggest enemy of Christianity was sitting in a hotel room in our city considering the claims of Christ, whom would we send to talk to him? In all likelihood we would select a well-known individual whose reputation and position in the church would be fitting for such a task. But not the Lord. He does not think like that. His master strategy is to use us all, from the least to the greatest. He is no respecter of persons and has a great burden to see all of his children vitally involved in proclaiming the gospel.

Ananias was apprehensive about the Lord's command. He had heard much about Saul of Tarsus. He knew how he had persecuted the Christians in Jerusalem. Ananias knew the chief priests had given Saul the authority to jail all who called upon the name of the Lord. So naturally Ananias wanted to consider his assignment carefully to confirm what the Lord wanted and to be sure that he was the man for the job. How typical! That is how men have reacted throughout history.

When God called Moses, he hesitated to obey. The same was true with Jonah, Jeremiah, and Gideon. We can understand their reluctance. But thank God for his love and patience with us. "As a father has compassion on his children, so the

Lord has compassion on those who fear him; for he knows how we are formed, he remembers that we are dust" (Psalm 103:13-14). God knows our weakness, but if we are willing to obey, he is willing to use us as he used Ananias.

Saul's New Life

After many days in Damascus Saul went to Jerusalem to join the disciples there, but "they were all afraid of him, not believing that he really was a disciple. But Barnabas took him in and brought him to the apostles" (Acts 9:26-27).

It is interesting to observe that Saul's first act was to go to the people who had stoned Stephen and take up the ministry of the man he had seen martyred. Saul "moved about freely in Jerusalem, speaking boldly in the name of the Lord. He talked and debated with the Grecian Jews, but they tried to kill him" (Acts 9:28-29). Stephen's ministry had made a lasting impression on Saul. So Saul went to this same group of Grecian Jews and resumed Stephen's ministry. Stephen had primarily opposed the Sadduccees, and Saul the Pharisee had sided with Stephen's opponents. So Saul returned to make amends for his past sin. He knew they would plan to slay him, but he was prepared to die. Later, Saul testified about this experience.

> When I returned to Jerusalem and was praying at the temple, I fell into a trance and saw the Lord speaking. "Quick!" he said to me. "Leave Jerusalem immediately, because they will not accept your testimony about me." "Lord," I replied, "these men know that I went from one synagogue to another to imprison and beat those who believe in you. And when the blood of your martyr Stephen was shed, I stood there giving my approval and guarding the clothes of those who were killing him." Then the Lord said to me, "Go; I will send you far away to the Gentiles" (Acts 22:17-21).

I'm sure that God was pleased with Saul's devotion, courage, and willingness to die. But God had a ministry to the Gentiles in mind, and Saul was his chosen instrument for that task (see Acts 9:15-16).

So Saul returned to Tarsus a new man. Because the arch-enemy was now a believer, the church enjoyed peace, and it continued to grow.

Meanwhile God continued to use Peter in a dramatic way. As a result of a miracle in the life of Aeneas, who had been a paralytic for eight years, amazing things continued to happen. "All those who lived in Lydda and Sharon saw him and turned to the Lord" (Acts 9:35).

Soon Peter received an urgent message to go to Joppa. An important disciple had died and they felt Peter might be able to help in some way. So he went and God used him to raise Dorcas from the dead. Why was she so important to the church at Joppa? Because she served the believers. She made robes and clothing for them (see Acts 9:39).

Here is an interesting lesson for us. Not everyone is called to be in the limelight. Some of us will work behind the scenes serving others. Why were the disciples in Joppa so upset over Dorcas' death? Because it is hard to find someone like her, "who was always doing good and helping the poor" (Acts 9:36). A disciple with a servant spirit is worth her weight in gold. The disciples at Joppa knew it. Dorcas' recovery had a powerful impact on many lives. "This became known all over Joppa, and many people believed in the Lord" (Acts 9:42).

SUMMARY:

Paul and Peter, the two major characters in Acts 9, were committed to Jesus Christ as the Lord of life. They—
- made a choice;
- forsook all;
- stepped out from the crowd;
- followed Jesus without turning back;
- made a lasting impact on the world.

Notes: 1. *Let the Earth Hear His Voice* (Minneapolis, Minnesota: World Wide Publications, 1975), page 1423.

10
Welcoming the Gentiles

CORNELIUS WAS ONE of the most important men who ever lived. Yet most people today could not identify him. Why was he so important? Because God chose him to be the first Gentile convert, and through his conversion the door of salvation was opened to the Gentile world. The apostles understood the commission Christ had given them. But until Cornelius was converted, they only preached to Jews and Samaritans. The apostles had not realized a Gentile could be brought into the body of Christ.

Cornelius was a centurion in the Roman army, responsible for more than a hundred men. He had been attracted to the God of the Jews and had begun to pray and give money. He was doing everything he knew to come into a personal relationship with God. but nothing worked. Yet God observed Cornelius and prepared the way for his salvation.

This process began with a vision of an angel who appeared and called him by name. Cornelius was startled, of course: "Cornelius stared at him in fear. 'What is it, Lord?' he asked. The angel answered, 'Your prayers and gifts to the poor have come up as a remembrance before God'" (Acts

10:4). Then the angel gave some instructions: "Now send men to Joppa to bring back a man named Simon who is called Peter. He is staying with Simon the tanner, whose house is by the sea" (Acts 10:5-6).

As we read what the angel said, we are struck with a question. Why didn't the angel tell Cornelius how to become a Christian? Why didn't the angel speak to him of repentance toward God and faith in our Lord Jesus Christ? Why didn't the angel share the gospel with him? Because God doesn't use angels to share the gospel. As we saw in Acts 2, he uses people like you and me.

After the angel instructed him to find a man named Simon Peter, Cornelius immediately called his personal aide and two servants from his household and sent them to Joppa where Peter was staying. The drama began to take shape. Here was a pagan soldier in Caesarea wide open to the gospel. All God had to do now was prepare someone to witness to him. As it turned out, this proved to be more difficult than getting the man ready to listen.

Is that true in your city? Are there more people ready to listen to the gospel than there are people ready to give it? Is that true in your neighborhood? Do you identify with that problem? In Jesus' day also, the harvest was plentiful, but the laborers were few. Even today, in spite of thousands of training clinics, workshops, and conferences, there is still a dire shortage of spiritually qualified laborers.

Preparing the Lord's Servant

But God did prepare a man to witness to this Roman centurion. Peter was on a rooftop praying. Under normal circumstances, Peter might not have responded to the invitation of the men from Caesarea. But as Peter was in prayer, the Lord prepared his heart through an unusual vision.

> While Peter was still thinking about the vision, the Spirit said to him, "Simon, three men are looking for you. So get up and go downstairs. Do not hesitate to go with them, for I have

sent them." Peter went down and said to the men, "I'm the one you're looking for. Why have you come?" The men replied, "We have come from Cornelius the centurion. He is a righteous and God-fearing man, who is respected by all the Jewish people. A holy angel told him to have you come to his house so that he could hear what you have to say" (Acts 10:19-22).

So, guided by the Holy Spirit, Peter agreed to go.

There are a number of important lessons for us in this event. God wanted his man to launch out on this mission in complete assurance of faith, with no misgivings. So he took the time to settle the matter in Peter's heart. Unless a person is absolutely convinced he is in the will of God, his life and witness bear little fruit and have little power.

Paul's constant declaration that he was an apostle by the will of God was more than just a means of assuring his readers he was ministering in the name of Christ and with his blessing. It contains one of the secrets of Paul's ministry. He was living in God's will and knew it. God used that fact to inflame Paul's spirit with courage and zeal.

If we want to be used by God, we must first ascertain how God wants to use us and then press on in that direction with great exuberance. This was the attitude with which the Lord wanted Peter to go forth.

Disciplemaking

The second lesson is in Acts 10:23: "Then Peter invited the men into the house to be his guests. The next day Peter started out with them, and some of the brothers from Joppa went along." Peter took some men with him when he went. Did he take them to carry the luggage? Did they go to run errands or to help with the travel arrangements? They may have done some of those things, but that certainly wasn't the main reason why Peter took them.

Peter's mission in life was making disciples. Jesus made that abundantly clear in his commission to the apostles. Peter had walked and talked with Jesus for three years. He knew the powerful effect that training by association had on his own life. It was all so simple—so unassuming.

There were no highly structured seminars, classes, institutes, or workshops like those we are so familiar with. There was no teacher equipped with an overhead projector, retractable pointer, charts, chalkboards, or outlines of systematic theology. Of course I don't decry such things. Whatever can be used to train men and women in the Christian life should be used.

But we are foolish or blind if we omit the basic training method Jesus used. He primarily trained his men by association on the job. To forget that—to do everything but that—and implement a training program that neglects the principle of association is the height of folly. Peter understood this principle of training, so he took some men along with him. He followed the pattern Jesus created when training the Twelve (see Mark 3:14).

One Man

Another lesson to observe is God's strategy in opening the door of faith to the Gentiles. God selected one man and started with him. This was consistent with God's plan down through the ages. Through Abraham he would bless the world. Through Moses he would deliver his people. Through Gideon he would defeat the Midianites. Through his son he would offer redemption to the world. This strategy is so profound in its simplicity that we miss it. We overlook the potential of one life.

When Dawson Trotman, the founder of The Navigators, visited us in our area ministries, his first question was, "Where is the man you are training?" I could show him my program. I could tell him all about our meetings. I could describe all of our activities, but he would always repeat one central question: "Where is your man?" We soon learned to make the approach suggested by that question the focus of our prayer and our ministry.

We sought the Lord to ask him for a man of like heart who would be eager to follow him. The letters W.H.A.T. suggested the focus for our search and our prayers. We prayed for a man who was *willing* to pay the price, had a *heart* for God, and was *available,* and *teachable.* People like that are gifts from God, so we prayed and kept our eyes open.

My first ministry assignment with The Navigators was in Pittsburgh, Pennsylvania. One night I was speaking to some young working and professional people at the First Presbyterian Church. I noticed a young man in the front row who seemed to be taking everything in. After the message I introduced myself. This young man was Bob Stephens, the engineer I mentioned in the previous chapter.

Since he was wearing a pin from an engineering fraternity I asked Bob where he had gone to school. He said the University of Maryland. I told him I had lived near that school for the past two years and, taking a wild chance, I asked if Bob knew a friend of mine, Dick Kirk. "Know him? He converted me!" exclaimed Bob. I didn't bother to correct his theology, but did mention that Dick and I had been meeting together regularly to share the word in Christian fellowship. I invited Bob to come to our home for a meal the following week so that I could get to know him.

Later, I learned that after Bob had met Christ, he had left college and gone to work at Pratt and Whitney's plant in Delaware. As a new babe in Christ he struggled and found the Christian life to be hard going on his own with no help from anyone. He began to drift back into his old ways until finally he found himself not living the Christian life effectively. His Christian life went from bad to worse until he prayed, "Lord, tonight I'm going to church one last time. If I don't find someone who can help me to be a real Christian, I'm giving up. It's tonight or never!"

The night I met Bob at church was the same night that he had prayed that prayer. The very same night I had prayed that the Lord would lead me to a man in whom I could invest some of the lessons God had taught me over the years. I was eager to share my life with someone who would have a real heart for God, and who would be available, teachable, and willing to pay the price. Bob was a very teachable individual. I have not discipled many men like him, but that is to be expected, for laborers are few. That evening at the church marked the beginning of a long-lasting friendship. Today Bob Stephens can look back at a personal ministry which God has used to raise up laborers for Christ on three continents.

It would take much more than one book to relate the blessings that Bob and other men like him have brought to our world. Just try to calculate the impact on the world of the conversion of a Cornelius—it would drive a computer wild!

Peter quickly explained to Cornelius how unusual it was for him to make such a visit to a Gentile's home. "You are well aware," he said, "that it is against our law for a Jew to associate with a Gentile or visit him. But God has shown me that I should not call any man impure or unclean. So when I was sent for, I came without raising any objection. May I ask why you sent for me?" (Acts 10:28-29).

The Jews regarded the Gentiles as unclean. They referred to Gentiles as dogs. In his prayers, a Jew thanked God daily that he was not a Gentile. If the shadow of a Gentile fell on a Jew, the Jew had to go to the temple to purify himself. To the Jewish mind the Gentile was less than nothing, filthy, and unclean. A Jew was forbidden by law to enter a Gentile's home. But Peter told Cornelius, "God has shown me some things, he led me here, and I am at your service. So what would you like me to do?" Cornelius gave his account of the story and concluded by telling Peter that his entire household had gathered to hear Peter's message from God.

God Is No Respecter of Persons

Peter's first remark was a mind blower to the men traveling with him. "Then Peter opened his mouth, and said, 'Of a truth I perceive that God is no respecter of persons: But in every nation he that feareth him, and worketh righteousness, is accepted with him'" (Acts 10:34-35 KJV). The Jews had always assumed that God was a respecter of persons. They believed God had chosen them, and rejected everyone else. They had missed God's great purpose for them and forgotten the clear teaching of Scripture. "For the Lord your God is God of gods and Lord of lords, the great God, mighty and awesome, who shows no partiality and accepts no bribes. He defends the cause of the fatherless and the widow, and loves the alien, giving him food and clothing. And you are to love those who are aliens, for you yourselves were aliens in Egypt" (Deuteronomy 10:17-19). Teachings like this can be found throughout the Old Testament, but the Jewish nation had neglected God's word. So there was Peter, in a Gentile's home, rather apprehensive and possibly not fully comprehending all that was happening. As he started his message, his main point was the great doctrine of the lordship of Jesus Christ. He is not just Lord, but "Lord of all."

The Lordship of Christ

Peter knew this truth from personal experience. He had walked with Jesus and observed his lordship in all areas of life. Once Peter had been one of the twelve frightened men in a small boat during a violent storm. They thought they were about to die. Yet while they worried, Jesus slept. So the Twelve awoke Jesus and showed him their predicament. He stood, spoke a few words, and the winds ceased and there was a great calm. They looked at one another and asked, "Who is this that even the wind and sea obey him?" (see Mark 4:35-41). He was Lord of the wind and waves.

When they landed, they were met by the demon-possessed man of the Gerasenes (see Mark 5:1-20). This poor man was completely dominated by Satan. A legion of demons possessed him and tormented him night and day. There stood Jesus and the demon-possessed man. Between the two of them stood as many as 6,000 demons from hell. With a word Jesus dispatched the demons and the man was delivered. Jesus had power over the demons of hell.

Upon their return to the other side of the lake, Jesus and

the disciples were met by Jairus, a ruler of the Synagogue. When Jairus saw Jesus, he fell at his feet and told him his problem. He "pleaded earnestly with him, 'My little daughter is dying. Please come and put your hands on her so that she will be healed and live'" (Mark 5:23). Imagine the joy that flooded Jairus' heart when Jesus agreed to go. But then a new problem arose and claimed Jesus' attention.

> A woman was there who had been subject to bleeding for twelve years. She had suffered a great deal under the care of many doctors and had spent all she had, yet instead of getting better she grew worse. When she heard about Jesus, she came up behind him in the crowd and touched his cloak, because she thought, "If I just touch his clothes, I will be healed." Immediately her bleeding stopped and she felt in her body that she was freed from her suffering (Mark 5:25-29).

Imagine what was going on in the mind of Jairus. His little daughter was not just ill, she was at the point of death. He no longer measured time by the minute but by the heartbeat. Every second was precious. Any moment it would be too late. If Jesus would only hurry. But no, there he stood, thronged by a crowd, talking to a woman. Just then the news he dreaded was announced. "'Your daughter is dead,' they said. 'Why bother the teacher any more?'" (Mark 5:35). If Jesus had just kept moving, maybe things would have been different. But now Jairus' world had fallen apart. His little girl was dead.

But Jesus turned to him and said, "Don't be afraid; just believe"(Mark 5:36). What do you think Jairus thought when he heard those words? Believe? Believe what? The girl was dead! That was no time for religious platitudes. It was time to face reality. Faith is all well and good, but at a time like this—what am I to believe? Jesus expected Jairus to believe the same thing he expects us to believe—God *can* do the impossible. When your world falls apart and there is no way out, God can do what is impossible for man. So Jesus went to the house and took command of the situation.

"After he put them all out, he took the child's father and

mother and the disciples who were with him, and went in where the child was. He took her by the hand and said to her, *'Talitha koum!'* (which means, 'Little girl, I say to you, get up!'). Immediately the girl stood up and walked around (she was twelve years old). At this they were completely astonished" (Mark 5:40-42). Jesus was Lord over disease and death.

Peter was one of those privileged to watch Jesus as he demonstrated his power over sickness and death, the demons of hell, and over the wind and the waves. From those experiences had come the conviction that Jesus was, in fact, Lord of all.

Share the Gospel

Peter's experiences with Jesus, and his submission to the lordship of Christ prepared him to be the man who unlocked the kingdom of God to the Gentiles during his visit with Cornelius. When he spoke in Cornelius' home, after making a few more introductory comments, Peter proclaimed the gospel (see Acts 10:39-41). The gospel is the power of God unto salvation (see Romans 1:16).

Some years ago Carrie, a friend of mine, was busy trying to reach her friends for Christ but with no success. She was talking with Nancy, another Christian, about this and Nancy asked, "What do you share when you explain the gospel to someone?" Carrie said she gave her testimony and explained how she had met the Lord. "Is that all?" Nancy asked. When Carrie said it was, Nancy exclaimed, "You're leaving out the power!" She then explained to Carrie that the power for salvation is in the gospel message. Then she taught her a clear and simple way to present the gospel to her friends. Soon many of them turned to the Lord in repentance and faith as Carrie shared the gospel message with them. Your testimony has the power to convince, but the gospel, the good news of the crucified and risen Savior, is the only message that has the power to convert.

After sharing the gospel, Peter went back to the foundations of our faith. He said God had "commanded us to preach to the people and to testify that he is the one whom God appointed as judge of the living and the dead. All the prophets testify about him that everyone who believes in him receives forgiveness of sins through his name" (Acts 10:42-43). The prophets and the apostles laid the foundations of our faith by their own lives and writings.

Paul wrote to the Ephesians about this too. "Consequently, you are no longer foreigners and aliens, but fellow citizens with God's people and members of God's household, built on the foundation of the apostles and prophets, with Christ Jesus himself as the chief cornerstone" (Ephesians 2:19-20). Our faith has good roots which go back to the beginnings of God's revelation of himself to man. Christianity is not a recent invention. The Christian life as we know it was passed on by men who were eyewitnesses to the ministry of Jesus, men who ate and drank with him after his resurrection. This is an essential truth for us to remember in a day when strange religious beliefs are found everywhere. It is good to remember the foundations of our faith are rooted in historic truth.

The Significance of Tongues

As Peter spoke, an unusual thing happened.

> While Peter was still speaking these words, the Holy Spirit came on all who heard the message. The circumcised believers who had come with Peter were astonished that the gift of the Holy Spirit had been poured out even on the Gentiles. For they heard them speaking in tongues and praising God. Then Peter said, "Can anyone keep these people from being baptized with water? They have received the Holy Spirit just as we have." So he ordered that they be baptized in the name of Jesus Christ. Then they asked Peter to stay with them for a few days (Acts 10:44-48).

Every Gentile in the room was immediately ushered into the kingdom of God! Again we have observed the dynamic power of the gospel and the receptivity of the audience.

This is not the first time we have observed tongues in our study of Acts. Many who read the Acts of the Apostles wonder about this phenomenon. We should consider I Corinthians 14:21. "In the Law it is written: 'Through men of strange tongues and through the lips of foreigners I will speak to this people, but even then they will not listen to me,' says the Lord." Here Paul quoted Isaiah 28:11-12. This passage contains the first mention of tongues in the Bible. Isaiah prophesied that through them God would speak "to this people." Who was "this people?" They were the Jews—the nation of Israel.

What was the purpose of these tongues? Paul wrote, "Tongues, then, are a sign, not for believers but for unbelievers" (1 Corinthians 14:22a). So God gave tongues as a sign for unbelieving Jews. As Paul commented, "Jews demand miraculous signs and Greeks look for wisdom" (1 Corinthians 1:22). If the Jews require a sign, God will give them one. He does not hide in the clouds and play hide and seek with us. He has an all-consuming desire to reveal himself to us and he will do whatever it takes to make himself known to us. Remember Acts 2? Many Jews had gathered in Jerusalem, and tongues were used as a sign for the benefit of the unbelieving Jews.

When the Holy Spirit came to the Samaritans, as described in Acts 8, were tongues manifested? No, because the Samaritans do not require a sign. Jews require a sign. In Acts 10, who was involved? Gentiles. Do Gentiles require a sign? No, Jews require a sign. So were tongues manifested? Yes! Yes? Surely we would have expected a negative answer. Gentiles do not require a sign and there was Peter in the midst of a house full of them.

What was the reason for the manifestation of tongues? To discover the reason, we must reread the passage carefully: *"The circumcised believers* who had come with Peter were astonished that the gift of the Holy Spirit had been poured out even on the Gentiles. For *they* heard them speaking in tongues and praising God" (Acts 10:45-46). What did God use to break through centuries of prejudice? What convinced those Jews that God had also granted the Gentiles repentance unto life? They were convinced by hearing them speak in tongues. So the sign was given, not for the Gentiles but for the Jews.

Acts 10 is filled with many unusual events: a vision of an angel, a great sheet descending from heaven, and the manifestation of tongues. But when we analyze this and consider it all carefully, what do we see? We see the purposes of God moving steadily forward from Jerusalem, into Judea, Samaria, and the Gentile world.

SUMMARY:

God has a great and exciting plan for taking the message of Christ to the ends of the earth. His method of accomplishing it is through men whom he has given to his Son as witnesses. They will reach others who will in turn teach others also. They are people who are—
- trained through association with godly people;
- open to God's direction;
- committed to the lordship of Christ;
- committed to sharing the gospel.

This plan continues today. May God grant us the joy of taking part in his grand plan—the Great Commission of Christ.

11
Peter
on the Carpet

TO THE JEWISH way of thinking, Peter committed three un-
pardonable sins. He had entered a Gentile's household, eaten
with the family, and to make matters worse, had baptized a
group of Gentiles into the church. The Jewish Christians felt
insulted because those Gentiles had not been circumcised
before they were baptized. For the Jews, such behavior was an
insult to God and a departure from the Scriptures and their national history.

To help them understand what he had done Peter "explained everything to them precisely as it had happened"
(Acts 11:4). He began with his vision in Joppa and explained
how God had led him to Caeserea where he met Cornelius.

> He [Cornelius] told us how he had seen an angel appear in his
> house and say, "Send to Joppa for Simon who is called Peter.
> He will bring you a message through which you and all your
> household will be saved." As I began to speak, the Holy Spirit
> came on them as he had come on us at the beginning. Then I
> remembered what the Lord had said, "John baptized with
> water, but you will be baptized with the Holy Spirit." So

if God gave them the same gift as he gave us, who believed in the Lord Jesus Christ, who was I to think that I could oppose God!' When they heard this, they had no further objections and praised God, saying, "So then, God has even granted the Gentiles repentance unto life" (Acts 11:13-18).

When the Jews heard that the Holy Spirit had been given to the Gentiles, in the same way he had been given to them on the day of Pentecost, they were convinced. It had been a long, uphill battle to bring the Gentiles into the kingdom. But once again the Lord had won the day. His kingdom of priests was finally on the move. It had taken some time, but progress is often slow.

In Colorado Springs, where I live, it takes a long time for spring to become summer. June may be rudely interrupted by an unexpected snowstorm. The sun appears briefly and the temperature warms up, but suddenly the north wind blows fiercely and we are scrambling for our overcoats again. At times like that it seems as if summer, real summer, will never come. When we look up at Pike's Peak towering above the city, it is as if a giant scoop of ice cream was just plopped on the summit—another reminder of winter. But slowly the snow melts, and warmer breezes finally dominate the weather. Summer has come, but not without a struggle.

So it was with God and his people. At long last he finally had them on track heading in the right direction—they understood that Gentiles as well as Jews should be welcomed into his kingdom. Apart from a few minor setbacks, the church became a lively witness to the Gentile world.

Now those who had been scattered by the persecution in connection with Stephen traveled as far as Phoenicia, Cyprus and Antioch, telling the message only to Jews. Some of them, however, men from Cyprus and Cyrene, went to Antioch and began to speak to Greeks also, telling them the good news about the Lord Jesus. The Lord's hand was with them, and a great number of people believed and turned to the Lord. News of this reached the ears of the church at Jerusalem, and they sent Barnabas to Antioch. When he arrived and saw the evidence of the grace of God, he was glad and encouraged them all to remain true to the Lord with all their hearts. He was a good man, full of the Holy Spirit and faith, and a great number of people were brought to the Lord. Then Barnabas went to Tarsus to look for Saul, and when he found him, he brought him to Antioch. For a whole year Barnabas and Saul met with the church and taught great numbers of people. The disciples were first called Christians at Antioch (Acts 11:19-26).

On the day of Pentecost people from many nations listened to the message. People from Cyrene were there and it is quite likely that some of them were among those who began to share the good news with the Gentiles. God blessed their ministry. Remember these were not the leaders of the church. They were laborers trained by the apostles. They were not the apostles, but their lifestyle bore a striking resemblance to that of the apostles. We reproduce spiritually after our own kind. That is what happened in the instance recorded in Acts 11. They proclaimed new life in the Lord Jesus Christ. The results? "A great number believed and turned to the Lord." Sounds familiar, doesn't it? The apostles had done their job. They had trained these laborers effectively.

Consider the city to which the Lord led this band of men. Antioch was known as the

Third City of the Roman Empire. Population, 500,000. Surpassed only by Rome and Alexandria. Mediterranean doorway to the Great Eastern Highways. 300 miles north of Jerusalem. Called "Queen of the East," and "Antioch the Beautiful." Embellished with everything that Roman wealth, Greek aestheticism, and oriental luxury could produce.

Its worship of Ashtaroth was accompanied with immoral indulgence and unbelievable indecency. Yet multitudes of its people accepted Christ. It became birthplace of the name "Christian," and center of organized effort to Christianize the World.[1]

Why would God send this missionary band to such a place? Surely there were some cities which could have been more easily reached, cities which would have provided a gentler training ground for those fledgling laborers. But why not Antioch? Who needs to hear the gospel more than immoral pagans? Also, if these disciples succeeded in such a setting, it would be a clear demonstration to everyone that the gospel could succeed anywhere.

Making an Impact for Christ

What do you think it would take to make an impact in such a city today? Exactly the same ingredients that it took then: the clear message of Christ and some witnesses who display the kind of attributes Jesus urged his followers to demonstrate. Let us consider three of them.

The first necessity is to be a fisher of men. "'Come, follow me,' Jesus said, 'and I will make you fishers of men'" (Matthew 4:19). I am not a fisherman in any sense of the word. The very thought of standing by a lake or sitting in a boat has no appeal to me at all. But I have a son who is a fisherman. By watching Randy, I have observed what it takes to be a good fisherman.

He usually fishes at Eagle lake—nine miles up a canyon from The Navigators' conference center at Glen Eyrie. My wife and I will plan a picnic lunch at the lake around noon the days Randy goes fishing. Randy and one of his friends will leave about dawn so they can spend the morning fishing. They leave filled with keen anticipation and lots of faith. They hope to catch many fish so there will be plenty of rainbow trout for lunch. Once they arrive at the lake, much skill and patience is required.

These two qualities give you a good picture of what it takes to fish for men also. The effective fisher of men is also characterized by anticipation, faith, hope, patience, and some know-how. Like the fisherman, the fisher of men must first go fishing if he hopes to make a catch. There may not always be a big catch when we fish for men, but there will be *no* catch unless we go fishing. To catch fish, you have to go where the fish are and throw out the bait. To catch men, you have to go where they are and share the gospel message.

This is where know-how comes in. A good fisherman doesn't leap into the lake, chase the fish around, and try to grab them so he can force the bait into their mouths. He tosses out something attractive that will lure a fish and eventually hook it. We must find out what interests our non-Christian friends and concentrate on that. With Jesus it was a comment about water in his conversation with the woman at the well. With Philip it was a question about what the Ethiopian was reading. A simple, natural comment or question can often open the door for a witness.

While traveling in Yugoslavia, we met a family from Venezuela. After a brief chat at lunch the lady asked if she could talk with my wife, Virginia. Later that afternoon they sat together for two hours discussing faith and what it means to know Christ personally. Randy, my son, also got into a conversation with her husband, and for more than an hour they talked about many things, including the gospel. Frankly, it all happened so naturally that we could not pinpoint a precise sequence of events. But my wife and son—two fishers— were alert and able to take advantage of the opportunities the Lord gave them.

We are called to publish, not to protect, the good news. When we follow Christ, we will fish for men because that is what he did. C.H. Spurgeon said, "True conversion is most fully displayed when it leads converts to seek the conversion of others." We often think that following Christ involves praying, reading the word, and having a quiet time. It does include each of those things. But it also means fishing for men.

Thomas Guthrie said, "I love your meetings for prayer. You cannot have too many of them. But, I would rather see a man who has been saved from the gulf below casting lifelines to others struggling in the maelstrom of death, than on his knees on that rock, thanking God for his own deliverance. I believe God will accept action for others as the highest possible expression of gratitude that a saved soul can offer."

The second necessity, or quality that should characterize our lives is salt. Jesus said, "You are the salt of the earth. But if the salt loses its saltiness, how can it be made salty again? It is no longer good for anything, except to be thrown out and trampled by men" (Matthew 5:13). What does that mean?

Probably the first thing that comes to mind when you think of salt is that it makes you thirsty. My wife loves popcorn. After eating a bowl of it she will have something to drink. Salted popcorn triggers a thirst. Now think of that in light of Revelation 21:6. "It is done. I am the Alpha and the Omega, the Beginning and the End. To him who is thirsty I will give to drink without cost from the spring of the water of life."

John also wrote, "The Spirit and the bride say, 'Come!' And let him who hears say, 'Come!' Whoever is thirsty, let him come; and whoever wishes, let him take the free gift of the water of life" (Revelation 22:17). Jesus is talking to people who are "thirsty." The old saying, "You can lead a horse to water, but you can't make him drink," is true. But if a horse is thirsty, there is no problem—he is eager to get his mouth down into a water trough. Our job as Christians is to be salt in the world, making people thirsty for God.

Empty the Saltshaker

Salt which is still in the shaker is ineffective. It has potential for good, but it is not doing good. To do its work it must be shaken out of its container. Our job is to penetrate society with the message of Christ. All too often the devoted Christian's greatest problem is that he is like salt trapped inside a container. He clings to some other Christians in an exclusive fellowship and remains isolated from the world.

But that was not how Jesus lived. "Now the tax collectors and 'sinners' were all gathering around to hear him. But the Pharisees and the teachers of the law muttered, 'This man welcomes sinners and eats with them'" (Luke 15:1-2). We must not overlook the significance of the word *into* in Christ's commission to us. "He said to them, 'Go *into* all the world and preach good news to all creation'" (Mark 16:15). There is the danger of isolation—we can be out of touch. But there's also another danger. If it is to do any good, salt must be distinctively salty. Jesus taught, "Salt is good, but if it loses its saltiness, how can it be made salty again? It is fit neither for the soil nor for the manure pile; it is thrown out. He who has ears to hear, let him hear'" (Luke 14:34-35).

There must be a redemptive difference in the life of the witness. A mild dose of religion is of little value. Christ's life in us brings about personal holiness and purity. We are in the world, but not of it. So we must be dispersed into the world but distinctively different from the men and women around us. If we are not in touch with the world, if we retreat into the safety of some warm but isolated Christian fellowship, we will become modern-day hermits. We need to be mixed in with the world to create a thirst for God among those around us.

The third quality that ought to characterize our lives is light. "You are the light of the world," said Jesus. "A city on a hill cannot be hidden. Neither do people light a lamp and put it under a bowl. Instead they put it on its stand, and it gives light to everyone in the house. In the same way, let your light shine before men, that they may see your good deeds and praise your Father in heaven" (Matthew 5:14-16). This light should be diffused into the world by our lives and by our message. Jesus spoke of our lives when he said men ought to see our good deeds.

Paul referred to our message when he wrote,

> The god of this age has blinded the minds of unbelievers, so that they cannot see the light of the gospel of the glory of Christ, who is the image of God. For we do not preach ourselves, but Jesus Christ as Lord, and ourselves as your servants for Jesus' sake. For God, who said, "Let light shine out of darkness," made his light shine in our hearts to give us the light of the knowledge of the glory of God in the face of Christ (2 Corinthians 4:4-6).

I know there are many who say, "But what can I do, I'm a nobody! If I had great wealth, a distinguished position, or great talents, maybe then somebody would listen to me." But that's not the issue. Don't worry about the size of your bank account, or how much power or prestige you have. If you will simply let Jesus Christ manifest himself in and through your life, you will become great in the kingdom of God.

I once received a letter asking if I would visit a young man in a veterans' hospital. Some friends of mine had visited this man who had suffered severe injuries when a land mine exploded. He had lost both of his legs, one arm, his jaw, and one eye. Yet daily he would roll himself out of bed and wheel himself up and down the wards talking to men about Jesus Christ. He was making an effort, he explained, "to keep them from getting too discouraged." So today, while some of us sit around wishing we had more wealth, prestige, or a better position in life, I'm sure this young man is still faithfully sharing the gospel.

On one occasion I heard a conference speaker at Glen Eyrie talk about a lady who was a dynamic witness for Christ. She contracted a strange disease and lost one leg, then the other. She began sharing the gospel by writing it out in letters to her friends. Then she lost her right arm. So she taught herself how to write left-handed and kept on sending out the gospel by mail until she lost her left arm. Then she taught herself how to write while holding her pen between her teeth. She is still communicating the gospel. She is a bright light in a dark world.

I'm sure the band of believers mentioned in Acts 11:20 also shined as lights in the world. When the apostles learned of that group's efforts, they soon sent them some helpers. When they decided to send Barnabas, they couldn't have chosen a better man. The people in Jerusalem trusted him completely. They had profited by his generosity. On the other hand, he was perfectly fitted to the work at Antioch. Cyprus, his home, was only sixty miles from there and he knew the territory well. "When he arrived and saw the evidence of the grace of God, he was glad and encouraged them all to remain true to the Lord with all their hearts. He was a good man, full of the Holy Spirit and faith, and a great number of people were brought to the Lord" (Acts 11:23-24, NIV).

Kept by God's Power

Barnabas "exhorted them all, that with purpose of heart they would cleave unto the Lord" (Acts 11:23 KJV). This thought poses an interesting question. Do we hold on to the Lord, or does he hold on to us? Is it our responsibility to stay close to him, or is it his responsibility to keep us close to him? What does the Bible teach us about these questions?

Peter wrote, "Blessed be the God and Father of our Lord Jesus Christ, which according to his abundant mercy hath begotten us again unto a lively hope by the resurrection of Jesus Christ from the dead, to an inheritance incorruptible, and undefiled, and that fadeth not away, reserved in heaven for you, *Who are kept by the power of God* through faith unto salvation ready to be revealed in the last time" (1 Peter 1:3-5, KJV).

According to Peter, we are kept by the power of God. But Jude wrote, "But you, dear friends, build yourselves up in your most holy faith and pray in the Holy Spirit. *Keep yourselves in God's love* as you wait for the mercy of our Lord Jesus Christ to bring you to eternal life" (Jude 20-21).

Does God keep us in his love, or do we keep ourselves in his love? The answer is that both are true. These two passages deal with two of the most important words in the Christian faith: *relationship* and *fellowship.* Our relationship with Christ can never be broken, but our fellowship with Christ can be broken—we must maintain daily fellowship with him. Let us take a closer look at these two words.

A Relationship with Christ

We enter God's family through spiritual birth. John wrote, "Yet to all who received him, to those who believed in his name, he gave the right to become children of God—children born not of natural descent, nor of human decision or a husband's will, but born of God" (John 1:12-13). If I have personally received Christ, I am a child of God in whom Christ dwells. When I receive Christ I am given the gift of eternal life. Jesus said, "I give them eternal life, and they shall never perish; no one can snatch them out of my hand" (John 10:28). Paul wrote, "Therefore, if anyone is in Christ, he is a new creation; the old has gone, the new has come!" (2 Corinthians 5:17). Those who have personally received Christ now live "in him." But that was not always true. Once we were "in Adam." Paul wrote to the Corinthians, "For since death came through a man, the resurrection of the dead comes also through a man. For as in Adam all die, so in Christ all will be made alive" (1 Corinthians 15:21-22).

When Adam fell into sin and death, we all fell with him. When Adam died, we all died. When Adam was separated from God, we were all separated from God. But since receiving Christ I have transferred my allegiance to Christ and I am now "in him." That is a great comfort because now I am as secure as Christ is. As long as he lives in harmony with the Father, I am kept in a secure relationship with God. So Paul wrote, "And God raised us up with Christ and seated us with him in the heavenly realms in Christ Jesus, in order that in the coming ages he might show the incomparable riches of his grace, expressed in his kindness to us in Christ Jesus" (Ephesians 2:6-7). As a Christian, my security does not depend on my feelings but on Christ.

Fellowship with Christ
Fellowship, on the other hand, is a different matter. This is what Barnabas was speaking about to the Christians in Antioch. We must take personal responsibility for our daily walk with Christ. He provides us with the means. He provides us with the motivation. His Spirit will encourage us and help us along the way. But he does not force us to pray or to read his word. He simply says, "Call to me and I will answer you and tell you great and unsearchable things you do not know"

(Jeremiah 33:3). God's invitation is, "O land, land, land, hear the word of the Lord!" (Jeremiah 22:29). So it is our responsibility to call upon him and to listen to him. The psalmist wrote, "I have considered my ways and have turned my steps to your statutes. I will hasten and not delay to obey your commands" (Psalm 119:59-60). We must obey God's commands.

I was discussing this idea once with some university students in Bandung, Indonesia. After I shared the gospel, one of the students asked me what would happen if he decided to receive Christ and then sinned. "Would I be required to accept Christ again?" he asked. My daughter was traveling with me so I pointed to her as an example while answering the question. Becky was born into my family and her relationship to our family would never change. She would always be my daughter. Our father-daughter relationship began at her birth. However, if she was disobedient, our fellowship would be interrupted and strained until she came to me to apologize and set our relationship right again.

The same is true of our relationship with the Lord. Sometimes we are good, while at other times we are bad. But good or bad, I am still his child. Our fellowship can be broken but not our relationship. When my fellowship with God is broken, it is up to me to confess my sin, forsake it, and accept his cleansing and forgiveness. "If we confess our sins, he is faithful and just and will forgive us our sins and purify us from all unrighteousness" (1 John 1:9).

Barnabas the Encourager

God blessed the ministry in Antioch and large numbers of people trusted the Lord. Barnabas needed help establishing these young believers in the faith. "Barnabas went to Tarsus to look for Saul, and when he found him, he brought him to Antioch. So for a whole year Barnabas and Saul met with the church and taught great numbers of people. The disciples were first called Christians at Antioch" (Acts 11:25-26). Barnabas was a warm, generous man. His very name meant "the son of consolation." He was full of heart, enthusiasm, inspiration, comfort, and encouragement. He held the truth warmly, and taught it warmly. He was a stimulator, a man of love and grace. But there came a time when another element of training was needed to strengthen and supplement his ministry. He needed a colaborer who was filled with zeal and logic, a man with an analytical mind, a man who could train the disciples in the great doctrines of the faith. So, Barnabas and Saul teamed up in Antioch.

Barnabas' willingness to work with Saul reveals some of the admirable traits in his life. He was humble enough to know when he needed help. He was not interested in empire building, gathering a group of people around himself who would revere him as a great leader. He knew his limitations and freely admitted them. Men like Barnabas are a great asset to a ministry and doubly so if they team up with a counterpart like Saul.

Here is a great principle of leadership. The leader must not merely surround himself with like-minded cronies—men who work, think, and act in a style similar to his own. The leader needs to bring in men who will complement his own gifts and abilities. If he does this, the ministry will deepen and double. But the devil fights against this strategy. He tries to get the leader to go it alone and refuse to admit his weaknesses and needs. If he attacked Barnabas in that way, the devil did not succeed. Barnabas was not concerned just about himself and his own reputation, but for all of the believers. Barnabas' love and dedication knew no bounds.

Subsequently, through the prophet Agabus, a need was made known regarding the Christians in Jerusalem. God revealed to the prophet that there would soon be a famine in the Jerusalem church. "One of them, named Agabus, stood up and through the Spirit predicted that a severe famine would spread over the entire Roman world. (This happened during the reign of Claudius)" (Acts 11:28). Immediately the disciples at Antioch responded and gave what they could.

Why do you think they responded so immediately and wholeheartedly? Because when the Christians in Antioch had experienced a need, the Christians in Jerusalem had sent help immediately in the person of Barnabas. The church at Jerusalem had proven their love for the Christians at Antioch. So naturally when the Christians in Antioch became aware of a need in Jerusalem, they responded in kind. When people receive help they want to return help.

Secondly, they believed the prophet. They gave by faith. There was actually no need at that precise time. They simply believed the prophet when he said there was going to be a need. They acted in faith. Why did the Lord speak through a prophet before the famine occurred? Because there is no food available during a famine. You can't eat money, but you cannot buy food without it. Money was sent so the people could stock up and prepare for what they knew was just around the corner. God was watching out for his people.

SUMMARY:

Large numbers were added to the church as these disciples launched out into the Gentile world. God used them as—
- fishers of men—casting lifelines to drowning souls;
- salt—penetrating the society and creating a thirst for God;
- light—illuminating the good news of Christ in a dark world.

Notes: 1. *Halley's Bible Handbook* (Grand Rapids, Michigan: Zondervan Publishing House, 1965), page 571.

12
Tough Faith and Leadership

ALTHOUGH GOD WATCHES over his people, that does not mean life will be a bed of roses. Troubles will come to us just as they came to the church in the first century.

> It was about this time that King Herod arrested some who belonged to the church, intending to persecute them. He had James, the brother of John, put to death with the sword. When he saw that this pleased the Jews, he proceeded to seize Peter also. This happened during the Feast of Unleavened Bread. After arresting him, he put him in prison, handing him over to be guarded by four squads of four soldiers each. Herod intended to bring him out for public trial after the Passover (Acts 12:1-4).

There was no panic or despair in the ranks. God used times of suffering and difficulty to strengthen the disciples. They developed a "tough faith."

Tough Faith
I saw an example of this some years ago at Maranatha Bible Camp near North Platte, Nebraska. The Navigators had a train-

ing program there which Walt Henrichsen was leading. I was visiting the program to meet with Walt and to speak to the trainees. Walt and I were sitting under a tree chatting when suddenly the silence was rent by an ear-splitting scream. One of the young men mowing the lawn had caught his foot in a power mower. It cut his shoe and foot. Blood flew in every direction. I panicked.

Over the camp's loudspeaker came an announcement calling for the nurse. In a few moments Rev. Ivan Olsen, the director of Maranatha, came out of his office, walked calmly to his car and started the engine. He gave instructions to wrap the young man's foot in a towel and put him in the car. Then he drove to the hospital. The speed limit on the camp grounds was ten miles per hour, and I noticed that Rev. Olsen drove out of the camp at that speed! I watched him behind the wheel—calm, solid, and in control of himself and the situation. In a couple of hours he brought the young man back to the camp. He recovered completely and was playing sports by the end of the summer.

I observed that Rev. Olsen had responded as a cool, steady man of God in the midst of an emergency that threw me into a fit. What was the difference? Rev. Olsen had walked with God for many years and had seen many troubles come and go. God used those times of stress to build endurance and a settled confidence in God into his life. He had a solid, tough faith.

There is a military organization called the Officers' Selection and Appraisal Center. The men who go there become numbers. All distinctions of rank are set aside. Each man is on the same level. The men are not tested on their knowledge or skills. They are observed to see how they react to the unexpected, to uncongenial conditions, to criticism, and crises. Each man is constantly interviewed, scrutinized, and tested to discern his potential for leadership.

As I heard about that program, it occurred to me that God has a similar program. The men who wrote the New Testament encourage us to participate joyfully in God's training program. James wrote, "When all kinds of trials and temptations crowd into your lives my brothers, don't resent them as intruders, but welcome them as friends! Realize that they come to test your faith and to produce in you the quality of endurance. But let the process go on until that endurance is fully developed, and you will find you have become men of mature character, men of integrity with no weak spots" (James 1:2-4, PH). Peter wrote, "I beg you not to be unduly alarmed at the fiery ordeals which come to test your faith, as though this were some abnormal experience. You should be glad, because it means that you are sharing in Christ's sufferings. One day, when he shows himself in full splendour, you will be filled with the most tremendous joy" (1 Peter 4:12-13, PH). Our faith will be tested. Rev. Olsen passed the test that day at Maranatha, and I failed.

A British general once said the first quality of a man in war must be robustness—the ability to stand the shocks and horrors of combat. I heard about a nation that has an interesting test for new weapons to be used in mountain warfare. If a new machine gun is under consideration, they take it to the top of a 100-foot tower and throw it down onto the concrete below. If it will still fire, they also test it for accuracy and see if it can be dismantled and reassembled easily. But it must first pass the shock test. They have learned that delicate weapons are of little value in actual combat. Combat weapons must be solid. They must have an above average breaking strength. In the Christian life we must be able to overcome the difficult tests we face by the power of God.

In Acts 12 we read an account of the two apostles James and Peter. They were suffering Herod's wrath.

Herod hit upon a scheme to win popularity with the Jews: murdering the apostles. After he realized that the Jews were pleased by James' death, he seized Peter also. "So Peter was kept in prison, but the church was earnestly praying to God for him" (Acts 12:5). A battle raged between Herod, with all his power and glory, and a band of Christians who were praying. But they were not just praying. They prayed earnestly and fervently. The word used to describe this kind of prayer is the word used to describe the intensity of pain one experiences while being pulled apart on a torture rack.

Fervent Prayer

Why did the disciples pray so intensely? Perhaps there were several reasons. First, they faced an impossible situation. It was physically impossible for Peter to escape. Because he had a reputation as a jailbreaker, sixteen guards were assigned to keep him. The authorities took no chances. A second possible reason for the intensity of their prayer was an incident in Peter's past. On a previous occasion when he had undergone severe testing, Peter broke down and failed. He had denied his Lord (see Luke 22:54-62). Now Peter was the leader of the Christian movement. If he were to fail again, it would have a devastating effect on the Christian community. So fervent prayer was offered to the Lord.

What is fervent prayer? James said, "The effectual, fervent prayer of a righteous man availeth much" (James 5:16, KJV). Luke referred to the same quality in his description of Jesus at prayer: "And being in anguish, he prayed more earnestly, and his sweat was like drops of blood falling to the ground" (Luke 22:44). Paul commended the way Epaphras prayed. "He is always wrestling in prayer for you" (Colossians 4:12). If we examine the different shades of meaning in the word fervent, we discover several differences between routine prayer and fervent prayer.

There is a difference in effort. The runner in a hundred-yard sprint and the man strolling in the park are both moving. But one of them puts forth more effort.

There is a difference in attitude. One man takes off a few weeks each year to work on his cabin in the mountains. The trapper works feverishly to finish the windows, door, and roof on his cabin before a blizzard strikes or he is surrounded by wolves and bears. Both men work hard, but there is a difference in their attitudes.

There is a difference in intensity. A mother cautions

a five-year-old not to jump off the bed as it will disturb the neighbors in the apartment below. The police officer talks to a man on the ledge of a high building to convince him not to leap to his death. Both conversations revolve around the idea of jumping, but one leap has greater consequences and there is a corresponding difference in the intensity of the conversation.

There is a difference in concentration. One pilot is landing his plane on a routine flight on a clear, warm, windless day. Another is landing a plane in a dense fog with his landing gear stuck. Both pilots are careful, but one concentrates much more.

The church in Jerusalem was offering *fervent,* earnest prayer to God. Did he answer their prayers? Did Peter pace back and forth, biting his nails, considering denial of his faith? No! "The night before Herod was to bring him to trial, Peter was sleeping between two soldiers, bound with two chains, and sentries stood guard at the entrance" (Acts 12:6). Suddenly a miracle occurred. I'm sure it was an answer to prayer. "Suddenly an angel of the Lord appeared and a light shone in the cell. He struck Peter on the side and woke him up. 'Quick, get up!' he said, and the chains fell off Peter's wrists. Then the angel said to him, 'Put on your clothes and sandals.' And Peter did so. 'Wrap your cloak around you and follow me,' the angel told him" (Acts 12:7-8).

Visualize the scene. What would have been your reaction? I would have said to myself, "Oh, no! Someone's come who doesn't even know how to organize a jailbreak!" Notice what happened when the angel woke Peter. First, a light shone in the jail. Secondly, Peter's chains fell clanging to the stone floor. Light and noise are not the order of the day while your guards are sleeping! The angel then told Peter to dress and put on his sandals.

I'm told three words are used for shoes in the New Testament. One of them refers to the shoes of the rich. Another word is used for the shoes of the ordinary people. The third word is used for the sandals of the extremely poor. The sandals of the very poor were simple wooden boards fastened on with a strap. This was the type of sandal Peter wore.

The angel told Peter to strap on his boards and they would clomp out of the cell. I would have preferred to carry my boards and sneak out on tiptoe. But that was not how the angel and Peter left. They clomped out together.

Why do you think Peter was able to sleep in jail? The answer has little to do with human courage but much to do with his confidence in God. Unless a Christian learns to sleep during times of stress there will be times in his life when he won't get much sleep! Being able to remain calm during times of stress is important, not only for our own welfare, but for the well-being of those around us. We communicate our faith best during difficult times.

When my wife and I went to the Midwest to begin the Navigator work, there were many times when money was practically non-existent in our home. It was my practice to have one of the men who was living with us for training in discipleship keep our financial records. They took turns bookkeeping from month to month. This gave them some training and prepared them for the time when they would be responsible for keeping their own ministry budgets and records. I remember the day one of those men took over on the first of the month. In a few days he came to me in a state of shock. "LeRoy," he said, "what are we going to do?"

"Do about what?" I asked.

"Our finances," he exclaimed. "I had no idea things were in such bad shape. What shall we do?"

"We will do what we have always done," I replied. "We will trust God." Then I shared 2 Chronicles 32:7-8 with him. " 'Be strong and courageous. Do not be afraid or discouraged because of the king of Assyria and the vast army with him. With him is only the arm of flesh, but with us is the Lord our God to help us and to fight our battles.' And the people gained confidence from what Hezekiah the king of Judah said."

There will be hard times. Jesus promised that. "I have told you these things, so that in me you may have peace. In this world you will have trouble. But take heart! I have over-come the world" (John 16:33). We must accept everything God sends our way thankfully and joyfully and keep on with our mission.

As soon as he was released, Peter went to see the Christians who had been praying. "When they opened the door and saw him, they were astonished. Peter motioned for them to be quiet and described how the Lord had brought him out of prison. 'Tell James and the brothers about this,' he said, and then he left for another place" (Acts 12:16-17). By visiting these Christians, Peter bolstered their faith and encouraged them in their praying.

Some time ago I began a campus ministry at the University of Pittsburgh. After getting some directions from the Lord as to how to go about the ministry, I began mustering prayer support. I went from church to church and asked the pastors for permission to take a few minutes at their prayer meetings to tell the people what God was leading us to do and to ask them for their prayer support. We visited many churches and were encouraged by the response. Many agreed to pray. Each week we would share the gospel in a fraternity house and make appointments with those who were interested and attempt to lead them to Christ. Soon I returned to the churches who were praying and took some of the converts with me.

I remember sitting in a prayer meeting with one of those new babes in Christ. When the pastor called for testimonies or answers to prayer, this student stood up. "I think I am an answer to your prayers," he said. Then he told them his story. He had gone from church to church in the city trying to find a way to God. But nothing had worked. Then one night in his fraternity house living room stood a man who explained the message of salvation and who had answers for his questions. He turned to the Lord in repentance and faith and became a new creation in Christ. So he thanked them all for praying and sat down. The place was electrified. I think it was the first time anything like that had ever happened and they were over-joyed. Answers to prayer produce joy and bolster our faith.

Leadership

Since Peter was a leader, it was his responsiblity to keep the people informed. Before any major campaign in World War II, Field Marshal Montgomery, the British General, informed all his men, including the cooks, about the purpose of the battle. He told everyone what to expect. He did that because information is one of the key factors in maintaining high morale. General Eisenhower also gave a great deal of attention to his troops' morale. He considered morale as the single most important factor in successful warfare.

A victorious army has high morale, but a defeated army has poor morale. Peter's release from prison was a victory for God. The heathen were raging. Herod had set himself against the Lord and his anointed. It was important for Peter to go to the troops and help them realize they were winning.

The Christians in Jerusalem were at war. They were in the thick of battle. As a good leader should, Peter kept them informed. When people are kept properly informed, they feel important to their leader.

Prudence

After visiting the Christians, Peter went into hiding. You always find a mixture of faith and prudence in the great men of the Bible. Peter had just walked out of prison. The guards did not wake up even though by all rights they should have. Doors were opened that should have remained shut. Peter could have said, "Well, I'll just go into the house, enjoy the fellowship, and when they come looking, I'll trust God for another miracle. I'll just ask him to make me invisible." But he didn't. He knew full well that God does not do for us what we can manage to do by ourselves. He does that which we cannot do. So Peter went into hiding. Luke doesn't say where Peter was hiding. He might not have known, but even if he did he probably would not have mentioned it. Quite possibly some of the believers were still using the same hideout at the time Luke was writing Acts. So the location of Peter's hideout was kept secret.

Pride

Acts 12 ends with an example of the danger of pride. Herod had gone to Caesarea to make a speech. They proclaimed him a god and he basked in their adulation, but only for a moment. "On the appointed day Herod, wearing his royal robes, sat on his throne and delivered a public address to the people. They shouted, 'This is the voice of a god, not of a man.' Suddenly, because Herod did not give praise to God, an angel of the Lord struck him down, and he was eaten by worms and died" (Acts 12:21-23). None of the Herods mentioned in the Bible were known for their humility. Humility is one of the prime attributes of a good leader and it is revealed in simple ways.

One day the president of a corporation stepped into the elevator to go to the penthouse on the top floor. The elevator was only half full, but the operator immediately began to close the door. The president smiled and said, "Let's wait for a few more people, we're only half full." That's terrific! He could have felt he deserved extra space because of his importance.

I remember reading about an incident in the life of Abraham Lincoln. He was entering a building and suddenly remembered he had left something he needed in another place. The doorman asked if he could fetch it for him, and since the doorman was eager to do that, Mr. Lincoln agreed. But before he left on the errand, Mr. Lincoln took the doorman's badge and did his job while he ran the errand.

Humility is the hallmark of truly great men, but it was not one of Herod's notable qualities. The Lord smote him, for God resists proud men.

Throughout those difficult times, God's word kept multiplying. Its influence in the believers' lives became ever greater as it spread throughout the land. Opposition will arise. Difficulties will come. Persecution may be intense. But the word of God is never bound. The good seed had been scattered (see Acts 8:1). It took root like any healthy plant and continued to grow and bear fruit. The difficulties experienced by the church promoted growth rather than stifled it.

There are three reasons why plants do not grow. One is

improper care. A second reason is poor conditions for growth, and third, a plant may have a wasting disease. Like plants, new Christians also require tender loving care and an environment which promotes healthy growth.

The believers were receiving proper care. The apostles watching over them knew they would give an account to God for the care of their souls. Were the conditions conducive to growth? The answer is yes. Strangely enough, the Christian church becomes fat and lazy during easy times but it flourishes when times are hard. They were a healthy group. Their minds were fixed on evangelism, discipleship, the word of God, prayer, and the Great Commission. So they grew strong and multiplied.

Acts 12 ends with the return of Barnabas and Saul from their mission of mercy in Jerusalem. They brought with them a young man named John Mark. He is the Mark mentioned earlier in the chapter: "He went to the house of Mary the mother of John, also called Mark, where many people had gathered and were praying" (Acts 12:12). He was a young man of great promise. Eventually he was mightily used by God to communicate the message of Christ to his generation and all future generations.

SUMMARY:

The good news of God continued to spread and the church grew strong even in the face of opposition. Their faithful God responded to—
- fervent prayer;
- a people with tough faith.

13
Developing
Workers

THE HOLY SPIRIT was still in perfect control of the church. Jesus had promised he would come to provide guidance, and the believers were eager to let him lead.

> In the church at Antioch there were prophets and teachers: Barnabas, Simeon called Niger, Lucius of Cyrene, Manaen (who had been brought up with Herod the tetrarch) and Saul. While they were worshiping the Lord and fasting, the Holy Spirit said, "Set apart for me Barnabas and Saul for the work to which I have called them." So after they had fasted and prayed, they placed their hands on them and sent them off (Acts 13:1-3).

The Holy Spirit commanded that Barnabas and Saul should be set apart, not to a place but to a work. He had a job in mind. If a person is trained to do the *work* of the ministry he can do it anywhere.

Let us say a young man is reached for Christ aboard a ship while serving in the Navy. He is instructed in the basics of the Christian life and begins to grow. He learns how to study his Bible, to read and memorize it, and to meditate on what God reveals to him through his word. He learns to pray and claim the promises of God. He gets involved in the Christian fellowship and begins an obedient walk with God. He begins to put Christ first in the major areas of his life and begins to separate from sin. He witnesses by giving his testimony to fellow sailors and learns how to share the gospel effectively. In short, he becomes grounded in the basics of the Christian life.

After some years, he leaves the Navy and enters a university. He has been studying and memorizing the Bible on a regular basis and has a growing prayer life. Now he is in a new environment. As he applies what he has learned, the Lord blesses his ministry at the university. After graduating, he goes to work as an engineer in a large corporation. He enters another new setting, but the basics of Christian living are still the same. His life in Christ deepens and his ministry for Christ keeps flourishing. He does his job heartily as unto the Lord and seeks first the kingdom of God. One promotion follows another. He gets married, joins a service club, and becomes established in his community. He has opportunities to serve the Lord in several different spheres now, but his life remains on the same track he learned years ago in the Navy. As the twig was bent, so grew the tree. He has a lifetime of joyful service in the kingdom of God. What was the secret? He was trained to be an effective worker for Christ.

So it was with Barnabas and Saul. We know much about Saul's background, but little about Barnabas. He may have been one of the seventy workers whom the Lord had selected and trained. We don't know. What we do know is that he was selected by the Holy Spirit for a great work in the cause of Christ.

Selecting a Worker

Two of the most vital elements involved in someone becoming a worker in the kingdom of God are careful selection and careful training. There were thousands who heard Jesus' call to repentance and faith. There were hundreds who followed him as disciples. But there were only seventy who were selected and trained to go forth as workers in the harvest. Even as he sent them out, Jesus reminded them of the shortage of laborers like themselves and admonished them to pray for still more (see Luke 10:1-2). What is the essential difference between a disciple and a laborer? Doesn't a disciple witness, read his Bible, and pray? Is there anything special about being a worker?

The difference is a matter of depth and degree. Let me list nine qualities that are found in depth in the life of a worker.

Hunger. He must hunger for a deeper walk with God, and want to experience a deeper reality of God in his life. He must hunger to learn and grow and be willing to pay any price to satisfy those hungers that God places in his heart.

Conviction. He must be convinced of the absolute necessity of having the basics of Bible reading, prayer, fellowship, and witnessing functioning in his life. He must be convinced of the reality of hell, the lostness of people without Christ, and the need for continuing personal growth in the Lord. He knows *why* he has a daily time alone with God. He knows *why* he studies and memorizes Scripture. He knows *why* he witnesses to others and *why* he maintains a consistent prayer life.

Ministry skills. He must be ever growing in the skillful use of the word in the lives of those to whom God leads him. Early in our Christian walk we often use the word like a club to browbeat people into line. A skilled worker in the kingdom is like a carefully trained surgeon who handles his instruments delicately and skillfully.

Personal holiness. The world does not squeeze the worker into its mold. Some months ago I was on the Island of Tioman in the South China Sea where the musical, "South Pacific" was filmed. Tioman is a beautiful, quiet, tropical paradise. One day my wife and I were walking along a path through the jungle and we came upon a rubbish heap. There were branches, limbs, egg shells, an oily rag, beer cans, and other rubbish that had been hauled out and discarded. In the middle of this pile of rubbish grew a lovely tropical flower. It stood straight, tall, alive, and pure in the midst of a pile of dead things. That's what a laborer is like. He blossoms for Christ in purity and holiness while living in the midst of this world's refuse and decay.

Concern for others. His interests gravitate to people rather than things. He has goals, objectives, and aims. He knows where he is going and how to get there. But he does not get there by using people as a ladder or staircase to success. He labors to help people in their walk with God.

A clear vision of the potential of others. He clearly understands God's master plan of evangelizing the world. He is convinced of the need for every Christian to be involved in that great task.

A servant heart. He knows that a servant heart is the basis for true leadership. He works at serving others rather than insisting on being served.

Cooperation. He does not go it alone but cheerfully bands together and works cooperatively with others. He does not have to be in charge or have a title or position that feeds his ego. He is content to roll up his sleeves along with the rest and pitch in wherever his life is needed. He is a team player.

Availability. If a job needs to be done, he echoes the prophet Isaiah's statement, "Here am I. Send me!" (Isaiah 6:8). He does not allow himself to get so busy with good activities that they prevent him from giving his life to what is best. He keeps his calendar clear enough so he is available whenever a real need arises. When the Holy Spirit spoke about separating Barnabas and Saul, they were available, ready, willing, and able to go. "The two of them, sent on their way by the Holy Spirit, went down to Seleucia and sailed from there to Cyprus. When they arrived at Salamis, they proclaimed the word of God in the Jewish synagogues. John was with them as their helper" (Acts 13:4-5).

On-the-Job Training
Once again we see the simple genius of God's plan for world

evangelization. Why did Paul and Barnabas take John Mark along? To help them with their luggage and travel plans? I'm sure he helped with those things, but certainly the primary objective of Paul and Barnabas was to see that John Mark received the exposure and training he needed to become an effective laborer for Christ. Remember this example and do the same thing in your own ministry. If you .want to train laborers for Christ, the best way to do it is to spend time with them and teach them the ministry "on the job." People learn best by example through association. Let people learn by associating with you.

Setbacks

Even though Paul and Barnabas were experienced trainers, their ministry was not without setbacks. They faced one here when Mark turned back. Likewise in our own ministries, setbacks are to be expected. The work of Christ is not like a set of numbers in a multiplication table, or made up of electrical machinery like an elevator which goes to the fourth floor when you push a button. It is not like a school of fish swimming up the same stream to the same spawning grounds century after century, or like a flock of swallows which always returns to Capistrano year after year.

God's work may have been much simpler if he had designed it around a mechanical device or a natural instinct of some sort, but in the councils of eternity, the Lord made his choice. His delight is in the sons of men (see Proverbs 8:22-31). He chose weak, human, foolish, sinful, self-centered, and fearful men and women. But praise God, we are transformable, redeemable, and teachable! Naturally it is more difficult to work with flesh and blood than with metal robots programmed to obey electronic commands, but God in his wisdom made this very choice. So to forward God's work, which Saul and Barnabas understood so well, they took Mark along to help him learn and grow. One day he would become a dedicated, competent worker in the ministry, and this was how he started.

As usual, there was opposition to the gospel. Here it appeared in the form of Bar Jesus, a sorcerer and false prophet. Saul described him: "You are a child of the devil and an enemy of everything that is right! You are full of all kinds of deceit and trickery. Will you never stop perverting the right ways of the Lord?" (Acts 13:10). He was a child of the devil who shared Satan's character, nature, and life. Jesus spoke about this in John 8:44: "You belong to your father, the devil, and you want to carry out your father's desire. He was a murderer from the beginning, not holding to the truth, for there is no truth in him. When he lies, he speaks his native language, for he is a liar and the father of lies." Bar Jesus was this kind of person. He perverted things, making bad seem good and wrong seem right.

The devil still tries to do this. He will tell you that the life of faith is too uncertain. He will promise you security—as if the Lord's ways were uncertain. He will tell you the Bible is too impractical and its teachings too demanding. He will tell you that serving the Lord is unpleasant, and unprofitable. "After all," he will remind you, "you've got to look out for yourself! If you don't, who else will?" He implies that God won't take care of you as he has promised.

So this was quite an opponent for this missionary team to face on their first journey. However, God had sent them, and Christ gave some reassuring promises to his followers. "When he has brought out all his own, he goes on ahead of them, and his sheep follow him because they know his voice" (John 10:4). Paul, filled with the Holy Spirit, addressed Bar Jesus. "'Now the hand of the Lord is against you. You are going to be blind, and for a time you will be unable to see the light of the sun.' Immediately mist and darkness came over him, and he groped about, seeking someone to lead him by the hand. When the proconsul saw what had happened, he believed, for he was amazed at the teaching about the Lord" (Acts 13:11-12). Unfortunately, this encouraging encounter was followed by a discouraging event. John Mark turned back. "From Paphos, Paul and his companions sailed to Perga in

Pamphylia, where John left them to return to Jerusalem" (Acts 13:13).

Why did that happen? Luke's account does not speculate, but we get a hint of something that might have touched it off. In Colossians Paul mentions that Barnabas and Mark were cousins (see Colossians 4:10). About this time, there was a change in the team's leadership. Previously it had been Barnabas and Saul. From then on it was Paul and Barnabas. Mark knew his cousin Barnabas had welcomed Paul into the fellowship in Jerusalem (see Acts 9:27), and Barnabas had brought Paul to Antioch (see Acts 11:26). He may have resented the idea of his cousin taking second place, or he may have chafed under a new style of leadership. Whatever the reason, he left them and went home.

Good News

But the work went on and Paul and Barnabas visited the synagogue in Antioch in Pisidia to preach Christ to the Jews there. Paul proclaimed, "From this man's [David's] descendants God has brought to Israel the Savior Jesus, as he promised" (Acts 13:23). He explained the gospel clearly.

> Though they found no proper ground for a death sentence, they asked Pilate to have him executed. When they had carried out all that was written about him, they took him down from the tree and laid him in a tomb. But God raised him from the dead, and for many days he was seen by those who had traveled with him from Galilee to Jerusalem. They are now his witnesses to our people (Acts 13:28-31).

Paul explained that God offers forgiveness and justification to all who believe. As usual, there was a clear warning to them not to refuse the marvelous good news of Christ.

It is interesting to note that Paul did not discuss social injustice, religious differences, political issues, economic problems, or intellectual questions. It was not that Paul was unaware of those issues or indifferent toward them. But he was a man on a mission. His commission did not concentrate on the transient issues of the day but on the eternal issues of the soul. Therefore he proclaimed the word of God. Evidently that was what they wanted to hear. "On the next Sabbath almost the whole city gathered to hear the word of the Lord" (Acts 13:44).

Note the varied reactions to the message. Some were jealous and "talked abusively against what Paul was saying. Then Paul and Barnabas answered them boldly: "We had to speak the word of God to you first. Since you reject it and do not consider yourselves worthy of eternal life, we now turn to the Gentiles. For this is what the Lord has commanded us: 'I have made you a light for the Gentiles, that you may bring salvation to the ends of the earth.' When the Gentiles heard this, they were glad and honored the word of the Lord; and all who were appointed for eternal life believed" (Acts 13:45-48).

These Gentiles believed the word of God and turned by faith to Christ. They received the gospel, not as a treatise on some new religion, not as a new philosophy, but as the amazing offer of salvation. For the first time, the Gentiles learned that they too had been chosen by God and were a vital part of his plan. They discovered that God loved them and had extended his salvation to them, and they rejoiced in that discovery.

Paul's Marching Orders

In Acts 13:47 Paul quoted Isaiah 49:6, which contained his marching orders. "I have made you a light for the Gentiles, that you may bring salvation to the ends of the earth." As far as Paul was concerned, from that day on he was free to concentrate on the Gentile world. He would not neglect the Jews or abandon them. He had orders not to abandon anyone. Every creature (see Mark 16:15) meant *every* creature in his day, just as it still means precisely that in our day. However, Paul had found the major goal for his ministry. He claimed this Old Testament Scripture, Isaiah 49:6, as his life verse. Through this key promise God redirected the course of Paul's life and ministry.

The Jews did not respond very well to Paul's comments. "But the Jews incited the God-fearing women of high standing and the leading men of the city. They stirred up persecution against Paul and Barnabas, and expelled them from their region" (Acts 13:50). Some of the leaders in Antioch stirred up a persecution and threw them out of town. So they went to Iconium. The last verse in Acts 13 is one of those bright little gems that shows up best against a dark background. "And the disciples were filled with joy and with the Holy Spirit" (Acts 13:52). In the midst of a persecution they experienced the joy of the Lord.

Twenty years after we first met Al and Margie Vail, my wife and I visited their home in Norfolk, Virginia. Al and Margie met each other while Margie was involved in our ministry in Pittsburgh, Pennsylvania. When we had dinner with them in Norfolk, Margie came downstairs with some assistance from one of her daughters. Margie was quite thin, weighing only about ninety-seven pounds. Her long battle with cancer had taken its toll. After dinner Margie and Virginia sat and shared about the joys of the Christian life and the glories of heaven that await us. Soon after our visit Margie died and entered the presence of her Lord. Margie spent her life helping others to enjoy their salvation and the life of discipleship. During Margie's last week on earth she spent some time helping a young lady with her Scripture memory, Bible study, and prayer. Margie Vail was a laborer, a worker in the kingdom of God to the end. In the midst of her trial, she had experienced the joy of the Lord.

A Change of Leadership

Barnabas provides another bright spot in Acts 13. Yes, the leadership of the team changed. Paul took charge. The circumstances in the ministry changed dramatically. Barnabas was no longer in the lead. Paul assumed command under the direction of God. But Barnabas did not change. His heart was still in the ministry. His zeal for God was not dampened. His spirit did not grow bitter. His ego was not crushed. He recognized and accepted God's leading.

While I was directing the Rocky Mountain Region for The Navigators, Bill Cole was the Navigator representative in Phoenix, Arizona. Bill is one of the finest Christians I know, a man from whom I have learned a lot. As we worked together, I became increasingly convinced that Bill would have a far greater ministry as a layman in the community than he would have as a member of our staff. We discussed this and Bill agreed. He resigned his staff position, and today is a high school teacher in Phoenix.

Shortly after Bill's resignation from our staff, there was a Navigator conference in Tucson, Arizona, at which I was speaking. Bill attended as a conferee. The collegians working on the registration desk did not know Bill, and they assigned him to an out-of-the-way room in one of the less comfortable buildings on the conference grounds. He just smiled, picked up his room key and cheerfully went off to unpack. "There's a big man!" I thought to myself as I observed Bill's reaction.

That was what Barnabas was like. Now it was no longer Barnabas and Saul. Now it was Paul and his companions. But that didn't matter to Barnabas. We must learn a lesson from his example. Positions are not important in the kingdom of God. The important thing is to find our place and fill it well. Find the assignment God has for you and do it with all of your heart.

SUMMARY:

The Holy Spirit selected Paul and Barnabas to broaden the scope of God's ministry in the world. God chose workers—
- trained for the task;
- equipped with a message;
- committed to a mission;
- humbly yielded to what God was doing.

14
Teamwork

"AT ICONIUM PAUL and Barnabas went as usual into the Jewish synagogue. There they spoke so effectively that a great number of Jews and Gentiles believed" (Acts 14:1). Paul and Barnabas functioned as a team. They were united in heart, vision, and purpose. We see this principle of teamwork throughout the Scriptures. Sometimes there were two men, at other times there were small bands of men, and occasionally we observe large groups. God is pleased when his children work together. The Bible teaches, "How good and pleasant it is when brothers live together in unity" (Psalm 133:1).

This unity took many forms in the Bible. In the Old Testament there were many family units such as those of Abraham, Isaac, and Jacob. Men like Moses, Solomon, and Nehemiah formed bands of coworkers around themselves. There were battle units for secular and spiritual warfare—such as the teams led by David, Gideon, Jesus, and Paul. The principle is included in 1 Samuel 10:26: "And Saul also went home to Gibeah; and there went with him a band of men, whose hearts God had touched" (KJV). We see it in Mark 6:7 and 30. "Calling the Twelve to him, he sent them out two by two and gave them authority over evil spirits. . . . The apostles gathered around Jesus and reported to him all they had done and taught."

Webster's New Collegiate Dictionary defines teamwork as "work done by several associates with each doing a part but all subordinating personal prominence to the efficiency of the whole."[1]

Paul used the idea of being yoked together like a team of oxen when he referred to one of his comrades as his "loyal yokefellow" (Philippians 4:3). Uzziah had a "host of men that went out to war by bands" (2 Chronicles 26:11). But teamwork includes more than that. Teamwork does not just describe men who are united with the same leader, but men who are linked to each other as well. This goes contrary to man's natural spirit. We resist uniting our hearts with others in order to accomplish some common goal. I am not speaking of a hastily formed posse, or an arbitrarily selected house-to-house visitation group. The concept I am describing is the kind of teamwork which includes at least five elements:

1. An accepted leader
2. A common objective
3. Basic agreement on activities
4. A strong, God-given love and loyalty among team members
5. A certain division of labor within the team.

Spiritual Unity

What is true spiritual unity and oneness? Some talk as if it were a kind of perfume which descends on people standing together holding hands. But that is not true. Spiritual unity cannot be absorbed passively. It comes to people who are engaged in the same battle together, when people serve together. Spiritual unity is forged in action.

There are several reasons for this. Only in action can the true value of things be known. Sameness of opinion is not unity. True unity is an identity of spirit. We all know how participation in some great cause or noble enterprise, especially when there is a hint of danger or some element of sacrifice, draws people together as nothing else can. When we are striving toward the same heroic goal, all else is forgotten and our hearts are knit as one. Identity of purpose, if we are in earnest, always leads to a unity of spirit. Godly men who join together with one purpose and one spirit to accomplish a great task requiring love and sacrifice acquire for themselves spiritual forces they have never felt before. They are carried along by a power and enthusiasm that is beyond themselves.

Some years ago our Navigator staff in the Netherlands was studying teamwork. Gert Doornenbal, the leader of the Dutch ministry, sent me a copy of their conclusion. As I read this over, I became convinced that they had identified the purpose, the function, and the spirit that is embodied in a team committed to the work of Christ. Here are the guidelines they were led to follow:

1. We must give ourselves to helping fulfill Christ's Great Commission.
2. We will do this by applying ourselves to equipping and multiplying laborers.
3. We will view every Christian as an important individual.
4. We will give ourselves to serving others.
5. We will strive for excellence in everything.

We will know that we have a functioning team when five things are true in our ministry:
1. When we have the same objective Jesus had—taking the gospel to every creature.
2. When we use the same method Jesus employed—multiplying laborers.
3. When we have the same vision that Jesus had regarding people—the importance of every individual.
4. When we have the same attitude toward people that Jesus had—he viewed himself as the servant of all.
5. When we are striving for the same standard Jesus had—excellence in everything.

To apply these guidelines we must ask five questions:
1. Does it help to make disciples?
2. Does it give us the most laborers?
3. Does it show the worth of the individual?
4. Can it be done in a better way?
5. Are we truly serving the body of Christ?

An Exciting Objective

Remember, all of this happens in action, not in a dreamy atmosphere or while we have a relaxed discussion about all things bright and beautiful. People must be challenged to lay down their lives. As we strive together toward a big, exciting, meaningful goal, our hearts will be knit as one. That's teamwork.

Billy Graham tells the story of a man who was offered a job at a fabulous salary but turned it down. The company manager asked, "Aren't we offering enough?"

"Oh, your salary is big enough, but your job is too small," the man replied. "I'm a missionary." He was consumed with helping to carry out Christ's mission in the world.

Paul and Barnabas were consumed with the same mission when they entered Iconium. Their message was well received, and a great multitude believed. It was not only what they said that prompted this response, but the way they said it. Luke writes that Paul and Barnabas *"spoke so effectively* that a great number of Jews and Gentiles believed" (Acts 14:1). What is it that makes people effective communicators? It is not just the content of the message, but the way it is given. This is true whether we are speaking to a crowd or to one person. Four things are conducive to effective communication.

Warmth and sincerity. A lady was telling her husband about an experience she had just had. An elderly man talked to her about her soul's destiny.

"Why didn't you tell him to mind his own business?" her husband asked.

"As I sensed the concerned tone of his voice, I knew it *was* his business," she replied.

Accurate content. You must do your homework. Have your facts straight and know what you are talking about. Don't try to fake it. If a question arises which you cannot answer, say so. But ask that person if he would be interested in discussing it further if you can find an answer. If he is, then do your best to find an answer to his question.

Composure. If a person is argumentative or abusive, don't respond in the same manner. Maintain a steady calm—in your manner and in your tone of voice. Remember that the fruit of the Spirit is self-control.

Friendliness. A warm handshake, a smile, and a friendly attitude all go a long way toward bringing someone to Christ. Remember, Jesus was a *friend* of publicans and sinners.

Although Paul and Barnabas communicated effectively and many believed, not everyone in Iconium liked what they had to say. "But the Jews who refused to believe stirred up the Gentiles and poisoned their minds against the brothers" (Acts 14:2). Notice how Paul and Barnabas reacted to the opposition: "So Paul and Barnabas spent considerable time there, speaking boldly for the Lord, who confirmed the message of his grace by enabling them to do miraculous signs and wonders" (Acts 14:3). We would expect this verse to read, "Therefore, they spoke cautiously." But instead we read that danger prompted boldness rather than timidity in these men. They relied on the Lord.

Soon, however, a plot arose to stone them to death, so they moved on to Lystra, "where they continued to preach the good news" (Acts 14:7).

In Lystra a man crippled from birth was healed, but when the people saw that miracle, "they shouted in the Lycaonian language, 'The gods have come down to us in human form!' Barnabas they called Zeus, and Paul they called Hermes because he was the chief speaker. The priest of Zeus, whose temple was just outside the city, brought bulls and wreaths to the city gates because he and the crowd wanted to offer sacrifices to them" (Acts 14:11-13).

When people are excited, happy, or startled, they immediately begin talking to one another in their own language. I may be sitting in a room filled with Dutchmen, Chinese, or Indonesians who are all talking with me in English. But if something humorous or exciting is mentioned, they will all instantly revert to their mother tongue.

Paul and Barnabas had no idea what was going on, so they did not try to stop the crowd at first. Quite naturally, since the people thought two of the gods were among them, they brought a sacrifice offering of flowers and oxen—the most costly and most honorable sacrifice they could offer. When Paul and Barnabas saw the oxen and the priest, they realized that they were about to be deified. This astonishing discovery sent a wave of overpowering fear through them.

> They tore their clothes and rushed into the crowd, shouting: "Men, why are you doing this? We too are only men, human like you. We are bringing you good news, telling you to turn from these worthless things to the living God, who made heaven and earth and sea and everything in them. In the past, he let all nations go their own way. Yet he has not left himself without testimony: He has shown kindness by giving you rain from heaven and crops in their season; he provides you with plenty of food and fills your hearts with joy." Even with these words, they had difficulty keeping the crowd from sacrificing to them (Acts 14:14-18).

Although Paul and Barnabas were able to quell this crisis, it was only a few days before another one of a very different nature cropped up.

You Can't Keep A Good Man Down

The enemies of the gospel never give up. "Then some Jews came from Antioch and Iconium and won the crowd over. They stoned Paul and dragged him outside the city, thinking he was dead" (Acts 14:19). People are fickle. One moment the crowd was going to offer sacrifices to Paul and Barnabas, and the next moment they were stoning Paul. They dragged what they assumed was his lifeless body out of town. Notice, when the people spoke of stoning him, Paul did not fly into a fit of fear and begin tearing his clothing, but when they spoke about deifying him he did. Paul knew that being worshiped by men was more dangerous than persecution.

The praise of men can lead to the poisonous belief that they are right. *Maybe I am an outstanding individual. After all, everyone says so,* the leader thinks to himself. That is one of the first steps towards becoming useless to God.

So there Paul lay in a crumpled, bruised, and bloody heap outside the city. Acts 14:20-23 contains a great truth—you can't keep a good man down!

> But after the disciples had gathered around him, he got up and went back into the city. The next day he and Barnabas left for Derbe. They preached the good news in that city and won a large number of disciples. Then they returned to Lystra, Iconium and Antioch, strengthening the disciples and encouraging them to remain true to the faith. "We must go through many hardships to enter the kingdom of God," they said. Paul and Barnabas appointed elders for them in each church and, with prayer and fasting, committed them to the Lord in whom they had put their trust.

Training Disciples

Notice that after leaving Derbe they returned to Lystra, Iconium, and Antioch. Lystra was where Paul was stoned and left for dead! Antioch and Iconium were the cities where those who stoned him were from! We read that and think to ourselves, *What a burden those men had for sharing the gospel! They were willing to return to hostile territory and risk their lives to preach the gospel of Christ.*

But that was not why they returned. Paul and Barnabas went back to establish the new believers in the faith. They willingly risked their lives to strengthen and encourage the believers. They did that because of their concept of world evangelization. Their mission did not depend on the welfare or success of a few professionals. The mission either succeeded or failed according to the faithfulness and dedication of the ordinary people. The people were the key to reaching the world. Therefore, the people must be helped, strengthened, encouraged, taught, and trained. So Paul and Barnabas returned to strengthen their souls and encourage them to continue in the faith.

Here we see the discipling process has three distinct aspects: strengthening souls, encouraging spirits, and teaching the truth about the cost of discipleship. Strengthening involves doing those things that would make a disciple strong in his daily walk. If you help a person learn how to get into the word and establish a strong prayer life, you have done much to strengthen him. Encouragement comes in many forms. If a person knows you are praying for him, he will be encouraged. If he has memorized a verse, completed a Bible study, or witnessed to his neighbor, commend him. Display the enthusiasm you feel in your heart. Let him know you are excited about his progress. Discipleship is not a stroll in a rose garden, so we shouldn't imply it is. Teach the truth about the cost.

Do you recall what Christ said of Saul of Tarsus when he became a Christian? He said, "I will show him how much he must suffer for my name" (Acts 9:16). What do you think Paul was thinking about as he was being stoned? Was he remembering Stephen?

In a sense, it is dangerous to listen to the gospel. One day you may be throwing rocks at the Christians, and the next day the rocks may be hurled at you. The gospel has the power to take us from the throwing to the receiving end. Saul the persecutor became Paul the persecuted.

Recently I met a man from a Hindu family. He had been an enemy of Christianity but became a follower of Christ through the witness of a friend. His mother was horrified by this so she went to a priest and explained what had happened. He told her to perform a rite over her son while he slept, guaranteeing that it would bring him back to the Hindu religion. Night after night she tried it, but it didn't work. God had given his angels charge over him to protect him, even while he slept. In despair she went to a priest of the Buddhist religion and explained her story. He sold her some leaves upon which he had cast a spell. If she put these in her son's tea he promised her they would do the job. But they didn't.

Her son kept on with his new found faith and began to grow in the Lord. He began memorizing the word. He joined a Bible study with some others in his school. He grew in his faith. His mother watched and finally had to admit his new life was genuine. His friends found it hard to believe that this young man who had once been the enemy of Christ had become his follower. So he became their enemy and endured the same persecution he used to initiate. Listening to the gospel may be dangerous.

The Refining Process

Paul reminded the disciples that "we must through much tribulation enter the kingdom of God" (Acts 14:22, KJV). The Greek word for tribulation, *thlipsis,* is from the ancient threshing instrument which separated chaff from wheat. Wheat from the field must pass through the threshing machine before being stored in the granary. What a picture of the believer's pilgrimage!

As good seed we are planted in God's field, the world. On our way to heaven, our final resting place, we will pass through God's great threshing machine. I don't know if you have ever seen a threshing machine in action, but it is quite a sight. It has no mercy on the grain. It threshes it around until the chaff is separated from the wheat. This gives us a picture of the Christian life.

However, God's threshing machine uses his mercy, love, and grace. It is not a cruel device but a gentle, loving means by which God works in our lives. At times God's ways may seem hard, and we may have a tendency to complain. But he knows what he is doing, and we can trust him. The hands that order our circumstances are pierced with nails. We must consider tribulation in the light of the cross. If you are in the midst of the threshing process, the refining process today, rejoice! God is at work in your life. He will see you through it all and perfect in you his great purposes. He will transform you into the image of Christ. It is not pleasant for one to feel the heat, but the smelting process must take place to release the gold. It is not pleasant for the wheat to be threshed, but it must be done to separate the chaff. Job knew this well. He said, "He knows the way that I take; when he has tested me, I will come forth as gold" (Job 23:10).

In each of the churches Paul's final act was to commit them to the Lord (Acts 14:23). The word *commit* conveys the idea of entrusting them to the Lord for his safekeeping. It is similar to the idea of depositing something in a safe.

In the summer of 1978 I was speaking at a training program for fifty men at a Christian camp north of Amsterdam in the Netherlands. I was assigned a room which had a door that did not lock. Three different groups were using the camps at that time. One of them was a non-Christian transcendental meditation society. I was reluctant to leave travel documents, airline tickets, and traveler's checks in an unlocked room, so the camp director put them in a safe. Paul did something similar for the Christians in Lystra, Iconium, and Antioch. He committed them to the Lord for his safekeeping.

That is what Paul did when he charged Timothy. "And the things you have heard me say in the presence of many witnesses entrust to reliable men who will also be qualified to teach others" (2 Timothy 2:2). Timothy was to entrust, commit, or deposit what he had learned from Paul with faithful men who would recognize the deposit's value and share it with others. Peter wrote, "So then, those who suffer according to God's will should commit themselves to their faithful Creator and continue to do good" (1 Peter 4:19). That was Paul's intent also. He commended them to the Lord for his safekeeping and for his enabling as they carried out his will.

Stay in Touch
Acts 14 ends with the return of Paul and Barnabas to the city where they began their journey. "From Attalia they sailed

back to Antioch, where they had been committed to the grace of God for the work they had now completed. On arriving there, they gathered the church together and reported all that God had done through them and how he had opened the door of faith to the Gentiles. And they stayed there a long time with the disciples" (Acts 14: 26-28). They had completed their mission, so they told their friends all about it.

If people are praying for you and backing your life and ministry, keep them up to date on what God is doing in your life. Tell them about your failures and victories. Thank them. It is all too easy to take their love and prayer for granted.

I learned this lesson the hard way. I am supported in my ministry by the prayers and gifts of many people. I try to send them news, keep them informed, and express my appreciation. One summer I became very busy. I was running here and there and completely neglected those who were giving and praying for us. By the end of the summer, our monthly income had dropped to one-third of what it was when the summer began. Many had stopped giving and worst of all, many stopped praying. So I learned my lesson. Wherever I am in the world, I try to keep the givers and prayers up to date.

Relax!
The second lesson here is the absolute necessity of an occasional retreat to recharge our spiritual batteries. If a car is on the freeway too long without refueling, it will eventually run out of power. This is also true in our lives. We need occasional times of rest and relaxation. We are human beings. This is especially difficult for highly motivated people. They think that taking a day off is a sin against the Lord.

In the early 1950s my wife and I worked with Ken Smith, a young pastor in Pittsburgh, Pennsylvania. Every Monday morning Ken headed for Butler, Pennsylvania, to play a round of golf. I was offended by that. *Aren't people going to hell on Monday also?* I thought. How could a pastor justify such an obvious lapse in his devotion to Christ? But Ken was very patient with me and eventually talked me into going along. After a while I saw the wisdom in his routine. After taking a day off to rest and relax he was recharged and ready to go.

Dr. Howard Hendricks, of Dallas Theological Seminary, says Christian workers are afraid to admit that they are also human beings. To admit that may seem to be coddling the flesh and giving in to our lazy, slothful nature. That is a danger. We must keep life in balance. The devil always tries to keep us off balance. A fighter in the boxing ring is an easy prey for his opponent if he gets off balance. The devil knows this so he will come to us and say, "Slow down." We tell him we can't slow down, so he says, "Okay, speed up." He will do anything to unsettle us. His concern is to keep us off balance in our Christian life.

SUMMARY:

God blessed the teamwork of Paul and Barnabas as they were—
- actively committed to Christ's mission to the world;
- clearly communicating the gospel;
- strengthening the believers;
- undergoing the refining process.

Notes: 1. *Webster's New Collegiate Dictionary* (Springfield, Massachusetts: G. & C. Merriam Company, 1979), page 1187.

15
Freedom in Christ

IN ACTS 15 some traumatic events occurred that transformed the work of Christ. It all began when Paul and Barnabas least expected it. They were back at their home base relaxing, enjoying the fellowship with their brethren and some well-earned peace and quiet. Then the unexpected happened.

"Some men came down from Judea to Antioch and were teaching the brothers: 'Unless you are circumcised according to the custom taught by Moses, you cannot be saved'" (Acts 15:1). Although the group was small, a great controversy resulted. It only takes a few to cause trouble.

My wife, my son, and I were in Geneva, Switzerland, for a few days during the peak of the fresh fruit season. We had been traveling in Eastern Europe for some weeks and had not seen much fresh fruit, so we were eager to sample some.

When we came across an outdoor market in Geneva, my son chose strawberries, and I chose cherries. The strawberries came in a small box, but the cherries were packed loosely in a large crate. The fruitseller spoke to us in French to ask how many cherries we wanted. We did not know how to answer him, so finally he said something, and, taking a shot in the dark, I nodded yes. He began filling a sack. He kept putting more and more in until the sack was almost full. He then put it on the scale and added some more.

I had not wanted to buy that many, but I did not know how to stop him. So I bought the whole sack thinking we would have cherries to enjoy for the next few days. We had some that night and they were delicious. The next day we enjoyed a few more, and there was still over half a sack left. We were not concerned since we thought they would be just as tasty the next day.

But on the third day, we discovered that most of them had rotted. Apparently a few rotten cherries at the bottom of the sack had affected the others. The same principle may be observed in the church, on an athletic team, or in a work crew. That was the situation which confronted Paul and Barnabas.

The men who arrived in Antioch from Judea brought the disturbing news that unless an individual kept the ceremonial law he could not be saved. Many of the Jews had hoped for a Messiah who would revive the Jewish nation's greatness and glory. The group which went to Antioch thought that if they could make the ceremonial law part of the Christian message, it would spread far and wide. Antioch was the key to their strategy, for Antioch was the headquarters of the missionary church. If they could convince the believers in Antioch, they knew they could convince them anywhere.

Prejudice Dies Hard

Old ways and prejudices do not die easily. There are people in the church today who are truly born again. They have abandoned their former conviction that the way to heaven is found by doing good works. They now know it is by grace through faith in the Lord Jesus Christ. But the idea that they can buy God's favor still lingers in the back of their minds. They still think God operates his kingdom on a point system. If they are good, they think he loves them. If they are not so good, he does not love them. So they spend their lives in a fruitless attempt to earn God's favor.

But the glorious truth is that God loves us with a steady, unchanging, everlasting love. He never changes. His love is strong, firm, and secure. Those who believe they must earn God's favor may not realize they have that attitude, or that it is wrong. Often it is a hangover from their lives as non-Christians, but it is an error and must be abandoned.

All of us are strangely inclined towards trying to turn our opinions and practices into rules for everyone else to follow. If something works well for me, then I try to impose it on everyone around me. This is true of good and bad habits. The jogger wants all of his friends to run with him. The dope addict tries to get others to join him in his addiction. The habitual drinker tries to get others to have one with him.

I was attending a conference in New Orleans with Hal Lindsey, author of the bestseller *The Late Great Planet Earth.* We were there at the invitation of Campus Crusade for Christ to speak at a winter conference. One evening the Crusade team took Hal and my wife and me out for a meal at a French restaurant. Our waiter was a tall, commanding gentleman dressed in a black suit and white shirt with a black tie and tails. He invited us to have a cocktail before our meal, and we declined. When he took our order he suggested some wine to go with our dinner. Again we declined. He seemed to take offense at this and said in a rather loud voice, "You can't enjoy a meal like that without wine!"

Hal glanced up at him, smiled, and said, "Just watch us!"

The waiter's problem was the same as the one we find in Acts 15. He enjoyed wine with his meals and presumed everybody else should too. In fact, as a good waiter, he did everything he could to encourage us to buy some. But we were a group that didn't enjoy wine with our meals.

My wife enjoys spending two hours or so each morning in prayer and Bible study. For her this is a great joy and something she looks forward to. Should she try to impose her practice on all of the ladies in our Sunday school class? What if she felt that because God had led her to do this, he wanted everybody else to do it? What if she began nagging and harassing the other ladies with the idea? She would be wrong, because what is right for her is not necessarily right for everybody.

If God has led you to memorize two verses of Scripture each week and you enjoy doing that, does that mean it is God's will for everybody? No! Let us be careful in our relationships. God will not necessarily lead others in exactly the same way he leads you. Biblical principles are universal, but practices are not universal. For example, while it is true that God desires fellowship with all of his children, the way I approach my personal fellowship with him is not necessarily the precise pattern for others to follow.

Paul found himself facing a difficult problem within the fellowship of the church. When he was faced with an angry crowd wanting to stone him, or the prospect of possible imprisonment, Paul hardly said a word. But when the welfare of new Christians was involved, he reacted strongly. "This brought Paul and Barnabas into sharp dispute and debate with **them**. So Paul and Barnabas were appointed, along with some other believers, to go up to Jerusalem to see the apostles and elders about this question" (Acts 15:2).

Why were Paul and Barnabas so concerned? Stated simply, these new believers were the secret to the success of the mission. Paul knew he could not evangelize the world single-handedly. Paul could not take the gospel to *every* creature. God's strategy was clear. Every Christian must be a missionary, and every person without Christ—in the family, in the neighborhood, in the city, in the land, in the world—is a mission field. But this wasn't the only reason Paul was concerned for these believers. Paul did not think of his brothers and sisters in Christ simply as cogs in the great machinery of world evangelization. They were individuals he knew intimately, loved dearly, and appreciated. He reminded the Thessalonians, "As apostles of Christ we could have been a burden to you, but we were gentle among you, like a mother caring for her little children. We loved you so much that we were delighted to share with you not only the gospel of God but our lives as well, because you had become so dear to us" (1 Thessalonians 2:7-8).

Paul loved them and did not want them to be shackled with a yoke of bondage. Later, he reviewed the incident described in Acts 15:1 with the church at Galatia (see Galatians 2:1-5). One of Paul's concluding statements made his views clear: "It is for freedom that Christ has set us free. Stand firm, then, and do not let yourselves be burdened again by a yoke of slavery" (Galatians 5:1).

Bondage was the issue and Paul opposed it forcefully. He knew it was not from the Lord. Christ had told his men to baptize the believers, not to circumcise them. Paul was not about to forget that command.

So they began their journey to Jerusalem to discuss the problem. "The church sent them on their way, and as they traveled through Phoenicia and Samaria, they told how the Gentiles had been converted. This news made all the brothers very glad" (Acts 15:3). When believers hear about others being converted to Christ, it causes great joy in the ranks. A writer in one of our national news magazines described the phenomenon of the increasing interest in historical Christianity that is sweeping the United States. He mentioned that Christians seem to enjoy sitting by the hour listening to how others were born again. This is true. If you want to breathe life into a meeting, have someone give his testimony.

When Philip first preached Christ in Samaria, it caused great joy in the city. The same Samaritans rejoiced over the conversion of the Gentiles. When I return from an overseas trip, I usually take some time to share some of the highlights with my Sunday school class, The Ambassadors, at First Presbyterian Church in Colorado Springs. I've noticed the class is only mildly interested in the places we visit, but whenever I share the stories of men and women who have come to Christ, the atmosphere becomes electric. Reports of lives changed by Christ produce joy among Christians.

At the meeting in Jerusalem the issue was clear. "Then some of the believers who belonged to the party of the

Pharisees stood up and said, 'The Gentiles must be circumcised and required to obey the law of Moses'" (Acts 15:5). There was much discussion among the elders and the apostles. Then Peter described his visit to Cornelius. Barnabas and Paul spoke next. "The whole assembly became silent as they listened to Barnabas and Paul telling about the miraculous signs and wonders God had done among the Gentiles through them. When they finished, James spoke up: 'Brothers, listen to me. Simon has described to us how God at first showed his concern by taking from the Gentiles a people for himself'" (Acts 15:12-15).

After some more comment and discussion, the apostles and elders drafted a letter to the Gentile believers in Antioch, Syria, and Cilicia. The letter did not ask the Gentiles to do anything beyond observing a few essentials: "It seemed good to the Holy Spirit and to us not to burden you with anything beyond the following requirements: You are to abstain from food sacrificed to idols, from blood, from the meat of strangled animals and from sexual immorality. You will do well to avoid these things" (Acts 15:28-29). The whole team, the apostles, elders, and brethren, agreed, and the issue was settled.

There are several lessons to learn from the debate over the Gentile believers in Acts 15.

Deal with Problems Openly
When the brethren came to Antioch with their proposal that a Gentile had to become a Jew before he could become a Christian, Barnabas and Paul acted wisely. First, rather than argue with these men, they took steps to bring the issue out into the open. We must remember this whenever a problem arises: get all of the facts out on the table. Consider them honestly and squarely and involve all of the parties concerned. Let everyone discuss those facts. Do not let problems or bitterness simmer below the surface.

One day a man stormed into Dawson Trotman's office. He said he could no longer work with one of the other staff members. Then he listed all of the other person's faults and problems. Dawson listened patiently to the complete story. Then he called in the man about whom this individual had been complaining. "OK," Dawson said, "Now tell him what you just told me."

Here is a great lesson. If you have anything against your brother, go to your brother. Don't talk *about* him, talk *to* him. We must strive to keep the unity of the Spirit in the bond of peace. Spirit-produced unity does not come automatically. We must work at it. There are times when we will agree to disagree, but let's ensure there is grace, love, and understanding when we do.

Man Cannot Purify Himself

Secondly, Acts 15:8-9 reveals a great truth about man's condition and the solution to his problem. "God, who knows the heart, showed that he accepted them by giving the Holy Spirit to them, just as he did to us. He made no distinction between us and them, for he purified their hearts by faith." These verses give us a glimpse of God's power. Jeremiah wrote, "The heart is deceitful above all things and beyond cure. Who can understand it?" (Jeremiah 17:9).

Man may be able to clean up the environment by preventing automobile exhaust or the pollution in rivers and lakes. But he will never be able to purify his own heart. Why? Mark 7:21-23 is very clear. "For from within, out of men's hearts, come evil thoughts, sexual immorality, theft, murder, adultery, greed, malice, deceit, lewdness, envy, slander, arrogance and folly. All these evils come from inside and make a man 'unclean.'"

While I was a student at the University of Washington in Seattle, I worked in a bakery. I washed pots and pans, cleaned the stove, and mopped the floors. One Saturday I washed the windows, but there was one spot I couldn't remove. I applied hot water and more and more soap but nothing worked. Then I saw my problem. The spot was on the other side.

Jesus says that is man's problem—evil originates within

our hearts. No amount of outward, external solutions will help. The only lasting solution comes when Jesus enters our hearts by his Holy Spirit and purifies our hearts from within. Only the power of God can purify something as rotten and deceitful as the human heart.

Men Are God's Method

The third lesson comes from the statement James made during the council meeting in Jerusalem when he quoted Amos 9:11-12: "'After this I will return and rebuild David's fallen tent. Its ruins I will rebuild, and I will restore it, that the remnant of men may seek the Lord, and all the Gentiles who bear my name, says the Lord, who does these things' that have been known for ages" (Acts 15:16-18).

The salvation of the Gentiles was God's idea. It was no mere afterthought. It was his plan from the beginning. It was not Peter's idea, or Paul's, or Barnabas'. It was God's idea. It was his work, and to accomplish that purpose he has chosen men and women like us. He uses people who are frail, foolish clay. As we view God's great eternal plan, and think of our own failings and foibles, we should fall to our knees to thank God for his patience, longsuffering, and love. We are the missionaries God is calling. He has chosen us to carry on his work. We are given the privilege of participating in his great eternal plan.

The last lesson is found in Acts 15:26, which describes the men to whom the apostles, elders, and brethren entrusted the vital mission of conveying the letter to the Gentiles in Antioch. They were "men who have risked their lives for the name of our Lord Jesus Christ" (Acts 15:26). They were tested, courageous, proven men who had fought many spiritual battles. This is what the church needs today: a band of men who will hazard their all to take the message of Christ to the world.

We must ask ourselves some hard questions: "Am I truly willing to give my life for Jesus?" This is what he demands. "Do I follow the Lord only so long as it causes me no personal hardship or discomfort?" David refused to offer God that which cost him nothing (see 2 Samuel 24:24). "Do I offer my Lord a whole heart, or one that is splintered and fragmented? Are my affections set partly on God and partly on earth?" Barnabas, Paul, Judas, and Silas, the letter bearers, were men who hazarded their all for the sake of Christ.

Now we come to a passage that is hard to believe. Earlier Paul and Barnabas had assured the people of Lystra that they were human, no different than other men. They now prove their humanity by fighting with one another and splitting up.

It began with a suggestion by Paul. "Some time later Paul said to Barnabas, 'Let us go back and visit the brothers in all the towns where we preached the word of the Lord and see how they are doing'" (Acts 15:36). Paul was not primarily interested in what they knew. He was more concerned with how they were doing. The whole purpose of the Christian ministry is to fit people for heaven by making them better people while they are on earth. The word of God is not given to supply us with facts, but to guide our lives and affect our behavior.

Paul's Missionary Heart

Paul's visit to Antioch is commonly referred to as his second missionary journey, but in a sense it was not really a missionary trip. A missionary plows new ground, and reaches out to new people, and new places. Paul was a pioneer, and reaching the unreached was much on his heart.

However, the journey he proposed to Barnabas was a journey designed to strengthen and edify the believers. For Paul, the new believers were the base upon which the whole missionary effort of the church would rise or fall. Paul wanted to see how those young believers were doing. I'm sure he was familiar with Proverbs 27:23: "Be sure you know the condition of your flocks, give careful attention to your herds." In Solomon's words, Paul thought, "Let us go early to the vineyards to see if the vines have budded, if their blossoms have opened" (Song of Songs 7:12). Barnabas was eager to make the trip and wanted to give his cousin Mark another chance to make good.

> But Paul did not think it wise to take him, because he had deserted them in Pamphylia and had not continued with them in the work. They had such a sharp disagreement that they parted company. Barnabas took Mark and sailed for Cyprus, but Paul chose Silas and left, commended by the brothers to the grace of the Lord. He went through Syria and Cilicia, strengthening the churches (Acts 15:38-41).

Why did Paul choose Silas? Because he was a man who had hazarded his life for the Lord Jesus. Paul wanted someone along whom he knew he could count on. Silas had already proven faithful and courageous under fire. He was also a Roman (see Acts 16:37). Paul knew having a Roman citizen along would be an advantage in their efforts to evangelize the Roman Empire.

Notice where Paul and Barnabas went after their disagreement. They both went home. Barnabas returned to Cyprus, and Paul left for Tarsus, the capital of Cilicia. Their actions remind me of an incident from my childhood. I was playing marbles with a friend when an argument arose. "I'm going to pick up my marbles and go home," he said to me. Something quite similar happened to Paul and Barnabas.

Which of them was right? Both were. Mark certainly deserved a second chance. We all need that. Later Paul commended Mark for his usefulness in the ministry. "Only Luke is with me. Get Mark and bring him with you, because he is helpful to me in my ministry" (2 Timothy 4:11). The action taken by Barnabas may well have been what salvaged Mark for a life of useful service which included writing one of the four Gospels. On the other hand, there is often too much at stake to risk trusting an individual who has behaved like a quitter in the past.

Barnabas and Paul had different temperaments, different personalities, and different ministry styles. But both men were profitable in the kingdom of God. Barnabas' heart was filled with love and compassion for young Mark, while Paul was consumed with the Commission of Christ. Even though there was a sharp disagreement, the devil didn't win the day, for now there were two teams in action: Barnabas and Mark, and Paul and Silas. I'm sure God blessed them all.

SUMMARY:

Even though disagreements arose concerning doctrine and men, God preserved the unity of his church.
- The basis of faith was preserved.
- The new believers were protected.
- God's men continued to persevere in God's work.

16
Recruiting
Laborers

PAUL THEN RETURNED to hostile territory. His previous visit to Lystra almost cost him his life. On this visit an event occurred that proved to be one of the greatest joys of his life. He met Timothy. "He came to Derbe and then to Lystra, where a disciple named Timothy lived, whose mother was a Jewess and a believer, but whose father was a Greek. The brothers at Lystra and Iconium spoke well of him" (Acts 16:1-2). Paul recruited Timothy and invited him to join the team. Timothy was a disciple with a good reputation among the believers. But was he the only disciple with a good reputation? No.

Why, then, did Paul select him to be the disciple he would train as a laborer for Christ? What did Paul see in Timothy's life that made him want to recruit him? I'm sure Timothy had lots of potential, yet it would take years for it to blossom.

Timothy's Qualifications
Let's examine the qualifications Timothy had for becoming one of Paul's colaborers.

He had a servant heart. "He sent two of his helpers,

Timothy and Erastus, to Macedonia, while he stayed in the province of Asia a little longer" (Acts 19:22). Timothy was one of Paul's helpers. To be a laborer for Christ we must be willing and eager to serve people. Whatever we do for Christ in this life must be done for people. Timothy demonstrated servant-hood, one of the qualities for which Paul was always on the alert. Servants are rare because most of us prefer to be served by others, instead of being their servants. The individual who only wants to be served makes a poor laborer in the cause of Christ—the supreme servant.

He was available. Timothy became one of Paul's compan-ions and was still available during the later stages of Paul's ministry. "He was accompanied by Sopater son of Pyrrhus from Berea, Aristarchus and Secundus from Thessalonica, Gaius from Derbe, Timothy also, and from the province of Asia Tychicus and Trophimus" (Acts 20:4).

He was teachable. This is evident from what Paul wrote in two New Testament books to this young man. In one of them he made the amazing statement that Timothy completely understood his teaching, way of life, and purpose (2 Timothy 3:10-11). Notice all of the things Timothy knew about Paul. Timothy obviously had a hunger to learn all he could from every aspect of Paul's life. He had an amazing desire to learn.

Recently I was asked to be a guest lecturer at the Canadian Theological College in Regina, Saskatchewan. One day I asked the class to explain why Paul felt so secure in sending Timothy to instruct the churches, especially in light of Paul's continual admonition to "be imitators of me." One of the men in the class put it very well. He said, "Timothy had spent so much time learning from the apostle Paul, that when Timothy was there, it was just as if Paul himself was present." This is a fan-tastic concept. Look for the person who is eager to put in the hours it takes to "fully know" what you are trying to impart from the Lord.

He was like-minded. "For I have no man like-minded, who will naturally care for your state" (Philippians 2:20, KJV). Paul saw that Timothy shared the goals God had burned into his own heart. They were of one mind and one heart on the great objectives of the Christian ministry.

He was faithful. "For this reason I am sending to you Timothy, my son whom I love, who is faithful in the Lord. He will remind you of my way of life in Christ Jesus, which agrees with what I teach everywhere in every church" (1 Corinthians 4:17). Timothy had spent so much time with Paul that he knew Paul's message and manner of life. But more than just knowing Paul's message and manner of life, Timothy was faithful to live it. He not only knew how to do what Paul did, he did it. Timothy was faithful—like a high fidelity record that faithfully reproduces the sound of the original.

He was a reproducer. Timothy not only patterned his life after Paul, he taught others to follow his lifestyle as well. Paul saw Timothy's potential as one in whom he could invest his life—one who would in turn establish, nurture, and train disciples to serve the churches faithfully. "We sent Timothy, who is our brother and God's fellow worker in spreading the gospel of Christ, to strengthen and encourage you in your faith" (1 Thessalonians 3:2). Timothy had the capacity to catch Paul's vision and approach to the ministry and share it with others. "And the things you have heard me say in the presence of many witnesses entrust to reliable men who will also be qualified to teach others" (2 Timothy 2:2).

These were some of the traits Paul may have seen in Timothy when he entered Lystra. Imagine Paul's elation at finding a man like this! All who have spent their lives recruiting and training laborers for the cause of Christ know the excitement that comes when you spot a person like that.

Principles of Recruiting

But then what? How do you go about recruiting a good man to the cause? Let me list a few lessons I have learned over the years.

Begin with prayer. Prayer is basic in the work of recruiting men to the cause of Christ. Some years ago I was traveling to a Navigator conference in Sioux City, Iowa. When

I arrived in Sioux City I stopped at a restaurant for something to eat. As I paid my bill I witnessed to the cashier. She looked startled and said, "You're the second person to talk to me about God today." When I inquired about who the other person was, I learned he was a young man on his way to our conference.

"Find that man!" I said to my traveling companions. Later we discovered that it was Jim North from Sterling College. For one year after the conference I prayed daily for Jim and asked the Lord for the privilege of colaboring with him. If Jim had the spiritual fire to witness to a cashier, I knew he would make a great contribution to our disciplemaking team. The following summer I visited Sterling College and talked with Jim. I asked him what his plans were for the summer. He told me he would be working in a fruit market.

"What did you do last summer?" I asked.

"Worked in a fruit market," Jim replied.

"And the summer before that?"

"Worked in a fruit market."

Then I asked him, "Jim, how long are you going to give your life to a fruit market?"

After pondering my pointed question, Jim decided that after graduating he would move to Lincoln, Nebraska, and join our disciplemaking team. He was an excellent addition. Today Jim leads the Navigator ministry in Indonesia.

Love them first. While directing a collegiate conference, I asked several of our staff to lead training workshops. Russ Johnston, who served on our staff at that time, led a workshop on "Recruiting." I was surprised to learn Russ used the time to lead a discussion on 1 Corinthians 13, the great New Testament chapter on love. However, I concluded that Russ had done the right thing. Love is a key factor in recruiting. Remember that the love of Jesus Christ drew us to him. "We love because he first loved us" (1 John 4:19). Love is very important when you are attempting to recruit a young leader.

My wife and I had the privilege of ministering to cadets at the United States Air Force Academy in Colorado Springs,

Colorado. They were above average academically, socially, and athletically. As we ministered to them spiritually, I learned that most of their teachers, coaches, and counselors during their high school years had held them in great esteem, but related to them from a distance. These young men were so bright and alert that their instructors never got too close to them. I deliberately attempted to do just the opposite. I did all I could to show them love and affection. Many responded, became involved in discipleship, and were recruited to the cause of Christ. Many are among my closest friends today.

Live the life of discipleship. Show them what it means to be a man or woman of God. There are hundreds of recruitable individuals who have a hunger to know more about living for Christ and how to do the work of Christ. Set the pace. Be an example for them. Remember 2 Chronicles 15:9: "Large numbers had come over to him from Israel when they saw that the Lord his God was with him." As Isaiah wrote, "Men of stature shall come over unto thee, and they shall be thine" (Isaiah 45:14, KJV).

Play a man's game, and men will come to play. If you play a child's game, you will attract children. Jesus did not coddle people. He was the most demanding leader the world has ever known. He demands our all. This is something I stressed while working with men at the Air Force Academy. Their schedules were demanding. Their days were long. Their courses were difficult. But I tried to communicate to them that life at the Academy was child's play compared to the challenge of following Christ for a lifetime. His standards of morality are the highest. His level of commitment is the highest. His work offers the greatest challenge, and his cause is the most important. His perspective on the world is the most accurate. His life was the greatest life ever lived. His words were the greatest ever spoken. Dawson Trotman used to tell us, "It doesn't take much of a man to be a Christian, it takes all of him."

Use them or lose them. If you involve someone by giving them a job to do, he will soon begin to speak of "our work" instead of "your ministry." Start with something small and simple. Increase his responsibility according to his faithfulness in those little things. Jesus began by asking Peter for the use of his boat for a few minutes while he taught the crowds. Later he asked for Peter's life. If men feel they are not needed, they will drift off to someone or something that offers them a sense of belonging. Put those you are recruiting to work, but be cautious. Men know immediately if they are just doing busywork. Their involvement must be real.

Apply the parade principle. Use the team to attract men to the team. On St. Patrick's Day in New York City, many of the bystanders watching the St. Patrick's Day parade wish they were Irish. As people watch the Irish marching by, singing songs about the "auld sod," dressed in green, laughing, and having a great time, in their hearts they think, *Wouldn't it be fun to be out there with them. They seem to be having so much fun. I'd love to be part of a gang like that.*

The early disciples displayed a similar spirit of gladness—and the people admired them (see Acts 2:46-47). The team is a recruiting tool. When a person observes the love displayed by the team, your effectiveness for Christ, and your joy in the ministry, he will eventually be drawn onto the team.

Meet their needs. Make sure they understand that it is more for their benefit than yours. In the late 1950s I met a young man named Johnny Sackett. He was an alert, enthusiastic young man to whom I was immediately attracted. He seemed to have great potential for Christ—which has proven true over the years. One day I sat with Johnny talking about the ministry and his involvement. After some thought he said, "Well, yes LeRoy, I think I'd like to help you out." At that point I tried to explain that we wanted to involve him primarily for *his* benefit, not ours. So we talked some more and he got the picture. Make sure that you minister *to* the man as well as with him. The experience must benefit him. I have seen leaders who gave lip service to this idea, but in reality their efforts were spent on themselves and their ministry. Men always know if they are just a means to accomplish the ministry or if they themselves are the ministry.

Relate them to the Great Commission. This was one of the most thrilling aspects of our ministry at the Air Force Academy. Since the United States Air Force has bases around the world, these men would have many opportunities to travel, and to develop world vision as a result of living, working, and ministering overseas. Many of the cadets we discipled have had a ministry for Christ around the world. So whether your recruit is a laborer, businessman, nurse, executive, or homemaker, show him or her how to relate to the Great Commission of Christ in the world.

Learn how to spot a good man. Learn how to tell the difference between a nice fellow and a real winner. One way to do this is to keep the team witnessing for Christ. This will attract the "warrior type," one who is interested in being out in the battle. If your team is fellowship-oriented, you will attract those who enjoy sitting around talking to each other. But if you thrust out in evangelism, you will attract those who want to be on the firing line for Christ.

Don't worry about the one who only wants to fellowship. There are many groups around the world who love to sit and discuss, argue, chat, and listen to new theories. So he will easily find a way to satisfy his need for fellowship.

But pity the individual who wants to get out there and get on with the job. He's the person you must provide with an outlet for the fire burning in his soul. He doesn't want to sit around or fill his time with busywork. He wants to plunge into the real thing. He wants to get going for Christ. So give him an opportunity and a ministry target. Provide the vehicle. If you do that, good men will flock to your door. The vehicle Paul provided for Timothy was the real thing—the Great Commission of Jesus Christ.

Hold your men loosely. When you work with men or women with leadership potential, hold them loosely. They do not like to be trapped in a cage. They are like Sylvester, our cat. He will sit on my lap purring all day long and remain still and contented as long as I don't interfere with him. But if I grab him and try to make him sit still, he will fight to get loose.

Young men and women with leadership ability are like that. If you grab them, they will run away.

Take your time. Don't hurry. Get to know them well. Learn what is on their hearts, and where their interests lie. Are they willing to pitch in when there is a need? How do they take instruction? Pray with them. Witness with them. Share the word together. Remember Paul's words, "Do not be hasty in the laying on of hands, and do not share in the sins of others. Keep yourself pure" (1 Timothy 5:22).

The Team Launches Out

After meeting Timothy and realizing his great potential, Paul recruited him to his team. One of Paul's first decisions regarding Timothy was intended to broaden his ministry and make Timothy more acceptable to more people. "Paul wanted to take him along on the journey, so he circumcised him because of the Jews who lived in that area, for they all knew that his father was a Greek" (Acts 16:3).

Although Paul was the apostle to the Gentiles, he still had a longing to see the Jews become Christians. He wrote, "Brothers, my heart's desire and prayer to God for the Israelites is that they may be saved" (Romans 10:1). Paul wanted Timothy to be completely acceptable to the Jews.

The decision reached by the Jerusalem Council in Acts 15 was obviously Spirit-directed, and met with acceptance as Paul's team conveyed their decision to the churches. "As they traveled from town to town, they delivered the decisions reached by the apostles and elders in Jerusalem for the people to obey. So the churches were strengthened in the faith and grew daily in numbers" (Acts 16:4-5).

When the people heard what was involved in becoming a Christian, they turned readily to Christ. The churches were strengthened in breadth and depth. The lost were won and the saved were edified. That is a great balance to strive for in any church program. All too often the pendulum swings either to one side or the other. The pastor preaches evangelistic sermons year after year, and the lost are won, but the Christians are not edified. Or, a pastor teaches the word, and people are built up, but there is no evangelism. In Acts 16:5 we see the perfect balance of evangelism and discipleship in the church.

The Team

As Paul and his companions continued their journey, it is clear that the Holy Spirit was very much in control. He was leading at every fork in the road. Jesus' promise of the Holy Spirit's guidance was being fulfilled exactly. Then an event occurred that changed the course of history. Paul learned that the Lord wanted him to go to Macedonia.

"During the night Paul had a vision of a man of Macedonia standing and begging him, 'Come over to Macedonia and help us.' After Paul had seen the vision, we got ready at once to leave for Macedonia, concluding that God had called us to preach the gospel to them" (Acts 16:9-10). Luke wrote, "*we* got ready at once . . . concluding that God had called *us*." Had God called Luke? No, Paul had seen the vision. So why did Luke write "we" and "us"? Because they were a team and Paul was the leader. When God spoke to him it was just as if God was speaking to the entire team.

The Team Breaks New Ground

What would you have expected if you were a member of Paul's team and learned that God had given specific directions to go to Macedonia to preach the gospel to them? I think I would have expected a brass band to welcome us and thousands lined up waiting to repent.

Whom did they find awaiting them in Macedonia? A woman, a demon-possessed girl, a beating, and a jail. Remember Isaiah 55:8-9: "'For my thoughts are not your thoughts, neither are your ways my ways,' declares the Lord. 'As the heavens are higher than the earth, so are my ways higher than your ways and my thoughts than your thoughts'" (Isaiah 55:8-9). God knew what he was doing. Lydia opened her heart to the Lord, the demon came out of the girl, and Paul and Silas were whipped and thrown into jail.

Why were they imprisoned? Because the demon-possessed girl was owned by some men who used her for their own personal gain. Such evil practices are still common in many parts of the world today.

While visiting an ancient temple in Indonesia, I was surrounded by beggars. Some were crippled and blind. After the beggars were given money by the tourists, some men came around, emptied the beggars' containers, and pocketed the money. Managing blind and crippled beggars was their business. They owned that pathetic group of people just as a farmer might own a herd of cattle. The beggars received practically nothing while their masters grew fat on their profits.

When the demon-possessed girl's owners realized they had lost their hope of gain, they made untruthful accusations. They complained that Paul's team had committed a civil offense, so Paul and Silas were prosecuted for a crime which they did not commit (see Acts 16:19-24).

Paul and Silas were "severely flogged." Once again, Paul was on the receiving end of the kind of punishment he used to inflict. As Paul said later, "I went from one synagogue to another to imprison and beat those who believe in you" (Acts 22:19). In Macedonia there was no mercy for Paul and Silas. The metal at the end of the leather thongs flayed them and laid their skin wide open. Then they were thrown into jail.

The jailer must have been a hard case since he was able to take two beaten, bleeding men and throw them into the inner cell, put their feet in the stocks, and then sleep like a baby. But notice the first act of this cruel, hardened, Roman jailer after his conversion. "At that hour of the night the jailer took them and washed their wounds; then immediately he and all his family were baptized" (Acts 16:33). When Christ entered his life his first act was one of compassionate love. He treated their wounds. True conversion has a compassionate impact in individuals' lives and on society.

A Tough Teacher

The next day the magistrates sent word to release Paul and

Silas. "But Paul said to the officers: 'They beat us publicly without a trial, even though we are Roman citizens, and threw us into prison. And now do they want to get rid of us quietly? No! Let them come themselves and escort us out'" (Acts 16:37). Paul's words alarmed the magistrates who "came to appease them and escorted them from the prison, requesting them to leave the city. After Paul and Silas came out of the prison, they went to Lydia's house, where they met with the brothers and encouraged them. Then they left" (Acts 16:39-40).

Why do you think Paul allowed the authorities to beat and imprison him unjustly? Luke does not explain his reason, but he may have done it for the benefit of the believers in Lystra. Perhaps the officials would be more cautious in the future. Perhaps there would be no more illegal, violent beatings if the magistrates learned their lesson. As a great teacher, Paul may also have realized the way in which the people of God would benefit by his sacrificial example. The first European church was established on a basis of courage and dignity in the midst of a wild and unlawful tumult.

SUMMARY:

Paul formed his team and led them into the battle. He—
- found good men;
- recruited them to the cause;
- led them as a team evangelizing the lost and building up the new believers.

17
Reactions to God's Message

"WHEN THEY HAD passed through Amphipolis and Apollonia, they came to Thessalonica, where there was a Jewish synagogue" (Acts 17:1). Why did Paul's team pass *through* Amphipolis and Apollonia? Didn't anyone live there who needed to hear the gospel? Of course they did. But Acts 17:1 is an illustration of the fact that need does not necessarily constitute a call. If I am governed by need, I can be easily overwhelmed, even crushed.

Dr. Richard Halverson, pastor of Fourth Presbyterian Church in Washington, D.C., says that during ministry trips to India he becomes so burdened by the obvious physical needs of millions of people that he must keep repeating to himself, "God is love, God is love." Dr. Halverson knows he cannot meet all of the needs he sees. He cannot plunge in and try to solve the problems of every beggar, cripple, or blind person that he meets. Only God could do that.

Needs abound everywhere. If I feel personally responsible for meeting all of the needs I see, I will be driven to despair. I must do what God has called me to do and trust him to meet many other needs through other people.

A missionary friend of mine provided an example of the devastating effects which an emotional response to human need can have. He taught in a boys' school. His teaching went well and many of his students came to Christ and grew in discipleship. But after some months the ever-present physical and spiritual needs of the land began pressing in on him. He saw the multitudes who were lost without Christ, and their lostness overwhelmed him. How could he eat a slice of bread when the streets were filled with starving men and women? How could he sleep while hundreds were dying without Christ? How could he play sport or relax when there was so much to be done?

He began trying to do everything. He went without sleep. He did not eat. He refused to relax. After some time the director of his mission board received a letter advising him to bring this man home because his overzealous exertions were exhausting him.

My wife and I were the first to greet him on his return to America. We were saddened by what we saw. Months without food or sleep, months of driving himself had taken their toll. Happily, he recovered his spiritual and physical balance and today is being mightily used by God. Beware of the problem of being devastated by the needs surrounding you. You are not God. You cannot meet every need.

We must determine what God's will for our individual lives is and then do it wholeheartedly. Give it all you've got. You will accomplish far more in your lifetime if you take this approach. A shotgun loaded with marshmallows will not penetrate a screen door, but a high-powered rifle will send a bullet through a tree. If you spread yourself too thinly you will attempt many things and accomplish very little. Your ministry will be like the Platte river that meanders through Nebraska—a mile wide and a foot deep.

The Word

When Paul arrived in Thessalonica, he followed his usual practice: "As his custom was, Paul went into the synagogue, and on three Sabbath days he reasoned with them from the Scriptures, explaining and proving that the Christ had to suffer and rise from the dead. 'This Jesus I am proclaiming to you is the Christ,' he said'' (Acts 17:2-3).

Actually, Paul had two practices which are mentioned in this passage. First, he went to the synagogue regularly, and second, he opened the Scriptures in an attempt to bring those present to Christ. Luke reminds us that Paul meticulously and plainly explained the gospel by sharing the word in an orderly fashion. The Scriptures were the source of all that Paul taught. Here is a key lesson for us in a day when man's ideas dominate so much of our thinking. The Bible gave depth, breadth, and height to Paul's message.

Notice that Paul gave his message in an orderly, understandable way. When you witness for Christ, make sure your message is biblical and Christ-centered. Make sure the gospel is *clear*. Ask God for wisdom to communicate those facts to the one to whom you are witnessing.

Are you a homemaker? What are the major concerns of homemakers today? What are their fears? What are their hopes and aspirations? What really troubles them in life? Think about those things and ask God to show you how the gospel relates to those issues. This approach will win a hearing for your message.

Are you a doctor, a lawyer, or a factory worker? What do your colleagues and coworkers talk about these days? Where do they hurt? Think about their problems, and then ask yourself, Does the gospel speak to that concern? If it does, how does it relate to that topic? Aim the gospel at a real target, a current felt need. Point it where your friends really live. Paul did. But we must be careful that we do not accommodate the gospel to their intellectual bent. Share the real gospel: repentance, faith, and the death and resurrection of Christ.

Make the gospel clear and present it within the context of real life. Remember that Paul's practice was to share the word and give his personal testimony. His testimony made his message real to his hearers, and the word of God gave his message power and life. "The word of God is living and active. Sharper than any double-edged sword, it penetrates even to dividing soul and spirit, joints and marrow; it judges the thoughts and attitudes of the heart" (Hebrews 4:12).

When you have an opportunity to witness for Christ, remember it is God who does the work in a person's heart. You are merely a channel through whom the Lord Jesus Christ has chosen to continue his ministry on earth by his Spirit. Think of Paul's example: "I will not venture to speak of anything except what Christ has accomplished through me in leading the Gentiles to obey God by what I have said and done" (Romans 15:18). Follow this pattern yourself.

This key passage teaches us that Christ did the work through Paul. Paul was the channel. Keeping that thought uppermost in your mind will help you to rest in the Lord. It is his work. You are just a channel through whom he has chosen to do it. This truth is also the solution to the problem of pride.

I was strolling along a river in Strasbourg, France, with a young man. He was a new believer through whom Christ was doing a mighty work on the university campus. He wanted to talk to me about the problem of pride.

As we were walking across an old bridge I pointed to a drainage pipe that carried excess water from the streets into the river. I asked him to look at the pipe and then said, "Alain, does it help you to know that is all you are? You are just like that pipe. The pipe has nothing to be proud of. Somebody else made it. Somebody else put it where it could do its job." Then we discussed Alain's life. He had not saved himself—God had. He had not directed his course in life to the university—God had. Now he was merely a channel whom God graciously placed at the University of Strasbourg to be an instrument through whom he could channel his love, mercy, grace, forgiveness, redemption, and salvation.

By recognizing that it is Christ who works through your life, you will be better prepared to share Christ and his word and to draw less attention to yourself in the process of sharing the gospel. This truth will also give you a greater boldness and freedom in witnessing. The gospel is not your ideas—it is God's message. He is the one who gave the world this message.

As I was writing this chapter, I was expecting a cablegram from a friend in the Middle East. When it came, the delivery boy did not apologize for its content or hesitate to bring it. He didn't write it. He just delivered it. We are to be the deliverers of God's message.

Paul realized that. He stepped right up to the door of the synagogue, entered, and delivered the message he had received from the Lord Jesus Christ. Paul was very clear about his part in proclaiming the message of salvation: "I want you to know, brothers, that the gospel I preached is not something that man made up. I did not receive it from any man, nor was I taught it; rather, I received it by revelation from Jesus Christ" (Galatians 1:11-12).

Regarding yourself as a channel of God's grace will also help you deal with feeling you are not good enough. Good enough for what? Can anyone be a good channel? Clearly none of us measure up to God's standards. But if he has chosen us, who are we to argue with him? Peter denied his Lord. Mark was a deserter in battle. Paul was a murderer. Matthew was a tax collector. But God used each of them. Paul wrote, "But we have this treasure in jars of clay to show that this all-surpassing power is from God and not from us" (2 Corinthians 4:7).

During Paul's visit to the synagogue in Thessalonica, the enemy launched a strong counterattack.

Some of the Jews were persuaded and joined Paul and Silas, as did a large number of God-fearing Greeks and not a few prominent women. But the Jews were jealous; so they rounded up some bad characters from the marketplace, formed a mob and started a riot in the city. They rushed to Jason's house in search of Paul and Silas in order to bring them out to the crowd. But when they did not find them, they dragged Jason and some other brothers before the city officials, shouting:

"These men who have caused trouble all over the world have now come here, and Jason has welcomed them into his house. They are all defying Caesar's decrees, saying that there is another king, one called Jesus." When they heard this, the crowd and the city officials were thrown into turmoil (Acts 17:4-8).

What is our reaction when opposition comes? I was speaking at a training program north of Amsterdam in the Netherlands. Most of the seventy-five trainees were responding quite enthusiastically to the message of discipleship. But when the team leaders met, they discovered a few men were having some real problems. They were arguing and stirring up dissension. The director of the program was quite concerned. As we discussed this matter I reminded him that there is always opposition. We are never out of the battle. We should rejoice when opposition comes! The Bible says, "Be joyful always; pray continually; give thanks in all circumstances, for this is God's will for you in Christ Jesus" (1 Thessalonians 5:16-18).

We should also rejoice since the enemy's opposition reveals that we are on the right track—we are doing what Satan hates and wants desperately to prevent. So take courage. If you find yourself in the midst of a fierce spiritual battle right now—if the conflict is raging around you—rejoice!

Singlemindedness

The enemies of the gospel provide an enlightening and interesting commentary on the effect of the ministry of Paul's team. They called the disciples, "These that have turned the world upside down" (Acts 17:6, KJV). The gospel was having a remarkable impact. What was the secret of its dynamic influence? I think these early believers succeeded because of the way they concentrated all their efforts in one direction.

One summer the director of a conference grounds asked me if my team would cut down a large cottonwood tree that was growing near his home. He asked us to cut it down, saw it up, and carry it away. I agreed to do the job, and we set to work. However, none of us were experienced tree cutters and we confronted an awkward set of circumstances. If we weren't careful, the tree would fall on the house. We tied some ropes around the tree's trunk and began sawing enthusiastically. We planned to pull the tree away from the house as soon as it began to fall. Some would pull on the ropes while others would push the tree away from the house. As the tree began swaying, we rushed into action. Wonder of wonders, our plan worked. The cottonwood fell and missed the house. The key to our success was that our efforts were all aimed in one direction.

Consider the church today. What do you see? Do you detect a united, strenuous, confident attempt to turn the world upside down? I don't. Some are pushing in one direction, others in another. We seem to be caught up in everything *but* turning the world upside down. Yet the apostles' primary thrust was just that—reaching the world for Christ. Even their enemies attested to the success of their mission.

Although many people in Thessalonica accepted the message Paul preached, most of the town was stirred up against Paul and his team. As a result, they had to leave Thessalonica for their own safety.

A contrast awaited Paul's team at their next stop—Berea. "Now the Bereans were of more noble character than the Thessalonians, for they received the message with great eagerness and examined the Scriptures every day to see if what Paul said was true. Many of the Jews believed, as did also a number of prominent Greek women and many Greek men" (Acts 17:11-12).

The Bereans were open-minded. When the message was given, they received it readily and were eager to listen and learn. Such an enthusiastic response is rare. A closed mind is something that a witness for Christ frequently encounters. People have a natural tendency to resist the gospel. Let me suggest four reasons why that is so.

First, the devil has blindfolded the unbeliever. "The god of this age has blinded the minds of unbelievers, so that they cannot see the light of the gospel of the glory of Christ, who is the image of God" (2 Corinthians 4:4). Whenever I encounter dishonest or illogical resistance while witnessing, I breathe a silent prayer to God that he will remove the blindfold from that individual's mind.

A second problem is stated in Romans 8:5: "Those who live according to the sinful nature have their minds set on what that nature desires; but those who live in accordance with the Spirit have their minds set on what the Spirit desires." Nonbelievers' minds are taken up with the things of the flesh—the sinful nature. They have a quiet, dignified, respectable love of sin. Wherever you are, sin is always present. Sin has very deep roots. It is difficult to eradicate. I have watched as people grew weary of its grip on their lives and attempted to overcome it by their own efforts.

The battle with sin is like my wife's relentless battle with the dandelions in our backyard. She pursues them vigorously with a tool that enables her to pull them up by their roots. But the war against dandelions is a losing battle, because you have to remove the entire root in order to prevent them from growing again. Usually a root breaks off and part of it is left in the ground. The broken root will start growing again and eventually the plant is back in full bloom.

The personal witness must trust God to show the non-Christian his truly helpless state and give him a desire to allow Christ to free him from sin's relentless grip.

A third problem which causes people to resist the gospel is curiosity. We are intrigued by side streets and love to explore the byways of life. Like sheep, we often go astray (see Isaiah 53:6). The minds of those exploring the byways of sin are often taken up with an obsessive curiosity that can lead to destruction. The way of Christ seems narrow, old-fashioned, and too restrictive, while the way of sin seems glamorous and appealing. That is because it appeals to our old nature. So in our personal witnessing we must help the non-Christian to see the pit at the end of sin's dark alley and pray that he will gain a desire to walk the bright highway of God.

The fourth problem is stated in Romans 8:7-8: "The sinful mind is hostile to God. It does not submit to God's law, nor can it do so. Those controlled by the sinful nature cannot please God." The carnal mind is at war with God. It does not want to subject itself to the word of God. At this point the mind and will join forces to sign a declaration of independence from God's law.

The mind sees Jesus Christ and declares it will not submit to him as Lord, much like the citizens in the parable Jesus told in Luke 19:12-14: "A man of noble birth went to a distant country to have himself appointed king and then to return. So he called ten of his servants and gave them ten minas. [A mina was about three months' wages.] 'Put this money to work,' he said, 'until I come back.' But his subjects hated him and sent a delegation after him to say, 'We don't want this man to be our king.'"

Such men declare war on God. The person witnessing knows that the only hope for them is to be overwhelmed by the love of God. The one who opposes God may persistently deny God's existence, rebel against God, and mock the word of God. In spite of all that, he may still hear the voice of God saying earnestly, "I love you," and be brought to the cross in unconditional surrender.

Acceptance

Although Paul frequently encountered such forms of resistance, the Bereans received the word gladly. They honestly desired to confirm that Paul's message agreed with the word of God. What a joy to meet people who accept the Bible as their final authority! I meet people like that frequently. There is a growing interest in knowing what the Bible teaches. Many men and women have grown tired of listening to endless theories about man and are eager to listen to the voice of God. Several simple, investigative Bible studies which are readily available worldwide have been mightily used by God to help people discover for themselves what the Bible teaches about man's need and God's provision of salvation in Jesus Christ.[1] Many neighborhood Bible studies also have provided an effective, encouraging way to investigate the Scriptures.

Although the Bereans received the word eagerly at first, their receptivity deteriorated after a hostile group arrived from Thessalonica. So Paul moved on to Athens. When he saw the extent of the idolatry that gripped Athens, he was moved to speak out for Christ in the synagogue. The people there showed a genuine interest in his message and some asked for a fuller explanation.

> A group of Epicurean and Stoic philosophers began to dispute with him. Some of them asked, "What is this babbler trying to say?" Others remarked, "He seems to be advocating foreign gods." They said this because Paul was preaching the good news about Jesus and the resurrection. Then they took him and brought him to a meeting of the Areopagus, where they said to him, "May we know what this new teaching is that you are presenting? You are bringing some strange ideas to our ears, and we want to know what they mean." (All the Athenians and the foreigners who lived there spent their time doing nothing but talking about and listening to the latest ideas) (Acts 17:18-21).

The people were intrigued by Paul's comments regarding Jesus and the resurrection. Paul was only too happy to give them a full explanation, and in Acts 17:22-31 we have the record of what he told them. Paul told his listeners that the unknown god they worshiped was, in fact, the God and Father of the Lord Jesus Christ.

> He is not far from each one of us. "For in him we live and move and have our being." As some of your own poets have said, "We are his offspring." Therefore since we are God's offspring, we should not think that the divine being is like gold or silver or stone—an image made by man's design and skill. In the past God overlooked such ignorance, but now he

commands all people everywhere to repent. For he has set a day when he will judge the world with justice by the man he has appointed. He has given proof of this to all men by raising him from the dead (Acts 17:27-32).

When Paul spoke of the resurrection, he provoked the same kind of reaction that we observe today. Some mocked. Others decided to put off making a decision until another time. But some believed. So if you witness to someone who scoffs at the gospel, take heart. You are in good company. It happened to Paul.

The first-century disciples faced physical opposition. They were beaten and stoned by unruly mobs. They encountered legal, religious, and intellectual opposition to the gospel. But the gospel prevailed. It prevailed in the first century and it will prevail in the twentieth century. As you consider your witness for Christ, it may seem hopeless. Many of the people in your office, plant, school, hospital, factory, or neighborhood do not believe. They all seem indifferent, even hostile, or sidetracked by strange beliefs. But take a lesson from the book of Acts. Take courage and keep sharing his message. He will not be defeated.

SUMMARY:

Paul and his team were singleminded—committed to their mission. Paul preached the gospel wherever God led him. Some people accepted what he had to say, but many opposed him violently. But as a channel of God, Paul kept passing on God's message:
- his text—the word of God
- his message—the Son of God
- his confidence—the power of God
- his guide—the Spirit of God.

Notes: 1. *Studies in Christian Living: Knowing Jesus Christ,* published by NavPress, is one such study.

18
Paul's
Training Syllabus

IN ACTS 18 we find the apostle Paul in Corinth. When I visited Corinth I quickly sensed its strategic importance. Its location controlled the trade routes between the Aegean and Adriatic seas. Greeks, Romans, and Middle Easterners met in Corinth to do their business. The apostle Paul knew that establishing a gospel witness there would spread the message far and wide. Paul went into action immediately after arriving in Corinth. "There he met a Jew named Aquila, a native of Pontus, who had recently come from Italy with his wife Priscilla, because Claudius had ordered all the Jews to leave Rome. Paul went to see them, and because he was a tentmaker as they were, he stayed and worked with them" (Acts 18:2-3).

He found a promising couple and began pouring his life into them. He was eager to share with them the lessons he had learned about following Christ. We have seen this pattern time and time again. Paul knew his job. He was to preach the gospel to every creature.

But he also knew his limitations. He was just one man. If he could train others to be his colaborers, he would double his effectiveness. Have you ever wondered what Paul did with those he trained? Wouldn't it have been exciting to have sat in the corner and listened to their conversations?

Fortunately, we do have a record of Paul's training syllabus. We have Paul's own summary of what he taught. He sent it to Timothy as a reminder. Paul wrote, "You, however, know all about my teaching, my way of life, my purpose, faith, patience, love, endurance, persecutions, sufferings—what kinds of things happened to me in Antioch, Iconium and Lystra, the persecutions I endured. Yet the Lord rescued me from all of them" (2 Timothy 3:10-11). Paul mentioned nine things.

Teaching. They learned his doctrine. As you thumb through Paul's letters, you immediately sense how his heart was burdened about many subjects: the word of God, prayer, holy living, stewardship, the Person of Christ, the Holy Spirit, the end times, discipleship, leadership in the church, faith, the gospel, justification, and many other related subjects.

Way of life. What is the best way to teach your way of life to someone else? By letting him see how you live, think, and work. The best way to do this is by allowing someone else to live with you, travel with you, and minister with you. That is how Paul trained Timothy, Priscilla, Aquila, and many others. Training by constant association and interaction was also Jesus' method of discipling others. Paul knew he could not improve on the methods of Jesus Christ.

Purpose. Paul had two God-given objectives in life and he was eager to share them. World evangelization was one. He lived to spread the gospel. Nothing diverted him from that task. He witnessed in the synagogue and marketplace. He witnessed to his jailers and to his shipmates on a sea voyage. No matter what the circumstances or situation, he witnessed.

Paul's second objective was to pursue an ever-deepening knowledge of Jesus Christ. He said, "I want to know Christ and the power of his resurrection and the fellowship of sharing in his sufferings, becoming like him in his death, and so, somehow, to attain to the resurrection from the dead" (Philippians 3:10-11). He knew he would never plumb the depths of the magnificent Person who had stopped him dead in his tracks on the road to Damascus, but he kept growing in his personal relationship with the Savior. The more he learned, the more he wanted to learn. He knew it was a progressive, step-by-step walk that Christ used to reveal more and more of his glory to his followers. "And we, who with unveiled faces all reflect the Lord's glory, are being transformed into his likeness with *ever-increasing glory,* which comes from the Lord, who is the Spirit" (2 Corinthians 3:18). Paul's two objectives could be summarized in the statement, "to know Christ and to make him known."

Faith. Now how would a person teach someone else faith? Paul lived by faith. He performed acts of faith. From prison he called on others to take courage and keep the faith. On board a storm-tossed ship he spoke words of comfort and faith. He displayed faith and courage in the midst of riots and tumult. He communicated faith by word and deed.

The two great enemies of faith are fear and doubt (see Mark 4:40 and 5:36). If you are presently in the midst of one of life's storms, you can help others to make it through the storm by affirming your confidence in God. Someone who needs your encouragement is always watching you. Remember that Paul and Silas were beaten and thrown into prison. What was their response? Their civil rights had been violated. Did they complain or sing protest songs? No! They sang hymns of praise to God—an act of faith. As they sang, "the other prisoners were listening to them" (Acts 16:25).

What kind of impression do we leave with others who observe us when we experience a test or trial? Is there a song of praise on our lips? Would Paul have been a soloist if I was his companion in jail?

Patience. The ability to keep your cool when being mistreated is a form of patience.

While checking into a hotel in Istanbul, Turkey, the clerk informed me their records showed I was supposed to arrive the day before. Since I was late, he said, I had lost my first night's deposit. I took a cable out of my briefcase that clearly showed the records were wrong—there had been a mix-up over the dates. But the clerk refused to acknowledge the mistake.

Finally the manager came, and I carefully explained everything to him. God gave me the grace to keep my composure and speak in a low, calm voice. I smiled and reasoned, but to no avail. They were convinced they were right. I committed the matter to the Lord and finished checking in.

Four days later when I went to the cashier's desk to pay my bill, the clerk said, "I see you have been credited with one night's deposit." I paid my bill and thanked the Lord. My patience had been rewarded.

Love. Love is the great identifying mark of a Christian. While the Lord was on earth he gave his followers a badge to wear that would mark them as his people. He said, "A new commandment I give you: Love one another. As I have loved you, so you must love one another. All men will know that you are my disciples if you love one another" (John 13:34-35).

Paul wore the badge of love openly every day. His love for God and his fellow man was obvious. To love is to give, and the apostle Paul gave himself selflessly to God and to people. His admonitions to the churches were always clear. "Be imitators of God, therefore, as dearly loved children and live a life of love, just as Christ loved us and gave himself up for us as a fragrant offering and sacrifice to God" (Ephesians 5:1-2).

Endurance. This is the Christlike quality that does not give in to the circumstances of life or give up when the battle rages. Endurance was one of Paul's key prayer requests for the Colossians: "We pray this in order that you may live a life worthy of the Lord and may please him in every way: bearing fruit in every good work, growing in the knowledge of God, being strengthened with all power according to his glorious might so that you may have great endurance and patience" (Colossians 1:10-11). It is through this quality of patient endurance that God perfects Christian character in our lives (see James 1:2-4, NASB).

Persecutions. Although Paul was continually opposed by the enemies of the gospel, he kept on the attack. Retreat was an unknown word in his vocabulary.

When the United States Marine Corps arrived on the battlefields of France in World War I, the allied forces were retreating. When he was ordered to retreat, the Marine Commander was shocked. "Retreat? We just got here!" he said, and with that his troops dug in and held the enemy's advance. During that battle the Marines earned the nickname "devil dogs" because they wouldn't give up. Paul was this type of tenacious warrior.

Sufferings. Christians are called upon to keep advancing in spite of sufferings or personal problems. Paul wrote to the church at Corinth about sufferings he faced and how he was able to overcome them.

> Five times I received from the Jews the forty lashes minus one. Three times I was beaten with rods, once I was stoned, three times I was shipwrecked, I spent a night and a day in the open sea, I have been constantly on the move. I have been in danger from rivers, in danger from bandits, in danger from my own countrymen, in danger from Gentiles; in danger in the city, in danger in the country, in danger at sea; and in danger from false brothers. I have labored and toiled and have often gone without sleep; I have known hunger and thirst and have often gone without food; I have been cold and naked. Besides everything else, I face daily the pressure of my concern for all the churches (2 Corinthians 11:24-28).

Although Paul also suffered from a thorn in the flesh, he was not deterred by it. When he prayed and asked God to remove it, God gave him a word of encouragement: "'My grace is sufficient for you, for my power is made perfect in weakness.' Therefore I will boast all the more gladly about my weaknesses, so that Christ's power may rest on me. That is why, for Christ's sake, I delight in weaknesses, in insults, in hardships, in persecutions, in difficulties. For when I am weak, then I am strong" (2 Corinthians 12:9-10).

Paul taught others how God supplied the strength to overcome the most difficult circumstances in his personal experience. He imparted the content of his training syllabus as much by life as by lip. These nine qualities were the basis for the instruction Paul gave growing believers like Priscilla and Aquila. The city of Corinth, where Paul lived with Priscilla and Aquila, was their unique training ground.

Historians have told us much about Corinth and its residents. Corinth was a byword in the ancient world for all manner of sin and evil. I think the best description of the Corinthians was given by Paul when he wrote,

> Do you not know that the wicked will not inherit the kingdom of God? Do not be deceived: Neither the sexually immoral nor idolaters nor adulterers nor male prostitutes nor homosexual offenders nor thieves nor the greedy nor drunkards nor slanderers nor swindlers will inherit the kingdom of God. And *that is what some of you were.* But you were washed, you were sanctified, you were justified in the name of the Lord Jesus Christ and by the Spirit of our God (1 Corinthians 6:9-11).

What a list! By reminding the Corinthians of their background Paul also gave us a very clear picture of what life was like in that strategic seaport.

When you begin to wonder if God can reach the people in the place where you work, with all the foul language and filthy stories, take heart. Read Paul's list again and remember the transformation that took place in the lives of the Corinthians.

Who were the most difficult people to reach—the religious Jews, or the Gentiles who lived in sin and debauchery? Luke's account of Paul's ministry in Corinth supplies the answer.

> Every Sabbath he reasoned in the synagogue, trying to persuade Jews and Greeks. When Silas and Timothy came from Macedonia, Paul devoted himself exclusively to preaching,

testifying to the Jews that Jesus was the Christ. But when the Jews opposed Paul and became abusive, he shook out his clothes in protest and said to them, "Your blood be on your own heads! I am clear of my responsibililty. From now on I will go to the Gentiles" (Acts 18:4-6).

In Corinth, the Jews gave Paul more trouble than the Gentiles.

When Paul turned to the Gentile world, he reminded the Jews that he was guiltless of the ruin they were bringing upon themselves. He had done his best, and they made their choice. Today we are often told that man is not responsible for his own actions. Man blames his environment, his parents, his friends, his schooling—anything but himself. But we are responsible for our actions. We are responsible for our decisions and the results they bring. Therefore, Paul warned the Jews of Corinth, "Your blood be on your own heads! I am clear of my responsibility" (Acts 18:6). He told them they could blame no one but themselves for the consequences of their refusal to receive the gospel.

When Paul encountered this opposition he received a word of comfort from the Lord. "One night the Lord spoke to Paul in a vision: 'Do not be afraid; keep on speaking, do not be silent. For I am with you, and no one is going to attack and harm you, because I have many people in this city!'" (Acts 18:9-10). God told Paul five things.

"Do not be afraid." Fear is the opposite of faith. Occasionally we encounter circumstances that produce fear in our hearts.

As I was leaving an Eastern European country, I reached the passport control desk at the airport, and the officer in charge said, "You are here on an expired visa!" There I was— just two feet from the departure lounge—but unable to leave. An officer with a rifle marched me to a steel cage and put me inside. I was scared to death. I had visions of being detained in jail. After all, I *was* a criminal in the officials' eyes.

My heart began pounding and my stomach knotted up. But I didn't want them to see my concern. So I smiled and said, "Well, let's do what we can to correct this problem." The officer called his superior and they talked for some time. Then they marched me to another desk and a man issued me a two-day extension. God had once again proven himself able to handle the situation. Had my faith remained strong I could have saved myself some anxious moments.

"Keep on speaking." This is hard to do when we are in a tense situation or facing strong opposition. It helps us to realize that even Paul needed an occasional word of encouragement to maintain his bold witness. When we find ourselves needing some encouragement to keep on sharing the gospel, we are in good company. In fact, Paul requested prayer for this very thing (see Colossians 4:3-4).

"I am with you." The emphasis is on the one who made this promise—the King of heaven, the Lord of all, Jesus Christ—he it is who said, "I am with you." It is so easy to lose sight of his promise. Problems seem so great, difficulties and opposition mount up, and we are terrified. At such a time we need to be reassured by the promise of his presence.

When I was a young Christian, I memorized some verses of Scripture such as John 16:13, Acts 2:25, and Hebrews 13:5, which spoke of the Lord's presence and guidance. Many times during the years since then, the Lord has spoken to me through those passages. Let me encourage you to memorize these passages of Scripture which promise his comfort and guidance.

"No one is going to attack and harm you." God had Paul in Corinth for a purpose and he would insure that his purposes were carried out. Temporary setbacks are all part of the battle. While a battle rages, it often goes one way and then the other. But we can take courage from the knowledge that Christ has already triumphed in the spiritual battle in which we are engaged. The Lord told Paul that he would be victorious in Corinth. As long as Paul was faithful to the mission Christ had given him, he would be safe.

"I have many people in this city." Notice the present tense of this statement. The Lord did not say he would even-

tually have many people in Corinth, but that he already had them. I'm sure as Paul looked around in Corinth and saw the people hellbent on their way to destruction—consumed by debauchery, greed, and lust—he wondered where Christ's followers were. Although Paul couldn't see them, they were there.

Like Paul, we too might feel lonely and discouraged where we live and work. When we do feel that way, we can take courage from the Lord's word to Paul. Today there are many villages, towns, and cities in which there are believers, even though they are not acquainted with one another or possibly are even prevented from fellowshipping together.

After spending a year and a half in Corinth, Paul took Priscilla and Aquila on to Ephesus where he left them and returned to Antioch. After staying in Antioch for some time, Paul resumed traveling around to encourage the disciples.

Now we meet Apollos, a fervent, eloquent man who had "a thorough knowledge of the Scriptures" and "taught about Jesus accurately" (Acts 18:24-25). Rarely do we meet someone as gifted and talented as Apollos who is also willing to learn and be taught. He only knew the baptism of John, so when Priscilla and Aquila "invited him to their home and explained the way of God more adequately" (Acts 18:26), Apollos was eager to learn. This was just what he needed to complete his ministry. When he went to Achaia, "he was a great help to those who by grace had believed. For he vigorously refuted the Jews in public debate, proving from the Scriptures that Jesus was the Christ" (Acts 18:27-28).

SUMMARY:

Paul continued to invest his life in faithful people who could teach others also.
- Paul lived and worked with Priscilla and Aquila.
- Priscilla and Aquila instructed Apollos.
- Apollos strengthened the church in Greece.

19
Results of
the New Birth

IN EPHESUS PAUL met twelve men whom Luke describes as disciples. As Paul got to know them he discovered something was wrong. They were not disciples of Jesus. They were disciples of John the Baptist. Paul told them, "John's baptism was a baptism of repentance. He told the people to believe in the one coming after him, that is, in Jesus" (Acts 19:4). They realized they needed to put their faith in Jesus. When they did, they received the Holy Spirit, spoke in tongues, and prophesied. They received the same sign of the new birth that God had given to other Jews.

How did Paul discern that these people had not been truly born again by the Holy Spirit of God? Luke doesn't tell us, but I'm sure many of us have had a similar experience. You meet someone and there seems to be something lacking—you sense that he is not a true believer, one of God's children.

I was sitting and talking in the midst of a large gathering one evening when our group was joined by a couple who arrived late. Immediately my wife and I sensed this couple was different. They were from the same part of the country, they dressed like everyone else, and talked like the others, but there was something different which we couldn't explain immediately. Perhaps it showed in their smiles. We wondered if they were fellow Christians. After the party we walked out to their car with them and turned the conversation to spiritual matters. They responded instantly. They were Christians! We spent the next half hour talking with them about the Lord and his work.

Born Again

Consider some of the things God does in us and for us when we are born again. How does it happen? Peter wrote, "For you have been born again, not of perishable seed, but of imperishable, through the living and enduring word of God" (1 Peter 1:23).

Jesus was in Jerusalem for the Passover and many believed in him when they saw the miracles he performed. "But Jesus would not entrust himself to them, for he knew all men. He did not need man's testimony about man, for he knew what was in a man" (John 2:24-25). These people were described as believers; "many . . . believed in his name" (John 2:23). However, Jesus discerned something was missing.

Shortly after that, Jesus talked with Nicodemus, who began the conversation with a brief statement of faith: "Rabbi, we know you are a teacher who has come from God. For no one could perform the miraculous signs you are doing if God were not with him" (John 3:2).

Instantly Jesus declared, "I tell you the truth, unless a man is born again, he cannot see the kingdom of God" (John 3:3). Nicodemus' faith, like the faith of those at the Passover, was a dead faith. It needed life. Jesus told Nicodemus, "Flesh gives birth to flesh, but the Spirit gives birth to spirit. You should not be surprised at my saying, 'You must be born again'" (John 3:6-7). We are born again by the Spirit through the word of God.

How does the transaction take place? Consider John 1:12-13: "Yet to all who received him, to those who believed in his name, he gave the right to become children of God—

children born not of natural descent, nor of human decision or a husband's will, but born of God." Believing in Christ's name is equated with receiving Jesus. I am born again by the Holy Spirit when I hear the word of God, place my faith in Jesus Christ, and receive him into my life. What happens in my life when that occurs? Let us examine eight aspects of the new birth.

I become a new creation in Christ. The Spirit of God brings a new song, a new hope, and a new purpose into my life. My former way of life becomes tasteless and repulsive. My old habits, old desires, and old pleasures pass away, and my life is renewed. "Therefore, if anyone is in Christ, he is a new creation; the old has gone, the new has come!" (2 Corinthians 5:17).

I am brought to life. Before this I was dead. I was alive in a sense, but I was alive to the wrong things. In the past I yielded myself as a servant of impurity. But now, as one who is alive to God, I have become a slave to righteousness (see Romans 6:19). "But because of his great love for us, God, who is rich in mercy, made us alive with Christ even when we were dead in transgressions—it is by grace you have been saved" (Ephesians 2:4-5).

I have a new source of power. God now lives in me through his Holy Spirit. He helps me to overcome my old habits and enables me to chart a new course under his guidance. I now live under God's control. Sin no longer rules. "He has given us his very great and precious promises, so that through them you may participate in the divine nature and escape the corruption in the world caused by evil desires" (2 Peter 1:4).

I am made complete. Many of those who live without Christ feel something is missing in their lives but they don't know what it is. They make valiant attempts to fill their emptiness with pleasure, things, adventure, fame, and fortune, but nothing works. They become frantic and turn to alcohol and drugs, but still remain empty. Many eventually become so despondent that they turn to suicide. The only one who can fill this vacuum is God himself. When Christ came into my life he filled the emptiness with a sense of contentment and completion. "For in Christ all the fullness of the Deity lives in bodily form, and you have been given fullness in Christ, who is the head over every power and authority" (Colossians 2:9-10).

I am satisfied. Jesus told the woman at the well, "Whoever drinks the water I give him will never thirst. Indeed, the water I give him will become in him a spring of water welling up to eternal life" (John 4:14). The water of life does not become a stagnant pond within us; it is a fresh geyser, constantly bubbling, gushing, and springing up within us. When we partake of the water of life and the bread of life that Christ offers us, our thirst is quenched and our hunger is satisfied. "I am the bread of life. He who comes to me will never go hungry, and he who believes in me will never be thirsty" (John 6:35).

I have everlasting life. Eternal life is not something I *will* have one day, it is a present possession. John wrote, "I write these things to you who believe in the name of the Son of God so that you may know that you *have* eternal life" (1 John 5:13).

Shortly after we were married my wife asked me, "What happens to us when we die?" I didn't know. At that time I thought there might be some sort of balance on which God would put our good deeds and bad deeds. Whichever way the balance tipped would determine our eternal destiny. Since I wasn't sure, I told my wife I would go to the library to see if there was a book on religion which answered her question.

When I asked the librarian for assistance, she showed me an entire section full of religious books. I chose one with a short title, hoping it would present the information I wanted simply so I could understand it. I read the book but it didn't answer my question—but I certainly enjoyed reading that novel, *Ben Hur*. It wasn't until I bought a Bible and read it that I learned eternal life is a present possession. I can know that I have it today!

Knowing we have eternal life will relieve our anxieties about what happens when we die. Jesus said, "I tell you the truth, whoever hears my word and believes him who sent me has eternal life and will not be condemned; he has crossed over from death to life" (John 5:24).

I am set free. I am freed from the grip of the prince of darkness and enter the light of the kingdom of God. "For he has rescued us from the dominion of darkness and brought us into the kingdom of the Son he loves" (Colossians 1:13).

Have you ever been lost in the dark? When I was serving in the Marine Corps during World War II, we were stationed on the island of Pavuvu in the South Pacific. I'd been relieved from guard duty and was making my way back to my tent. It was an extremely dark night and I was picking my way slowly along the path trying to find my tent. I became totally lost and had no idea of where I was. I entered what I thought was my tent but soon found out I was in the wrong one. I stumbled around for a long time before I found a landmark that helped me to become reoriented and I found my way to the right tent. Being lost in the dark can be a frightening experience.

As Christians we can live without fear, in the light. Christ promised, "I am the light of the world. Whoever follows me will never walk in darkness, but will have the light of life" (John 8:12).

My name is written in the book of life. When we are transferred from death to life, from the power of Satan to the power of God, from darkness to light, our names are recorded in heaven. "If anyone's name was not found written in the book of life, he was thrown into the lake of fire" (Revelation 20:15).

These eight results of being born again took place in the disciples of John when they met Paul in Ephesus, and they can affect your life today if you receive Christ as your Savior.

Friendly Persuasion

After meeting the disciples of John, Paul went to the synagogue and "spoke boldly there for three months, arguing persuasively about the kingdom of God" (Acts 19:8). Again Paul gave a bold witness to his faith in Christ. Here we learn two things about how he witnessed. He reasoned, and he gave Scriptural answers to the questions people had. This is an approach we must use. If someone raises a question which you can't answer, don't worry. It is not a sin to be unable to answer something.

But don't let it happen twice with the same question. Go to work. Start digging. The Bible has an answer. Talk to your pastor; ask for his advice. Do whatever you can to find an answer. As Peter said, "Always be prepared to give an answer to everyone who asks you to give the reason for the hope that you have" (1 Peter 3:15).

Paul persuaded his audience of the truth. The two most persuasive forces in the world are the Holy Spirit and the Holy Bible. Our responsibility is to share the word—to show the danger of delay, and the danger of rejection. The danger of delay is clear: "Do not boast about tomorrow, for you do not know what a day may bring forth" (Proverbs 27:1). No one knows what is waiting around the next bend. Paul reminded the Corinthians, "As God's fellow workers we urge you not to receive God's grace in vain. . . . I tell you, now is the time of God's favor, now is the day of salvation" (2 Corinthians 6:1-2).

For thousands who are alive at this moment there will be no tomorrow. So God says, "Come now!" When we declare these truths, the Holy Spirit does his work of convincing a person of his need to heed them. Although the apostle Paul did not pressure people unduly, he was not above using some friendly persuasion. Likewise, we need to persuade people from the Scriptures of the urgency of responding to Christ.

The Way
Acts 19:9-10 is packed with important truth. Christianity is again referred to as "the Way." Christianity is the way to heaven! Jesus said, "I am the way and the truth and the life. No one comes to the Father except through me" (John 14:6).

Christianity is also a way of life. We have a God-given lifestyle that the world cannot understand or appreciate. As a non-Christian I couldn't understand Christianity either. If this world is all there is, if there is no God to whom I am accountable, it makes no sense at all to live like a Christian. But there *is* a God to whom I must render an account. There *is* a judgment for sin. There *is* a heaven and a hell. Christianity is a way of thinking, a way of living, and the way of salvation.

Paul presented this way of thinking, living, and salvation to the Jews for three months. However, they rejected all that Paul offered them. So Paul left them.

Paul and the disciples then met daily in the school of Tyrannus and discussed the things of God. The result of these discussions in Ephesus was staggering. Paul "took the disciples with him and had discussions daily in the lecture hall of Tyrannus. This went on for two years, so that all the Jews and Greeks who lived in the province of Asia heard the word of the Lord" (Acts 19:9-10). Paul did not rush. He invested two years of his life, but it was worth it. If you invest your life passing on to others the lessons God has taught you, you will be involved in the most explosive and dynamic adventure in the world.

We are now confronted with another aspect of life in Ephesus: "curious arts"—magic, sorcery, and witchcraft. Certain "Ephesian letters," chants spoken to demons, were sent all over the world to practitioners of the Ephesian-style witchcraft. A similar fascination with magic still prevails.

Some young men I know rented a home in Boulder, Colorado. They found some strange markings on the basement walls. They knew that a group of devil worshipers had lived in the house before them, so they decided to whitewash the walls. They put several coats of whitewash over the strange markings, but all to no avail. When they checked each morning they discovered the markings had burned through and were still plainly visible. Eventually they moved and rented another home.

Many young men and women have become involved in

the occult with disastrous results. One young man told me how he had fallen further and further into the grip of fear and helplessness. He was under the power of Satan and he knew it. Finally, out of desperation, he cried out to God and in a miraculous way met a man who led him to Christ. Thank God the power of Christ is greater than anything the forces of hell can muster!

The magicians in Ephesus also learned the power of the name of Jesus. "Many of those who believed now came and openly confessed their evil deeds. A number who had practiced sorcery brought their scrolls together and burned them publicly. . . . In this way the word of the Lord spread widely and grew in power" (Acts 19:19-20). However, although this was a great victory for God, the disciples could not fall back and rest after it.

Spiritual warfare can be discouraging. Just as you win a battle on one front, new skirmishes break out on another. The devil is a relentless foe. While Paul was still in Ephesus he encountered some more trouble. A silversmith named Demetrius made silver shrines for the tourists and those who made religious pilgrimages to the temple of Artemis. He had a lucrative business, but quickly realized his business was threatened by Paul's effective preaching.

Therefore, Demetrius gathered up the craftsmen and workmen and said, "You see and hear how this fellow Paul has convinced and led astray large numbers of people here in Ephesus and in practically the whole province of Asia. He says that man-made gods are no gods at all" (Acts 19:26). Demetrius also pointed out that the temple of Artemis was being discredited and endangered by this onslaught from the Christian religion. Whenever avarice and greed are combined with religious fervor and a nationalistic spirit, they produce a powerful evil force. Demetrius stirred the people to riot.

Finally, after much confusion, they rushed into the great theater and chanted their devotion to the goddess Artemis for two hours. Fortunately, the town clerk restored order and the crowd was dismissed.

It is interesting to observe Paul's reaction to this dangerous, threatening event. "Paul wanted to appear before the crowd, but the disciples would not let him. Even some of the officials of the province, friends of Paul, sent him a message begging him not to venture into the theater" (Acts 19:30-31). Paul was a soldier at heart and he wanted to march into the arena and try to persuade the people. However, he wisely listened to his friends' counsel and was spared to fight another day.

Here is an important lesson. We must do everything we can to keep the total picture of God's worldwide mission in mind. It would have been so easy for Paul to have been caught up in the excitement of the moment. But all of the factors must be weighed carefully and our decisions must be made in light of the total picture. There was much of the world still to be reached. Rome was still a long way off. Spain was much on Paul's heart. So he listened to his friends' counsel.

Some may be called to burn out for the Lord—their lives may be short yet powerful. They expend their energies in a great thrust of religious zeal and their ministry ends quickly. But the majority of us are placed on earth to plod. We are not the great heroes of the battle. We are the faithful foot soldiers who simply keep at it day to day and do our jobs. If that's your calling, be encouraged by this glimpse of Paul and keep plodding. The Lord's "Well done," awaits the plodder and the hero alike.

Warren Myers, a missionary and close friend of mine, wrote a letter about the importance of plodding in the life of William Carey, the father of modern missions. In the same letter Warren also highlighted how Carey's sister, another faithful foot soldier in the Lord's army, prayed regularly for her brother's ministry.

Many books have been written about William Carey; but as far as I know, none have been written about his bedridden, "useless" sister. She and William were very close, and he wrote her extensively about his struggles in translating the

Bible, printing readers, training teachers, establishing converts. Others heard the broad outlines; she received the details and hour after hour lifted them to the Lord from her bed.

God used this self-educated shoe repairman and his two partners to translate and print the whole Bible in eight Indian languages and the New Testament in 25 more—a record unequaled in mission history.

Add to this their establishing schools and newspapers, conducting catechism classes, starting a seminary, plus Carey supporting himself by a secular job.

William Carey had two mottos: "I am not gifted but I can plod." "Attempt great things for God, Expect great things from God." And he had a bedridden sister who prayed.

When I wonder who really gets the credit for what the Lord did through Carey, 1 Samuel 30:24 comes to mind, "As his part is that goes down to the battle, so shall his part be who remains by the baggage. They shall share alike."[1]

We need to follow these same examples: plod and pray. Paul decided to keep away from the trouble so he could keep plodding. Therefore, he let the town clerk quell the riot.

I am impressed by the town clerk in Ephesus. He was quite a man, able to quiet a frenzied mob with a few brief remarks. What did he say that calmed them down? Four things stand out.

First, he reminded them that they were shouting about something everybody already knew. No one, he said, denied the greatness of the Ephesians' goddess. So why was there such a fuss?

Second, Paul and his companions had really done nothing to upset the Ephesians. They hadn't robbed the temple or blasphemed their goddess.

Third, if Demetrius wanted to fight about something, let him fight his own battles. The courts would take care of him.

Fourth, the Romans would clamp down on the city if they kept up the disturbance.

The crowd listened attentively, settled down, and

disbanded. What had the town clerk done to command the situation as he did? He kept his cool, reasoned with the crowd, and helped them to see it was in their best interests to end the disturbance. That's leadership: *motivating people to want to do what is good for them.* The town clerk wisely helped the people to see that the best choice for everyone was to calm down and go home. If you can bring people to the place where they are eager to do the right thing, instead of feeling they *have* to do it, you too will experience success in leadership.

SUMMARY:

Paul and the disciples continued to plod along in the face of opposition, persuading people all over Asia Minor, by the power of God's word, to—
- be born again;
- accept the Christian way of life.

20
Characteristics
of a
Spiritual Leader

PAUL AND HIS seven companions traveled through Macedonia and Greece preaching to the people and encouraging them. However, it is easy to focus just on Paul and forget about the others with him. "He was accompanied by Sopater son of Pyrrhus from Berea, Aristarchus and Secundus from Thessalonica, Gaius from Derbe, Timothy also, and from the province of Asia Tychicus and Trophimus" (Acts 20:4).

Why did Paul take these men with him? Paul knew he was not the answer to world evangelization. The key was the band of men whom God would touch through him. Therefore, Paul spent much time training these men who would oversee the ministry. As you reflect on Paul's example, think about your own life—what steps can you take to help others grow spiritually and become effective workers for the Lord? Think in terms of four stages.

A healthy convert. Help the believer receive the assurance of his salvation.

A growing disciple. Help him begin to grow in grace, fellowship regularly with other believers, and worship God. Show him how to set aside time daily for morning prayer and

Bible reading, and how to give his testimony to his relatives and friends. This will help him begin a life of discipleship.

A mature disciple. Help him come to a real commitment to Christ and become fruitful in his witness for Christ. Show him how to share the gospel in a clear, Christ-centered manner. Teach him how to enjoy a steady intake of the word through Scripture memory and Bible study, and how to develop a prayer life that grows in depth and breadth. Help him to live for the Lord, not for himself, and to become a man of faith, whose life is pure and useful in the work of the kingdom of God.

A worker. Help him take his place in the ranks of those who labor in the harvest. Teach him not only how to help others come to Christ, but also how to help them grow in the grace and knowledge of Jesus Christ. Help him develop his ministry skills and personal convictions. Help him to know why he is committed to following Christ and teach him how to help others.

Let me suggest a few training tips that may prove useful as you help others grow and develop in their walk and work for Christ.

Keep in mind the strategic value of training others. A mission organization or ministry team which helps develop the workers' gifts and abilities will invest its resources wisely. Make it your objective to help each disciple you train become a strong, devoted, effective man or woman of God.

To do this you must personally set the pace in the ministry and be an example to others in holy living and devotion to Christ.

Provide a way for others to get involved. Have a means of outreach where those you train can join others to witness for Christ and grow in the Lord. A small Bible study fellowship or a weekly witnessing outreach in the neighborhood will keep people in the battle and train them as workers for God.

Initially, this can be accomplished through a small group. But, if you want to train a skilled worker you must spend individual time with that person. Skilled, dedicated workers are not trained in bunches. You must train them individually, as well as in groups, to function as a team. You are not training superstars, but team members.

Paul's own example illustrates the correct approach: "For you know that we dealt with each of you as a father deals with his own children, encouraging, comforting and urging you to live lives worthy of God, who calls you into his kingdom and glory" (1 Thessalonians 2:11-12). Jesus ministered to the masses, but trained twelve men.

Paul concentrated on the men who traveled with him as well. As he continued his journey, an incident occurred that gives us a glimpse into Paul's heart. In a meeting of the disciples in Troas, Paul preached so long that Eutychus went to sleep and

> fell to the ground from the third story and was picked up dead. Paul went down, threw himself on the young man and put his arms around him. "Don't be alarmed," he said. "He's alive!" Then he went upstairs again and broke bread and ate. After talking until daylight, he left. The people took the young man home alive and were greatly comforted (Acts 20:9-12).

Paul's heart was full and he had much to share. He preached all night!

Paul continued traveling toward Jerusalem. Upon his arrival in Miletus, Paul called the elders of the church to come and meet with him.

> When they arrived he said to them: "You know how I lived the whole time I was with you, from the first day I came into the province of Asia. I served the Lord with great humility and with tears, although I was severely tested by the plots of the Jews. You know that I have not hesitated to preach anything that would be helpful to you but have taught you publicly and from house to house. I have declared to both Jews and Greeks that they must turn to God in repentance and have faith in our Lord Jesus. And now, compelled by the Spirit, I am going to Jerusalem, not knowing what will happen

to me there. I only know that in every city the Holy Spirit
warns me that prison and hardships are facing me. However, I
consider my life worth nothing to me, if only I may finish the
race and complete the task the Lord Jesus has given me—the
task of testifying to the gospel of God's grace. Now I know
that none of you among whom I have gone about preaching
the kingdom will ever see me again. Therefore, I declare to
you today that I am innocent of the blood of all men. For I
have not hesitated to proclaim to you the whole will of God"
(Acts 20:18-27).

Paul reviewed with the church leaders all he had done
among them. He gave them a profile listing seven qualities of
spiritual leadership which he exemplified.

A humble mind. Pride kills leaders. Paul warned Timothy
about selecting leaders. "Not a novice, lest being lifted up
with pride he fall into the condemnation of the devil" (1
Timothy 3:6, KJV). The leader keeps in step with God and
functions by his power. God resists the proud.

I am a member of an outstanding church. If you were to
ask the members of our church who has the finest pastor in
town, they would undoubtedly answer, "We do." If you were
to ask who has the finest choir in town, again they would
answer, "We do." They would speak in glowing terms about
our youth program, our Sunday school, and our missions program. Does that mean we pity all the other churches in town?
Of course not. Experiencing God's blessing should cause us to
go to God in a spirit of humble thanksgiving. This is true of
anything in life. Being a good singer can prompt either pride
or humility. Are you a talented teacher, a good mother with
well-behaved children, or a successful businessman? Go to
God with humble thanks. Paul did.

A tender heart. Paul was a man of deep emotion. He loved
the Ephesians, and they loved him. When his visit ended, a
touching, revealing scene occurred: "He knelt down with all
of them and prayed. They all wept as they embraced him and
kissed him. What grieved them most was his statement that

they would never see his face again. Then they accompanied him to the ship" (Acts 20:36-38).

Our pastor told a story about a boy whose sister was in an accident and lost a lot of blood. The boy was the only one who had the right blood type for the transfusion his sister needed. The doctor explained the girl's need to her brother. The young boy asked, "Will my sister die if I don't give her my blood?"

"Yes," the doctor replied, "It is very likely that she will." The boy thought about it for a while and then said he would do it. After they took some of his blood he remained on the hospital bed lying quiet and very still. A nurse observed him lying there with a puzzled, faraway look in his eye. She approached him to ask if anything was wrong.

"Well," he said, "I was just wondering when I am supposed to die." He had presumed that he would die if he gave his sister his blood. That is a picture of Paul's heart. He would gladly give his life for those he ministered to. He loved them deeply with a tender, loving heart.

A strong will. Paul was severely tested by the threats to his life, and by opposition and difficulties in various forms. But he kept going. Jesus also constantly encountered opposition but pressed ahead. He set his face to go to Jerusalem and in spite of many attempts to sidetrack him, he arrived. Love, humility, and a strong will are rarely combined as effectively in one person's life as they were in the life of Jesus.

It is all too easy for a strong-willed individual to be a clever, cold-hearted producer who is not tempered by love and compassion. These qualities were perfectly balanced in the life of Christ. He had a determined will, a heart of love, and a compassionate spirit. By spending much time in fellowship with Christ, these attributes can become ours as we reflect more and more of his life to others. A strong will is an essential, God-given attribute of a leader. He must lead the way in spite of difficulties. He must keep going. He is responsible for keeping the mission on course.

The courage to say what needs to be said. Paul said,

"I have not hesitated to preach anything that would be helpful to you but have taught you publicly and from house to house. I have declared to both Jews and Greeks that they must turn to God in repentance and have faith in our Lord Jesus" (Acts 20:20-21).

What needs to be said must be said. Sometimes the leader is misunderstood and feelings are hurt, but that is the risk the leader must take. I remember a painful situation I had to deal with as a leader. One of the men was forever saying the wrong thing at the wrong time. Although he had greatly offended several people, he was oblivious to the problem. I talked with him about it, but he laughed it off as a joke. He completely misunderstood the situation. I knew we could not overlook his problem, so my wife and I, and two other close friends of his, met with him to share our concern.

Each of us described an incident in which we had seen this problem. Although he remembered each incident, he had no idea that anyone had been offended. We explained that we wanted to alert him that his effectiveness for Christ would be endangered if he continued to speak thoughtlessly to others. Finally he understood and agreed to change his behavior.

We shared that an excellent way to control one's speech is to memorize and pray over Psalm 141:3: "Set a guard over my mouth, O Lord; keep watch over the door of my lips." I remember how difficult it was to confront our friend. But there are occasions when what needs to be said must be said, and we must have the God-given courage to say it.

The courage to do what needs to be done. Some years ago I was working with a very dedicated young man who had a great heart for God and wanted to go to the mission field. Yet it was obvious to me that the organization he was with would never send him overseas. He maintained high hopes, but his gifts and abilities did not match their overseas objectives or needs. For years he longed to serve with them.

One day we took a long walk and I challenged him to review his life—his ambitions, dreams, gifts, and abilities. Then we discussed some specific applications. It would be in his best interests if he dropped everything, enrolled in a graduate course at a Bible college, and associated himself with a mission group that truly needed him and would be able to use his skills and gifts. After some months of careful consideration, he did just that.

Today he serves as a highly respected, valuable missionary in a very needy area of the world. If he had lacked the courage to change his life's course, he would still be dreaming about serving God on the mission field. Because he dared to change and do what needed to be done, he is on the mission field today.

As we study the lives of the apostles, we can learn to be as decisive and courageous in our actions for the gospel as they were. Paul, especially, had a pioneer spirit (see 2 Corinthians 10:15-16).

A clear objective. Paul had a clear objective: "I consider my life worth nothing to me, if only I may finish the race and complete the task the Lord Jesus has given me—the task of testifying to the gospel of God's grace" (Acts 20:24). Paul spoke of the task God had given him. God also has a special task for you. He has a unique opportunity where you can serve, and it is something only you can do.

Paul was determined to complete the work God had given him to do. This was one of the notable qualities in the life of Jesus. "My food," said Jesus, "is to do the will of him who sent me and to finish his work" (John 4:34). Toward the end of his ministry he said, "I have brought you glory on earth by completing the work you gave me to do" (John 17:4). The work Jesus referred to was the great work of preaching the gospel, helping people to follow him in a life of discipleship, sending some out as laborers, and training the twelve apostles. Finally, Christ accomplished the work of redemption. His last words on the cross were, "It is finished" (John 19:30).

Paul echoed the same joyful testimony at the end of his days: "I have fought the good fight, I have finished the race, I have kept the faith" (2 Timothy 4:7). He encouraged others to set a similar goal for their own lives:

Do you not know that in a race all the runners run, but only
one gets the prize? Run in such a way as to get the prize.
Everyone who competes in the games goes into strict training.
They do it to get a crown that will not last; but we do it to
get a crown that will last forever. Therefore I do not run like
a man running aimlessly; I do not fight like a man beating the
air (1 Corinthians 9:24-26).

Paul told the Philippians, "Brothers, I do not consider
myself yet to have taken hold of it. But one thing I do: Forget-
ting what is behind and straining toward what is ahead, I press
on toward the goal to win the prize for which God has called
me heavenward in Christ Jesus" (Philippians 3:13-14). Paul
knew where he was going.

A clear conscience. "I am innocent of the blood of all
men. For I have not hesitated to proclaim to you the whole
will of God" (Acts 20:26-27). Paul left the Ephesian elders with
a clear conscience. Like all of us, I am sure he could think of
things he could have done better and some things that were
left undone. But he knew he had done his best, and that is all
that the Lord asks of anyone. Only God is perfect in all that he
does and is. We often make mistakes—but if we have done our
work in his power, by his grace, and for his glory, he will
delight in us.

After reflecting on the ministry God had given him, Paul
turned to give the leaders a final challenge.

Guard yourselves and all the flock of which the Holy Spirit
has made you overseers. Be shepherds of the church of God,
which he bought with his own blood. I know that after I
leave, savage wolves will come in among you and will not
spare the flock. Even from your own number men will arise
and distort the truth in order to draw away disciples after
them. So be on your guard! Remember that for three years I
never stopped warning each of you night and day with tears.
Now I commit you to God and to the word of his grace,
which can build you up and give you an inheritance among all
those who are sanctified. I have not coveted anyone's silver

or gold or clothing. You yourselves know that these hands of mine have supplied my own needs and the needs of my companions. In everything I did, I showed you that by this kind of hard work we must help the weak, remembering the words the Lord Jesus himself said: "It is more blessed to give than to receive" (Acts 20:28-35).

In Acts 20:28 Paul refers to the leaders as "overseers." In Acts 20:17 he called for the "elders" of the church. The word *overseer* describes the work, and the word *elder* describes the man. As an overseer, a man was charged with making sure that people did their work properly. The term *elder* signifies that an individual has a mature walk with God and is experienced in the work of the ministry.

Notice that Paul reminded the leaders that the flock belongs to God. It was not their church, but God's church. He exhorted them to be shepherds—they were to feed, protect, and guide the flock. They were to keep alert for anything that would harm the flock and steer them away from possible danger while staying alert to all that would build them up.

The leaders were to follow the same course in their own lives. The shepherd can never assume he is immune to danger. A roaring lion is lurking outside the fold, waiting for an opportunity to attack, planning to smite the shepherd and scatter his flock. A prerequisite to usefulness in the life of another is first to care diligently for yourself.

Acts 20:29 conveys a warning: the flock is always in danger of attack. The Great Shepherd was not spared. It is certain his flock will not be spared either. Often these attacks come in totally unexpected ways.

Recently, I was talking with a Christian leader who has served the Lord on two continents. "LeRoy, my family is in trouble," he told me. His eldest son was frantically rebelling against everything. It was as if the man was rowing his family across a lake in a rowboat and the boy was busy boring holes in the bottom. What he was doing made no sense. He loved his father, mother, brothers, and sisters, but was taking a course that would hurt them all. It had all the marks of an attack by the devil. Satan is a foul, rotten, vicious fighter who loves to kick us when we are down.

Acts 20:30 warns us that trouble can also come from within the church itself. Years ago I listened to a Christian leader describing another man's ministry. He had visited the man's church and was challenged by the Christ-centered message and the fruitful evangelism. Years later another friend asked me if I knew of this man's ministry. I told him that while I had never observed it, I had heard it was a good work.

As we talked I was shocked to hear what my friend said. Apparently there had been a subtle change, hardly noticeable at first, but as the months passed it became evident that the ministry was taking a new course. Christ was no longer the center. People were no longer being saved and established in the faith. This pastor had led his church down a path that killed their effectiveness for Christ.

Paul warned the believers, one by one, in person, for three years, day and night, to watch for an attack from within.

Acts 20:32 is surprising. We would expect Paul to commend a group of babes in Christ to the Lord and his word, but he was speaking to leaders! We all need to be reminded from time to time to be faithful to God and to feed upon his word.

Not long ago I was talking with a Christian leader who told me he had not opened his Bible for weeks. The Scriptures had become dry. He had not prayed for weeks. His spiritual life was in the doldrums. This can happen to any of us.

When I feel myself becoming spiritually dry, I have a plan that works for me. I spend a day alone with the Lord. I read my Bible, sing hymns, and pray. I often take along a biography of one of the great heroes of the faith—an evangelist or missionary who has been greatly used of God. After a few hours of praying, meditating on the Scriptures, and reading excerpts from an inspirational book, I begin to revive. My spiritual batteries are soon recharged.

In Acts 20:33 Paul reminded the group that their attention must be directed toward heaven, not things on earth.

Covetousness and self-interest have no part in the individual who follows the one who lived a life of self-sacrificing love. When self-sacrifice controls our lives, God gives us strength to help our weaker brothers and sisters become strong in their walk with the Lord. Paul ended his talk with a challenge on giving and highlighted the example of the Lord Jesus.

Giving was a much-needed emphasis in Ephesus. The leaders and the priests of the temple of Diana were the keepers of a great storehouse of gold and silver which they used for their own pleasure. In Acts 20:33-35 Paul gave an object lesson that contrasted starkly with the religion the Ephesians were familiar with when he said, "I have not coveted anyone's silver or gold or clothing. You yourselves know that these hands of mine have supplied my own needs and the needs of my companions. In everything I did, I showed you that by this kind of hard work we must help the weak, remembering the words the Lord Jesus himself said: 'It is more blessed to give than to receive.'"

The religion of the goddess Diana was characterized by magic, secrets, mysteries, and personal pleasures. Paul reminded the elders that Christianity and the message of the gospel is characterized by the open, public declaration of God's word—a message that brings light and inspires men and women to join in the self-sacrificing work of advancing the mission of Christ in the world.

SUMMARY:

Paul exhibited effective spiritual leadership.
- His eyes were on the masses of the world—but he also trained his leaders.
- He gave himself to people—but he stuck to his objective.
- He adhered to tough standards—but he had a tender heart.

21
The Marks
of Maturity

AS LUKE POINTS out in Acts 21:1, Paul found it difficult to tear himself away from the Ephesian elders. A deep bond of love existed between Paul and those men. Love has a way of binding us together and making separations difficult. Paul wrote to the Colossians about compassion, kindness, humility, gentleness, and patience but stressed love above them all. "And over all these virtues put on love, which binds them all together in perfect unity" (Colossians 3:14).

Still on the move, Paul's first stop was Tyre where his ship was to unload its cargo. Luke then reports,

> Finding the disciples there, we stayed with them seven days.
> Through the Spirit they urged Paul not to go on to Jerusalem.
> But when our time was up, we left and continued on our
> way. All the disciples and their wives and children accom-
> panied us out of the city, and there on the beach we knelt to
> pray. After saying good-by to each other, we went aboard the
> ship, and they returned home (Acts 21:4-6).

When I was a fledgling Navigator on my first assignment, I received a letter from Dawson Trotman. He signed the letter,

"In the Bonds, Daws." I had never seen a letter signed like that before. Daws was communicating something important. We were not just united in an organization—there was something deeper. He did not look on me as a cog in a machine, but as a person with whom he was united by the Spirit of God in the bonds of the love of Christ.

There would be far fewer problems in Christian work if our ministers, missionaries, Christian workers, and laymen and women were all united in the love of Christ rather than a denomination, doctrine, purpose, or organization. Unity on a superficial level may quickly give way to disunity.

Tyre was known as a market place for the world. It was high on Paul's priority list. If strong, robust disciples could be developed in Tyre, their influence would be felt around the world. All too often we are caught up in the opportunities or difficulties of the moment and forget to see how they fit into the big picture. Does this activity contribute directly to the evangelization of the world? Does this plan help us train the most disciples in the best way and in the least amount of time? Paul clearly kept these things in mind and structured his ministry accordingly.

Leadership

Paul was not an inspector coming to unearth some minor difficulties and major on them for a week, or a cold supervisor coming to square them all away with a heavy hand and brittle logic. He was a man whom they loved.

A leader must do two things with people. First, he must treat them like disciples of Christ and help them in their spiritual life and ministry. He must bolster them in their doctrine and sharpen them in their service for Christ. Second, he must also treat them like human beings and meet their personal needs. He may spend an entire day teaching them how to do Bible study, but if a person is thinking about his financial problems or a sick child, it will all be to no avail. Leaders must help those they work with to cope better with their work and their family life—in addition to training them spiritually.

Paul's next major step was Caesarea. This visit brought together an interesting group: Luke, Paul, Philip the evangelist, Philip's four daughters who had the gift of prophecy, and Agabus the prophet. What a gathering! Luke—the author of two New Testament books; Philip—who twenty years earlier served as a table waiter in the ministry at Jerusalem, and his four daughters who ministered the word; Paul—author of most of the New Testament, a great theologian and strategist; and Agabus—a man mightily used by God to minister to the needs of the church in Jerusalem.

Spiritual Gifts

This group illustrated the truth of Paul's words to the Corinthians:

> There are different kinds of gifts, but the same Spirit. There are different kinds of service, but the same Lord. There are different kinds of working, but the same God works all of them in all men. Now to each one the manifestation of the Spirit is given for the common good (1 Corinthians 12:4-7; see 12:8-31 also).

Each man and woman in that group had his or her own gift and calling from God. No individual was more important than any other in the sight of God. Keep that in mind the next time you are tempted to wish you were somebody else. The all-wise, all-loving God knows what he is doing. He made you the way you are, and he has placed you where you are for a purpose.

Philip was one of the most exciting members of the group. What a thrill to see him still going strong for the Lord. One wonders if the other members of his table-serving, dishwashing crew ended well. We know Stephen did, but how about the others? We can only hope they finished well too.

How to Keep Going

In Norway I visited two good friends, Dagfinn and Graethe Saether. We first met fifteen years earlier in Oslo, Norway.

During our latest visit someone asked Dagfinn what had kept him going all these years in the Christian life. Both he and his wife are still as fired up about their ministry and as deeply devoted to Jesus Christ as ever. Dagfinn's answer to the question was classic: "It has not been what I have done. Our endurance is not due to our enthusiasm or our perseverance. It is all a result of God's faithfulness." How true! Year after year Dagfinn and Graethe have basked in the warmth of God's love and faithfulness and their lives have been a radiant testimony to thousands. They are a trophy of God's grace and mercy. We can learn from their example. We too must trust God to keep us going and growing.

The words Agabus spoke to Paul at Caesarea are highly significant. Through his words Paul knew precisely what he was getting into by going to Jerusalem. Remember the Lord had already forewarned Paul of the dangers he would face. At the very beginning of Paul's Christian life the Lord promised, "I will show him how much he must suffer for my name" (Acts 9:16). Paul marched forward knowing full well what he was to face. After Agabus spoke, Paul replied, "Why are you weeping and breaking my heart? I am ready not only to be bound, but also to die in Jerusalem for the name of the Lord Jesus" (Acts 21:13). Paul was not taken by surprise. No doubt the most surprised people were the folk in Caesarea when Paul later returned to minister to them again (see Acts 23:23 and 24:23-27).

Let Him Decide

Acts 21:14 contains an interesting truth: "When he would not be dissuaded, we gave up and said, 'The Lord's will be done.'" There comes a time when we must simply say to a person, "Do what you must do." Even though it is obvious to us what the results will be, we must take our hands off and let him follow his course.

I was talking with a Christian leader who had been grooming a young man for an important role in the Lord's work in that country. One day the young man walked into his office and told him he was leaving the country and planning to marry a foreigner. The leader was shocked but kept his head and remained calm and collected. They talked this over for several weeks. The leader did everything in his power to help the young man see the far-reaching consequences of his decision. But the older man's efforts were all to no avail. So, when it became evident the young man would not be persuaded, the leader simply said, "The will of the Lord be done." Even though it made no sense and broke his heart, he simply trusted the Lord in the matter and committed it to him. This leader knew how to let go and trust God for the eventual outcome.

As usual, Paul took some disciples with him when he left for Jerusalem. "After this, we got ready and went up to Jerusalem. Some of the disciples from Caesarea accompanied us and brought us to the home of Mnason, where we were to stay. He was a man from Cyprus and one of the early disciples. When we arrived at Jerusalem, the brothers received us warmly" (Acts 21:15-17). Mnason was described as a mature follower of Christ. What did Luke have in mind when he described him as a mature disciple? What are the marks of maturity according to the Bible? If we examine the apostle Paul's prayers for the first-century believers, we will find the answer.

The Marks of Maturity
In his prayer for the Colossians, Paul reveals seven marks of a mature disciple. "For this cause we also, since the day we heard it, do not cease to pray for you, and to desire that ye might be filled with the knowledge of his will in all wisdom and spiritual understanding; That ye might walk worthy of the Lord unto all pleasing, being fruitful in every good work, and increasing in the knowledge of God" (Colossians 1:9-10, KJV).

He can discern God's will for himself. A mature disciple does not depend on others to guide him in every decision in life. How important it is for a leader to help people reach this stage of growth! Babies are dependent on others for everything. A mark of maturity is the ability to exercise discernment, initiative, and sound judgment. Paul prayed this for the young Christians he helped along the road to maturity.

His life is pleasing to the Lord. It is not just his spiritual life which honors the Lord, but also the so-called secular side of life as well. He not only maintains his integrity in the family of God, but he also walks wisely and conducts his affairs wisely among non-Christians.

His life is filled with good works. Although we are not saved by good works, we are brought to life in Christ to do them. I think of my wife in this regard. She has helped with a variety of good causes ranging from a Child Evangelism Good News Club to bring the message of salvation to the children in our neighborhood to giving her time calling door-to-door to collect money for the Heart Fund.

He has a deepening knowledge of God. Paul wanted this for himself and for others. This is where many fail. They learn much about how to work for Christ, but they fail to grow in their knowledge of God.

He keeps growing stronger in the Lord and in the power of his might. This is a must if we are to be victorious in our spiritual warfare. Weakness is not one of the attributes of God. We serve the Lord God *Almighty.* Admittedly, we are always weak in ourselves, but God's strength finds an outlet through our weaknesses. "But he said to me, 'My grace is sufficient for you, for my power is made perfect in weakness.' Therefore, I will boast all the more gladly about my weaknesses, so that Christ's power may rest on me" (2 Corinthians 12:9). Remember—it's God's strength, not ours (see Ephesians 6:10).

He displays steadfastness and patient endurance. This is certainly a mark of maturity—the will and the ability to keep going in spite of obstacles, difficulties, testings, tribulations, and hardships.

While I was watching my granddaughter play with her tricycle, she hit something on the driveway, got stuck, became frustrated, and cried for help. Her behavior was perfectly natural for a child. But when she becomes a young lady, all of that will change. Obstacles are challenges to overcome. Endurance is a sign that one is growing up.

He exhibits joyful thankfulness. The mature disciple is thankful for good experiences and difficult trials. He is joyful and thankful in everything (see 1 Thessalonians 5:16-18).

Philippians 1:9-11 adds four more marks of maturity. "And this is my prayer: that your love may abound more and more in knowledge and depth of insight, so that you may be able to discern what is best and may be pure and blameless until the day of Christ, filled with the fruit of righteousness that comes through Jesus Christ—to the glory and praise of God."

He abounds with love based on knowledge, common sense, and spiritual insight. It is easy to love those who are lovely, but difficult to love the unlovely. Abounding love, even for the unlovely, is a mark of maturity.

He can discern the best from the good. Paul longed to see growing Christians mature in their ability to put first things first. Children do whatever is put in front of them. They rarely follow an orderly plan of action. Something I was taught early in my Christian life has been very useful through the years. It is the simple practice of thinking through all you have to do in a particular day and numbering those activities in the order of their importance. Then you simply do those things according to your listing of priorities: first things first.

We all make such choices all the time. A student must decide if he should waste time in the student union playing ping-pong, or prepare for the test he must take tomorrow. The decision he makes reveals his level of maturity. A housewife has a floor to scrub, windows to wash, and a meal to prepare, but her favorite show is on television. Her decision will reveal her level of maturity. Paul prayed that the young believers he knew would discern what was best for them and do it.

He lives a sincere, pure life that gives no offense in anything. One of the pains of growing to maturity is cutting away old habits and practices from one's past. This is never easy, but when old habits disappear and new ones replace them, we are maturing.

He is filled with Christ's righteousness. This is quite different from the self-righteousness that fills the world. Becoming more and more like Jesus is an essential mark of maturity for any believer.

Paul's prayer in Ephesians 3:14-19 illustrates this same point.

> For this reason I kneel before the Father, from whom his whole family in heaven and on earth derives its name. I pray that out of his glorious riches he may strengthen you with power through his Spirit in your inner being, so that Christ may dwell in your hearts through faith. And I pray that you, being rooted and established in love, may have power, together with all the saints, to grasp how wide and long and high and deep is the love of Christ, and to know this love that surpasses knowledge—that you may be filled to the measure of the fullness of God.

Here Paul prays that the Christians in Ephesus would be strengthened in their inner beings. He wanted the Christians to strengthen their new spiritual natures while their old natures were becoming weak and anemic. The nature we feed the most will become strongest. The sinful pleasures, books, magazines, and movies that were once a part of our regular diet as non-believers must be replaced with Christian fellowship, prayer, and the word of God. When we begin to do this, it is both a mark of maturity and a means of growing stronger in the Lord. As we do this, Christ himself occupies more and more of the recesses of our hearts and we become **more** like him.

Peter provides us with another checklist on maturity.

> Make every effort to add to your faith goodness; and to goodness, knowledge; and to knowledge, self-control; and to self-control, perseverance; and to perseverance, godliness; and to godliness, brotherly kindness; and to brotherly kindness, love. For if you possess these qualities in increasing measure they will keep you from being ineffective and unproductive in

your knowledge of our Lord Jesus Christ. But if anyone does not have them, he is nearsighted and blind, and has forgotten that he has been cleansed from his past sins (2 Peter 1:5-9).

Here we are given a great promise. When these qualities are present and growing in our lives, we will be effective and productive in our knowledge of Christ.

As we consider these marks of maturity, we should ask ourselves some questions. Am I effective in my service for Christ? Am I unproductive? Is my knowledge of Christ growing daily? If not—go over Peter's list carefully and see which of those qualities is alive and well in your daily experience. If some are not, select one that needs the most work and pray over it. If possible, do a Bible study on it and ask God by his Spirit to enable you to apply to your life whatever he reveals to you.

As we think about what made Mnason a mature disciple, I'm sure that it was qualities like those mentioned by Paul and Peter that played an important part in his growth.

Immediately upon their arrival in Jerusalem, Paul and his companions went to see the brethren. "When we arrived at Jerusalem, the brothers received us warmly. The next day Paul and the rest of us went to see James, and all the elders were present. Paul greeted them and reported in detail what God had done among the Gentiles through his ministry" (Acts 21:17-19).

Paul's report was not filled with what he had done, but with what *God* had done through his ministry. This is something more than just a technical point or a way of showing humility: it is an important key to walking in the joy of the Lord. The burden of striving for personal success is lifted. We are free. It is God's work. With glad, eager spirits we simply let him accomplish what he wants to accomplish through us. If we can learn to do that, life becomes much more pleasant, and, I might add, much more productive.

After listening to Paul's report, the brothers described a problem to him and suggested a possible solution (see Acts

21:20-26). Paul had a great hunger to see the work of Christ done in peace and harmony; so he agreed. He knew the unity of the Spirit and the bond of peace would not be achieved without effort.

Maintaining unity and peace is one of the leader's responsibilities. Quite often it takes much prayer and effort to keep peace among colaborers. Causing dissension in the ranks is one of the devil's typical and most common methods of attack. Satan's work will go on unhindered if he can get the Christian forces to battle with each other. Therefore, the believers were willing to go to great lengths to maintain peace and unity.

The disciples' very efforts to ensure peace among the brethren, however, sparked a riot among the Jews.

> When the seven days were nearly over, some Jews from the province of Asia saw Paul at the temple. They stirred up the whole crowd and seized him, shouting, "Men of Israel, help us! This is the man who teaches all men everywhere against our people and our law and this place. And besides, he has brought Greeks into the temple area and defiled this holy place." (They had previously seen Trophimus the Ephesian in the city with Paul and assumed that Paul had brought him into the temple area.) The whole city was aroused, and the people came running from the temple, and immediately the gates were shut. While they were trying to kill him, news reached the commander of the Roman troops that the whole city of Jerusalem was in uproar. He at once took some officers and soldiers and ran down to the crowd. When the rioters saw the commander and his soldiers, they stopped beating Paul (Acts 21:27-32).

The Asian Jews who knew and hated Paul spotted him in the temple and assumed he had brought one of his friends there and had polluted the place. Again we are reminded of how distorted the people's view of the temple had become—they did not think of it as a house of prayer for all people. So they attacked Paul and tried to beat him to death.

The commander in charge quickly moved in with his men and stopped the attempted murder.

Then an incredible thing happened. Paul seized this as a witnessing opportunity! Imagine that! There was a wild, bloodthirsty mob screaming for his death. They had beaten him. The air was filled with hatred and violence. But Paul viewed his attempted murder as an open door for preaching the gospel and giving his testimony. He certainly had a battle mentality. While most of us would have fled for our lives and taken comfort in our rescue by the soldiers, Paul saw it in a completely different light. He saw this fanatical mob screaming for his execution as an opportunity to give a word of personal testimony. Acts 21 ends with Paul ready to speak to the people.

SUMMARY:

Paul displayed the marks of a mature disciple. His life yielded to whatever God might bring forth, Paul went to Jerusalem—
- ministering to the church along the way;
- committed to peace and unity among the believers;
- ready to preach the gospel at any opportunity.

22
Paul's Last Message in Jerusalem:
A Guide for Witnessing

A STRANGE HUSH fell over the crowd when Paul began to speak. They became very quiet. Just before he spoke they were in a mad frenzy, emotionally out of control, and bent on murder. Now they were absolutely silent listening to the man they had wanted to kill. Why? Let me suggest four reasons.

The power of God. It may have been God's supernatural power at work as he made one more attempt to reach the people of Jerusalem with his message of salvation. The Lord had a willing witness on the scene ready to speak, so he quieted the crowd to make it possible for Paul to witness. But how did God do that? First, we are told they became quiet when they heard Paul speak in their own language.

One summer our oldest son, Larry, worked on a ranch which had a program for teenage evangelism. At the end of the summer one of the staff at the ranch called me and said Larry had led more of the teenagers to Christ that summer than anyone on their staff. Larry had the wonderful ability to move alongside a teenager and win his friendship and confidence so he could share the gospel in an interesting, winsome way. Many gave their hearts to Christ through his witness.

The senior staff was more experienced, but Larry had the advantage of being closer to the teenagers in age. He spoke their language. He knew their pop music heroes and identified with them easily. The effective witness will be the person who understands and identifies with those to whom he witnesses. A factory worker in Birmingham, Alabama, would not normally be as effective in sharing the gospel with a Montana cattleman as would another cattleman.

The way Paul spoke. When Paul said, "Brothers and fathers," there may have been a certain tone in his voice that made them listen. We have already seen Paul's great love for these people. When a person witnesses to someone he loves, his message comes across differently than when he is witnessing to a stranger. When a girl talks to her mother about the plan of salvation, it will be different than when she is discussing Christ with her history teacher at college. Her words may be essentially the same, the message is not changed, but the way it is delivered will be different. In Acts 22 Paul was speaking to a people for whom he was greatly burdened. His audience may have sensed his love and concern for them.

People recognize the ring of truth. As Paul continued his testimony, the people remained quiet. There is something about a man who tells the truth that commands attention.

I have sensed this in my own witness. When I talk with individuals about their need for Christ, and share Christ's love for them, they listen. When I share about his death on the cross, people listen attentively. I have talked to people who claim to believe nothing, but who listen carefully when I tell them Christ loves them, wants to enter their lives, forgive their sins, and give them a new life. I have never heard anyone laugh at the gospel message.

But imagine what would happen if I told a group of collegians that the Easter bunny was standing at the door of their heart, knocking, and waiting to be invited in. They would laugh, of course. Why? Because they don't believe in the Easter bunny. Why don't they laugh when I tell them Christ is there? They claim they don't believe in him either. But somehow, when they are confronted with his presence and love they listen quietly. They sense the ring of truth.

I spoke to a gathering of students at the University of Auckland in New Zealand. Some of the students had advertised the meeting, and when I arrived in the lecture hall hundreds of students were pouring into the room. I was nervous. *What if they heckle me?* I thought. *What if someone disrupts the meeting? What if? What if?* My mind began conjuring up all sorts of things. Finally I was introduced and I went to the podium. A hush fell over the meeting.

At first I thought they were putting me on. Usually one must spend some time getting the audience's attention in such a meeting. But those students literally leaned forward in their seats, waiting to hear what I had to say. I was startled and for a moment I thought there was a conspiracy to demonstrate an apparent interest, only to break up the meeting a few minutes later. But they continued to listen earnestly throughout my address. I shared God's word and very carefully explained to them how they could be born again. They listened to my whole lecture with an amazing level of intensity. They, too, sensed the ring of truth.

A farewell speech commands attention. Paul's words may have been delivered in an unusually urgent tone of voice if he sensed this would be the last time he would ever speak to his fellow Jews in the Holy City of Jerusalem. This was a very memorable occasion for Paul. There is something about a person's farewell speech that makes it very different from any other. A professor who has taught the same class for years senses something unique when he approaches his desk to teach his students for the last time. An inaugural address has a distinctive ring to it, but a farewell address has a greater emotional intensity about it. It is often more memorable because of its greater depth of feeling. The people may have sensed this and listened more intently than usual.

Paul had not lost his faith in God's power to convert the people of Jerusalem. There is an urgency connected with witnessing to loved ones. If they do not respond immediately, it may seem as if they will *never* respond. It is easy to become discouraged—to lose hope—to wonder if the devil has won the battle. But notice Paul's eagerness to share the gospel with them one more time. He did it with the air of a man who believed God would work.

I visited a young friend's home in Great Britain. As his mother served us afternoon tea, I caught the young man's longing for his mother's salvation. He had known Christ for about six years, but there had been little response on the part of his parents. But he has not given up. He makes frequent trips home from his work in Birmingham. He keeps them up to date on his activities and demonstrates his love to them. He is confident that God will one day break through their shell of complacency and bring them to himself.

We can learn much from Acts 22 about being an effective witness for Christ. Paul identified completely and thoroughly with the Jews. The first thing Paul did was to make them understand that he was a thorough-going Jew. "I am a Jew," he said, "born in Tarsus of Cilicia, but brought up in this city. Under Gamaliel I was thoroughly trained in the law of our fathers and was just as zealous for God as any of you are today" (Acts 22:3). This is a great witnessing principle. The witness must not stand aloof. I saw this demonstrated early in my Christian life and it made a lasting impression on me.

While I was a student at Northwestern College in Minneapolis, Minnesota, every week I went down to skid row to witness with a team of students at a rescue mission. We would sing, testify, and present the gospel. Men would come forward to accept Christ. I observed a difference between the staff of the mission and the students who visited each week. When we counseled with a man, we were very much aware of his untidy appearance. But the staff of the mission knelt with the man, and put their arms around his shoulders, despite the smell of liquor, or the sweat.

The greatest act of identification ever recorded is the incarnation of God's Son described by John in the first chapter of his Gospel:

In the beginning was the Word, and the Word was with God,
and the Word was God. He was with God in the beginning.
Through him all things were made; without him nothing was
made that has been made. In him was life, and that life was
the light of men. . . . The Word became flesh and lived for a
while among us. We have seen his glory, the glory of the one
and only Son, who came from the Father, full of grace and
truth (John 1:1-4, 14).

When the Son of Man came among us, touched us, loved
us, wept for us, healed us, and gave himself for us, he identified with us totally. Paul completely identified with his audience and communicated his kinship with them.

The next thing we see is Paul's conciliatory manner. He
quickly commended them for their zeal for God. Amazing! He
put their attempt to murder him in the best possible light. He
did not scathe them with harsh words about the riot and attempted murder, but he soothed them with words carefully
chosen to calm them down so they might listen to the message
of Christ. To calm them, he remained calm. He complimented
them. Paul's talk was warm and courteous. He was generous.
He equated their fanaticism and frenzy with zeal and dedication to God. Paul assured them he understood completely. He
was always loving and gracious in his witness.

In another obvious attempt to calm their spirits and win a
hearing, he referred to the Christian faith in the term used by
the Jew. He called it "the Way." He said, "I persecuted the
followers of this Way to their death, arresting both men and
women and throwing them into prison" (Acts 22:4). He left no
stone unturned in his attempt to get them to listen.

Certain terms have either a calming or an explosive effect
on the hearers. In some circles using words like *saved* or *born
again* is helpful, while in other groups it might be better to
talk about following Christ or serving the Lord and explain
what repentance and faith involve. Know your audience.
Know what will communicate effectively and what will not.
There is no sense using a term that will provoke your hearers.

Your mission is to get them to listen—not to argue.

Paul then reminded his audience of something they might already have known. After mentioning the arrests he added, "as also the high priest and all the council can testify. I even obtained letters from them to their brothers in Damascus, and went there to bring these people as prisoners to Jerusalem to be punished" (Acts 22:5). Some of the members of his audience might even have been there twenty years before when he left Jerusalem for Damascus. In any event, Paul said, it was common knowledge at the time. Then he described the event which was the greatest turning point in his life.

> About noon as I came near Damascus, suddenly a bright light from heaven flashed around me. I fell to the ground and heard a voice say to me, "Saul! Saul! Why do you persecute me?" "Who are you, Lord?" I asked. "I am Jesus of Nazareth, whom you are persecuting," he replied. My companions saw the light, but they did not understand the voice of him who was speaking to me. "What shall I do, Lord?" I asked. "Get up," the Lord said, "and go into Damascus. There you will be told all that you have been assigned to do." My companions led me by the hand into Damascus, because the brilliance of the light had blinded me. A man named Ananias came to see me. He was a devout observer of the law and highly respected by all the Jews living there. He stood beside me and said, "Brother Saul, receive your sight!" And at that very moment I was able to see him. Then he said, "The God of our fathers has chosen you to know his will and to see the Righteous One and to hear words from his mouth. You will be his witness to all men of what you have seen and heard. And now what are you waiting for? Get up, be baptized and wash your sins away, calling on his name" (Acts 22:6-16).

In his testimony Paul highlighted three things:

First, he saw a light and heard a voice from heaven. Paul knew that the Pharisees definitely believed in visions and revelations from God. Once again he spoke within a framework which they could accept. Paul said the only reason he had gone about teaching and preaching his message was because the word had come to him from heaven.

Second, he explained he was simply acting in obedience to what God had told him to do. It was not his choice, but God's. Since God had spoken, he had no choice. This was another point on which his listeners could agree. Men must obey the word of God.

Third, Paul focused on the fact that God's command had been given to him through the revelation of Jesus Christ. Paul knew that everything he said—everything he did—stood or fell based on the truth of the death, resurrection, ascension, and revelation of the Lord from heaven. It was the one thing that gave his life validity. Without it, his view of life was wrong. His hope of eternal life was false. His preaching was a lie. His life's work was based on an unsound foundation. His apostleship to the Gentiles was of human origin. All of his life and ministry depended on the truth of the revelation of Jesus Christ that came to him on the road to Damascus.

As Paul explained his conversion to the Jews, he gave some insight as to why the others who were traveling with Paul on the road to Damascus were not converted (see Acts 22:9). While they saw the light he saw, they did not hear the voice he heard. They may have heard something, but they did not hear the message. Paul's experience, and his companions' inability to hear the voice which spoke to him, was similar to an incident which occurred during Jesus' ministry.

Jesus said, "Now my heart is troubled, and what shall I say? 'Father, save me from this hour'? No, it was for this very reason I came to this hour. Father, glorify your name!" Then a voice came from heaven, "I have glorified it, and will glorify it again." The crowd that was there and heard it said it had thundered; others said an angel had spoken to him" (John 12:27-29). They heard, but they did not truly hear. Since faith comes by hearing, not by seeing, the people with Paul were not converted. Here is another guideline for witnessing for Christ. Make sure people actually hear your words and understand what you say. Often some members of an audience hear a speaker's voice but do not hear his words distinctly. Use familiar terms and speak in a way that will make them want to listen.

In Acts 22:12 Paul told them that his first steps in this new life were guided by Ananias, a devout man who observed the law, and had a good testimony among the Jews. Paul's initial encouragement to follow Christ did not come at the urging of a Gentile, but through Ananias, a Jew. Paul majored on the facts that would keep his audience with him.

As Paul developed his testimony, he tried to explain that he had not deserted the Jewish religion but was simply following God's command to take this message to *all men*. In fact, Ananias had told him, "The God of our fathers has chosen you to know his will and to see the Righteous One and to hear words from his mouth. You will be his witness to all men of what you have seen and heard" (Acts 22:14-15). Paul's ministry was a result of God's appointment and in accordance with his will. He had seen the just one— Christ—and had heard his voice. Paul's ministry was to "all men"—Greeks, barbarians, Jews, Gentiles, wise and unwise, bond and free.

By this time I am sure the apostle Paul was much encouraged. He had told them of his religious background and they had listened. He had told them of his conversion to Jesus Christ and they had listened. But the atmosphere changed.

> When I returned to Jerusalem and was praying at the temple, I fell into a trance and saw the Lord speaking. "Quick!" he said to me. "Leave Jerusalem immediately, because they will not accept your testimony about me." "Lord," I replied, "these men know that I went from one synagogue to another to imprison and beat those who believe in you. And when the blood of your martyr Stephen was shed, I stood there giving my approval and guarding the clothes of those who were killing him." Then the Lord said to me, "Go; I will send you far away to the Gentiles." The crowd listened to Paul until he said this. Then they raised their voices and shouted, "Rid the earth of him! He's not fit to live!" (Acts 22:17-22).

Paul may have been on the verge of reminding them of his love and reverence for the "holy place" which they thought he had profaned. He had arrived in Jerusalem and gone to the temple to pray. While he was praying in the temple in the midst of Jerusalem, God's call came to Paul—not in some obscure part of the world. Here, in Jerusalem, God had told him to go and preach to the Gentiles. However, when they heard of his call to the Gentiles, the people's mood changed dramatically. Even mention of the Gentiles drove them into a rage.

Naturally, since Paul was speaking Hebrew, the commander of the Roman troops had no idea what was happening. All he saw was a sudden outpouring of emotion. So he acted promptly.

> As they were shouting and throwing off their cloaks and flinging dust into the air, the commander ordered Paul to be taken into the barracks. He directed that he be flogged and questioned in order to find out why the people were shouting at him like this. As they stretched him out to flog him, Paul said to the centurion standing there, "Is it legal for you to flog a Roman citizen who hasn't even been found guilty?" When the centurion heard this, he went to the commander and reported it. "What are you going to do?" he asked. "This man is a Roman citizen." The commander went to Paul and asked, "Tell me, are you a Roman citizen?" "Yes, I am," he answered. Then the commander said, "I had to pay a big price for my citizenship." "But I was born a citizen," Paul replied. Those who were about to question him withdrew immediately. The commander himself was alarmed when he realized that he had put Paul, a Roman citizen, in chains (Acts 22:23-29).

The words, "I am a Roman," were revered and honored all over the world—even among barbarians. They guaranteed protection and exemption from being thrown into jail. So Paul avoided a merciless scourging, not because he was afraid of pain, but because in all likelihood it would have killed him. He had been severely beaten by the mob, and another beating at this time would probably have ended his life. Paul demonstrated that suffering for the sake of suffering is not a Christian virtue. The commander immediately released Paul from his bonds and took steps to get at the truth. "The next day, since the commander wanted to find out exactly why Paul was being accused by the Jews, he released him and ordered the chief priests and all the Sanhedrin to assemble. Then he brought Paul and had him stand before them" (Acts 22:30).

SUMMARY:

Paul's last message to the people of Jerusalem gives us a guide for witnessing.
- Rely on God.
- Relate to the audience.
- Show compassion toward them.
- Share the truth about the life, death, and resurrection of Jesus Christ.

23
Demonstrating God's Love

PAUL WAS TAKEN before the high priest. The last time he had seen the high priest, Paul was his hatchet man. "Saul was still breathing out murderous threats against the Lord's disciples. He went to the high priest and asked him for letters to the synagogues in Damascus, so that if he found any there who belonged to the Way, whether men or women, he might take them as prisoners to Jerusalem" (Acts 9:1-2).

However, now Paul was the one who was bound in Jerusalem for his allegiance to the name of the Lord Jesus. The tables were turned. But Paul was far happier on this occasion, in spite of his chains. He had discovered life in all its fullness in Jesus Christ. He was no longer Saul of Tarsus but "Paul, a servant of Christ Jesus, called to be an apostle and set apart for the gospel of God" (Romans 1:1). He now had a new name, a new calling, and a new life.

Why was Paul so determined to bring the message of hope to the members of the Council? This was the fifth opportunity that God had given them to hear the message of Christ. They had already heard it from Jesus himself. "Every day he was teaching at the temple. But the chief priests, the teachers of the law and the leaders among the people were trying to kill him. Yet they could not find any way to do it, because all the people hung on his words" (Luke 19:47-48).

The Council heard the message during their encounter with Peter and John following the incident with the lame man at the Beautiful Gate of the temple. They had heard the apostles (see Acts 5:27-32). They had listened to Stephen's testimony, and now they listened to Paul. Was he determined to give these people another opportunity to hear the truth because they were such wonderful, loving, kind, and generous people? No. The Sadducees were hard, unprincipled dictators. They were motivated by greed, cruelty, and a craving for power. The temple priests received tithes from the people, but the Sadducees stole them. The members of the Council were powerful, brutal, lawless rascals who robbed the ordinary priests and cheated the common man. Paul knew all of this and yet he gave himself unreservedly to the work of bringing them the message of love, hope, and salvation.

What about the Pharisees? Possibly Paul's determination to take the gospel to them arose from his knowing them so well. After all, he was one of them. Were they people whose lives were filled with virtue—kindness, love, mercy, and generosity? Certainly not! The Pharisees were hypocrites of the worst kind. They imposed rules on people that made life unbearable, but they refused to bear the heavy burdens they imposed. Everything they did was done to win the praise of men. They craved positions of honor and prestige. Secretly they stole from the helpless, from widows, the weak, and the unprotected. But in public they were known for their long prayers. They made much of incidentals, but completely neglected the truly great principles of their religion—justice, mercy, and faith. They were like a serving bowl that is clean on the outside but filthy inside. The Pharisees were a proud, self-indulgent, self-centered gang of hypocrites.

Following Christ's Example
Paul knew all this. Why, then, did his spirit burn to bring to

them the message of redemption? Why was he willing to suffer and bleed to do this? Even the Gentiles to whom he
ministered were no more filled with peace and love than were
the Sadducees and Pharisees. The Gentiles were also a
murderous, immoral people. Yet Paul was willing to bleed
under the whip, willing to go without food and sleep, willing
to travel hundreds of miles by land and sea, willing to spend
and be spent for an undeserving people. Why? Because he was
a follower of Christ—who had left him an example. As Paul
wrote, "You see, at just the right time, when we were still
powerless, Christ died for the ungodly. Very rarely will
anyone die for a righteous man, though for a good man
someone might possibly dare to die. But God demonstrates
his love for us in this: While we were still sinners, Christ died
for us" (Romans 5:6-8).

On some occasions a man will give his life to save someone else. I'm sure many of the slaves freed after the Civil War
would have given their lives to save President Lincoln. But
would they have been equally as willing to sacrifice
themselves on behalf of the captains of the slave ships who
had forced them to leave their homes and families, confined
them to the hold of a ship, beaten them, starved them, and
treated them like animals? Of course not. But that is precisely
what Paul was willing to do.

When he wrote to the Romans, Paul said non-Christians
are powerless, or without strength, and ungodly. I once heard
an Anglican minister describe the root meanings of those
words. He said the term *without strength* was used to describe
a putrefying illness so foul that one could hardly dare to stay
in the same room as the one who was diseased. He added that
the word *ungodly* was a word used to describe one who is so
morally corrupt that no one could stand to be in his presence.

Rarely, thank God, do we meet anyone like that, but I
have a friend whose life once matched that description. He
had graduated from Georgetown University and joined the
Diplomatic Corps, but when the Second World War broke
out, he entered the Navy as an officer. His life was so corrupt

that when he went on liberty he avoided his friends so that he would not contaminate them with his foul and ugly way of life. However, someone eventually shared the gospel with him and his life was transformed by the power of Christ. When released from the Navy after the war, he graduated from one of the finest seminaries in America, and his life since then has born fruit for Christ on two continents. Today Bill is a trophy of the grace of God and a perfect example of the results of Christ's dying for the ungodly.

Helping the Hopeless

Let us set this incredible picture in a different context. Suppose you knew the person who had caused your grandmother's death by driving her from her home and robbing her of her only means of sustenance. What would your attitude toward that person be? Would you spend your fortune trying to show him kindness and love? Would you suffer beatings and the weariness of long and arduous travels? Would you give your life that he might live a life of joy and comfort? That is the picture of what Paul was doing. It stemmed from his love for Christ—the one who had shown him the way of self-denying love.

As Paul stood before the Council, an incident occurred that reminds us of the time when the high priest questioned Jesus about his disciples and his teaching.

> "I always taught in synagogues or at the temple, where all the Jews come together. I said nothing in secret. Why question me? Ask those who heard me. Surely they know what I said." When Jesus said this, one of the officials nearby struck him in the face. "Is that any way to answer the high priest?" he demanded. "If I said something wrong," Jesus replied, "testify as to what is wrong. But if I spoke the truth, why did you strike me?" (John 18:20-23).

The Authority of the Word

The servant is not above his Lord. If they struck the Lord Jesus without cause, they certainly felt free to do the same to one of his spokesmen.

> Paul looked straight at the Sanhedrin and said, "My brothers, I have fulfilled my duty to God in all good conscience to this day." At this the high priest Ananias ordered those standing near Paul to strike him on the mouth. Then Paul said to him, "God will strike you, you whitewashed wall! You sit there to judge me according to the law, yet you yourself violate the law by commanding that I be struck!" Those who were standing near Paul said, "You dare to insult God's high priest?" Paul replied, "Brothers, I did not realize that he was the high priest; for it is written: 'Do not speak evil about the ruler of your people'" (Acts 23:1-5).

In his reply Paul quoted from the book of Exodus. In doing this he clearly demonstrated that his life was governed by the authority of the word of God. This is an important point for the disciple to stress in both his life and his witness, for today there is a widespread rebellion against authority.

While speaking to a group of students at a university in the Netherlands, I stressed the importance of submitting to the authority of Christ and his word. Immediately, half a dozen of the students stiffened in their seats. They sat bolt upright and stared at me in amazement. They couldn't believe what they heard. So I amplified my statement. If their professor assigned a certain book to be read, they must read it. If their boss at work assigned a certain task to be done, they must do it.

It is no different with the word of God. When God assigns a certain task, we must march off and do it in obedience to Christ and his word. The apostle Paul was a man under authority. He was a man on a mission. His Lord had spoken and he obeyed his commands. He had been given the task of evangelism and he took it up wholeheartedly. Again, we see another of the foundation stones for a life of discipleship. The example is too clear to miss, and too important to take lightly. Wholehearted obedience to the word of God should mark every area in the life of a disciple.

The Lord's Encouragement

I am sure Paul was not pleased with the outcome of his interview with the Sanhedrin. No doubt he was somewhat dejected and discouraged. So the Lord gave him a special and somewhat unusual word of encouragement: "The following night the Lord stood near Paul and said, 'Take courage! As you have testified about me in Jerusalem, so you must also testify in Rome'" (Acts 23:11).

It is interesting to note why God encouraged Paul. The Lord still had work for him to do. Humanly speaking, we might have expected the Lord to say, "Cheer up, Paul. Soon it will all be over. Shortly you can retire to a pleasant villa overlooking the Mediterranean Sea and spend the remaining years of your life enjoying a well-earned rest." But no. His word was, "Cheer up, there are still many miles left to travel and much work still to be done."

When you think about it, this makes sense. Jesus had performed his most important work during the last moments of his life. He did not come to earth, teach the multitudes, train the apostles, and then spend his last years in retirement. His greatest act was his death on the cross and his resurrection. Should we expect something different? I doubt it. He has work for all of us, all along the way. The setting may change, but the work of winning the lost and helping people to grow in grace goes on.

So God continued to protect and encourage Paul, but the Jews did not give up. Since they could not get the job done by legal means or by mob action, they cooked up a plot based on lies and deceit that would lead to murder.

It is interesting to note how the plot was thwarted. On one hand was all the power of the Sanhedrin. On the other hand stood a small boy, one of Paul's nephews. The Lord used him to deliver Paul from the murder plot. When we read about that incident, it reminds us of Paul's comment to the Corinthians: "But God chose the foolish things of the world to shame the wise; God chose the weak things of the world to shame the strong. He chose the lowly things of this world and the despised things—and the things that are not—to nullify the things that are" (1 Corinthians 1:27-28).

God's ways are not our ways. Who would have thought of defeating the giant Goliath with one smooth stone shot from the sling of a shepherd boy? Who would have thought of defeating an entire army with a swarm of locusts? Who would have planned the redemption of the world through a baby born in a manger?

When you face what appear to be insurmountable odds, take heart. One person with God is a majority. The situation may look hopeless, but it is not. God will see you through and he will often use what appear to be insignificant and unusual means to accomplish his will.

The Obedience of Love
When the commander heard of the plot to murder Paul, he took action immediately. Why was he so determined to save Paul's life? Simply because it was his duty. Paul was a Roman citizen, so the commander had no choice. It was not Paul's moral character or his loving spirit that prompted his action; it was simply his responsibility to insure the safety of a citizen of Rome.

As we have seen, Paul responded in much the same way as the commander. Paul was a man on a mission. He was under orders from God. He had a duty to perform without hesitation or argument. He said, "I am obligated both to Greeks and non-Greeks, both to the wise and the foolish. That is why I am so eager to preach the gospel also to you who are at Rome" (Romans 1:14-15).

Frankly, in our time, we hear little about our responsibility to God. However, we should not carry out our responsibility merely from a sense of duty. Paul wrote, "For Christ's love compels us, because we are convinced that one died for all, and therefore all died" (2 Corinthians 5:14). Our love for Christ is what ought to compel us to carry out our responsibility to God.

Humanly speaking, it seemed that Paul's situation went

from bad to worse. He was about to fall into Felix's hands.
History tells us Felix was a cruel, greedy, and sensual man.
Once again the situation seemed dark. But God was in control.

SUMMARY:

Paul's life demonstrates why God was able to use him so
mightily.
- He gave himself to anyone—the ungodly, unlovely,
  and the unreceptive.
- He wholeheartedly obeyed the word of God.
- He was committed to the end—to a *whole* life of service, all because of his compelling love for the God
  who loved him and died for him.

24
A False
Accusation

WHEN THE JEWS arrived, they brought a lawyer and professional orator named Tertullus with them. It is interesting to
see how he described Paul: "We have found this man to be a
troublemaker, stirring up riots among the Jews all over the
world. He is a ringleader of the Nazarene sect and even tried to
desecrate the temple; so we seized him" (Acts 24:5-6).

Tertullus said Paul was a troublemaker. This was a very
accurate analysis of Paul's activities from one point of view.
Paul had a communicable disease—the gospel—and he spread
it wherever he went. He was like a plague except he spread
healing rather than sickness. The Lord's great desire for all of
us is that we might communicate the gospel as effectively as
an infected person spreads a communicable disease.

We should ask ourselves, "Why don't we do that? Why
are we not more actively communicating our faith in Christ?"
Often it is because we face two problems. Many of us are in an
isolation ward. We do not get out and about in society
witnessing for Christ. The only time most of us are vocal
regarding our faith is when we are with other Christians. Then
we freely testify to our love for the Savior, sing his praises, and

quote his word. But we are silent whenever we are among non-Christians. Although we know the gospel must be audible (for faith comes by hearing), we don't speak about the gospel in our contacts with the lost. We just do not spread the life of Christ to others.

Another problem is that many people have not caught the real thing. They have a few of the symptoms perhaps, but they are not true carriers of the transforming message. They know a few hymns, can quote a few Scriptures, can tell people when they were baptized or confirmed and when they joined the church, but they have not actually been born again. Millions are in this pathetic condition. They neither enjoy the temporal pleasures of this world nor the joys of eternal life. They are in a state of religious limbo. Since they have not caught the real thing, they certainly cannot spread it. Paul, on the other hand, was definitely a "troublemaker." He vigorously spread his new life in Christ to others wherever he went.

The second accusation made by Tertullus was inaccurate. Paul had not stirred up riots; his enemies had. The Asian Jews were continually dogging his heels and stirring up the people. Paul's constant comments regarding the resurrected Christ angered some, and their anger led to public disorder and bloodshed. But it was Paul's blood that was shed; it was Paul who was mistreated; it was Paul who suffered.

Third, Tertullus called Paul a ringleader. This meant he was the man out front who led the others. This was true. Paul was a leader in the finest sense of the word.

I spent the summer of 1978 in Europe. My first assignment was to speak for a week at a Navigator summer conference near Strasbourg, France. One hundred thirty-two newly converted, enthusiastic young French men and women attended and the Lord gave us a marvelous time together. The schedule showed that a meeting of the *Anamatures* would be held every morning at 7:30. I learned that the *Anamatures* were the discussion group leaders. This is the word from which our word *animation* is derived. The *anamature* is the person who brings the meeting to life. *What a great definition of leadership,* I thought; *the person who breathes life into a group.*

Following my time in France, I went to Norway, the Netherlands, and Great Britain. While in London, England, I had the privilege of listening to the Archbishop of Canterbury speak to a gathering of bishops from around the world. He said he felt the finest leader was a stimulator—someone like the French *anamature.* I listened with keen interest and went to my Bible later to verify that idea.

Two verses came to mind. One was 2 Peter 3:1: "Dear friends, this is now my second letter to you. I have written both of them as reminders to *stimulate* you to wholesome thinking." The other passage I thought of was Hebrews 10:24: "And let us consider how we may *spur one another* on toward love and good deeds." Both verses accurately describe the ministry of the apostle Paul. He kept people stimulated and on the move. He was definitely a ringleader.

When Paul began his defense, he started by setting the facts straight. Then, typically, he got right to the central issue. Yes, it was true that he was a Christian, a follower of the Way. He was a believer, one who believed all that was written in the law and the prophets. "However, I admit that I worship the God of our fathers, as a follower of the Way, which they call a sect. I believe everything that agrees with the Law and that is written in the Prophets" (Acts 24:14). This statement is important in the light of the widespread unbelief in the church today.

The Word of God

In New Testament times it was a virtue to be a believer. Now it is in vogue to be an unbeliever, a doubter. Today it is considered clever when someone picks and chooses what he will and will not believe. It is fashionable to say, "Yes, I go along with the Bible on that point. No, I do not go along with the Bible on this point." Whoever behaves like that sets himself up as a judge of the word of God. This is the opposite of Paul's approach to the Scriptures. He believed every word. Sometime ago I was accused of believing the Bible from cover to cover. However, that accusation did not go far enough; for I believe the cover, too, which says, "Holy Bible."

One of the keystones of faith, and a foundation for discipleship, is believing what the Bible claims for itself. It is the word of God. Instead of being selective in my belief in the word of God, I need to believe what Jesus said to his Father: "Your word is truth" (John 17:17). We must believe the Bible to be what it claims.

The Son of God
But not only that, we must also believe *Christ* to be whom he claims to be. "I am the way, and the truth and the life. No one comes to the Father except through me" (John 14:6). Jesus is the Son of the living God, the King of kings, and Lord of lords. Paul stated it clearly and beautifully to the Philippians in Philippians 2:10-11. "At the name of Jesus every knee should bow, in heaven and on earth and under the earth, and every tongue confess that Jesus Christ is Lord, to the glory of God the Father."

Faith in Christ and faith in his word are the twin foundation stones of discipleship. It is neither clever nor wise to think differently. Jesus himself said it was foolish: "How foolish you are, and how slow of heart to believe all that the prophets have spoken!" (Luke 24:25).

Spiritual Training
In Acts 24:16 Paul made a statement that needs to be applied in our day and age. He said, "So I strive always to keep my conscience clear before God and man." The word *strive* conveys the idea of hard work. It is often used to describe an athlete's training for an important event. As we examine this example from Paul's life, let's consider these questions: What can we learn from an athlete? What does an athlete do that applies to discipleship? What is there in an athlete's life that we can apply?

One passage of Scripture guides our thinking.

Do you not know that in a race all the runners run, but only one gets the prize? Run in such a way as to get the prize. Everyone who competes in the games goes into strict training. They do it to get a crown that will not last; but we do it to get a crown that will last forever. Therefore I do not run like a man running aimlessly; I do not fight like a man beating the air. No, I beat my body and make it my slave so that after I have preached to others, I myself will not be disqualified from the prize (1 Corinthians 9:24-27).

Compete to win. I am not competing with my brothers and sisters in Christ to see if I can be a better Christian by winning more people to Christ, or memorizing more verses than they do, or praying more hours, or reading my Bible more often. I compete with my own slothful nature, which fights me at every turn. I must gain the victory here through Jesus Christ. "But thanks be to God! He gives us the victory through our Lord Jesus Christ" (1 Corinthians 15:57).

Exercise self-control in everything. Here is the idea of a strict diet. University athletes eat at a training table. The cooks prepare nourishing foods which will build muscle and stamina instead of sluggish fat.

The disciple must learn to feed on the word of God. Paul wrote about "wholesome words, *even* the words of our Lord Jesus Christ" (see 1 Timothy 6:3, KJV). The Scriptures must be a staple ingredient in the disciple's diet. This is how a disciple becomes "nourished up in the words of faith and of good doctrine" (1 Timothy 4:6, KJV). Regularity in Bible study, prayer, worship, Christian fellowship, and witnessing all contribute to the well-being of the disciple. They provide him with a diet that leads to victory, not defeat.

Apply discipline. The athlete goes nowhere without rigorous discipline. Many boxers have come and gone, some honorably and some dishonorably. Those who did well were disciplined men. But occasionally the newspapers would print a picture showing a boxer in a bar drinking a beer with his friends before a fight. Usually such a man did not do well. His lack of discipline was his downfall. Discipline is also a mark of discipleship. You must learn how to "train yourself to be godly" (1 Timothy 4:7).

The simplest way to achieve a disciplined life is to think through what you believe God wants you to do with your life, then set some short-range goals to help you achieve your objectives. Break your goals down into simple daily practices, and then stick with them. Like Paul, you will find you must buffet your body and make it serve you. Discipline is not always pleasant, and many people hate it. It is easier to be an undisciplined person; but discipleship is not a matter of comfort or personal satisfaction.

The following passage also illustrates the kind of striving which Paul speaks of in Acts 24:15, and provides three more essentials for the disciplined Christian life: "Therefore, since we are surrounded by such a great cloud of witnesses, let us throw off everything that hinders and the sin that so easily entangles, and let us run with perseverance the race marked out for us" (Hebrews 12:1).

Throw off every sin and hindrance of any kind. No runner arrives at the starting line dressed in a heavy overcoat, a large pair of boots, and carrying a bulky pack on his back. When he prepares to run, he strips for action.

Many people do not run well as Christians because they are toting too much extra baggage. Jesus said, "Others, like seed sown among thorns, hear the word; but the worries of this life, the deceitfulness of wealth and the desires for other things come in and choke the word, making it unfruitful" (Mark 4:18-19). If you are going to do well in the race, there are things you must set aside and leave behind. There are sins that should be forsaken. There are weights that must be cast away.

Run with endurance. The race is not won in the first few seconds, but in its last moments. The competitors begin a long-distance event fresh and strong, but by the end of the long, grueling race, some begin to falter. Then endurance pays off. Weariness or pain is not an issue. Every runner experiences fatigue. The issue is endurance—who will make it over the long haul and finish well? Endurance is the result of a strict diet, propeɪ training, and the right mental attitude—this is as true in the spiritual realm as it is in the physical. Peter said, "Prepare your minds for action" (1 Peter 1:13). So when your flesh says "Give up," or "Give in," your mind must take charge and set your course to do what God wants.

Compete according to the rules. In sports there are both training rules and rules of competition. One rule that must be followed in discipleship training is to keep things in their proper perspective. When the new Christian takes his initial steps in discipleship, he does not fully understand everything. He may begin memorizing some verses, but it may be years before their full impact and blessing is realized. It may be difficult for him to rise for morning prayer, but later in life he will thank God it became a built-in routine in his first years as a Christian. Such disciplines are like learning athletic skills. The Christian may hurt now, but he will rejoice later. His lungs may burn and his muscles may ache, but if he stays at it and keeps his goal in view, all else is forgotten when he wins the race.

Competing according to the rules is just as important as training according to the rules. Those who do not obey the rules will be disqualified. Openness, honesty, daily confession of sin, and daily fellowship with God are the rules of discipleship. Purity of life, a walk of faith, and a standard of excellence are the marks of a disciple in action. Paul lived such a life: striving to finish, striving to win.

Paul's Audience with Felix

As we know, Felix was a clever man. He was well aware that the only "crime" of which Paul was guilty was being a dedicated Christian—and that was no crime. Other believers were not hassled by the Jews. Felix knew Paul should have been freed immediately. But, not wanting to offend the powerful Jews, Felix said he would wait until Lysias the commander arrived to get more facts. But Lysias never came.

Felix, of course, was in no hurry to discuss the case. The Jews knew they had a weak position so they were not anxious to press the matter. So there Paul sat.

Now we are introduced to Drusilla, Felix's wife. She was the daughter of Herod Agrippa, the man who slew the apostle James and tried to kill Peter. She was a Jewess and, quite naturally, she was curious about this new doctrine which was well known throughout the world. Paul knew Felix had taken Drusilla from her first husband. He was a skilled evangelist and preached the message of Christ so effectively that it stirred their consciences. He found an open nerve. Felix and Drusilla "listened . . . as he spoke about faith in Christ Jesus. As Paul discoursed on righteousness, self-control and the judgment to come, Felix was afraid and said, 'That's enough for now! You may leave. When I find it convenient, I will send for you'" (Acts 24:24-25).

Paul spoke to them about righteousness, temperance, and the mastery of fleshly appetites. He knew Felix was governed by tyranny and sensual lust. Felix and Drusilla wanted to be entertained and satisfy their curiosity, but instead they were convicted of their sin. This is a very clear passage which will guide us in our personal evangelism. Find the open nerve that leads to an individual's conscience and approach him along that road. It does little good to speak to anyone about something which he does not understand. But if we can speak to a real need, he is likely to relate to what we have to say.

Felix listened to Paul. However, he did not respond to his message. Instead he let Paul sit in the palace under arrest for over two years. What was Felix trying to do? For one thing, he was trying to make some money from the situation. "At the same time he was hoping that Paul would offer him a bribe, so he sent for him frequently and talked with him" (Acts 24:26). One of his basic motives was greed. Paul had told him that he was a courier of alms and offerings (see Acts 24:17). So Felix may have assumed Paul was either a rich man or one who had access to large sums of money. But Felix misread Paul; he didn't understand him. Admittedly, Paul could have tried to win his freedom by scraping up enough money to buy his way out of jail, but Paul was more interested in winning Felix to Christ than he was in winning his own freedom. He was a man on a mission, and Felix was his newest mission field.

The second reason why Felix kept Paul under arrest for two years was his craving for personal glory, popularity, and the adulation of the Jews. "When two years had passed, Felix was succeeded by Porcius Festus, but because Felix wanted to grant a favor to the Jews, he left Paul in prison" (Acts 24:27). He was a man-pleaser.

As we see these attributes in the life of Felix, we should take warning. Those qualities are not reserved just for sinners. They can also be found in the life of the Christian. Personal glory and selfish gain have been the downfall of some good Christian men. Paul's admonition in 1 Corinthians 10:12 is a timely reminder: "So if you think you are standing firm, be careful that you don't fall!"

SUMMARY:

Paul stood before Felix as a living testimony of what God can do with a man. He was a committed disciple—
- infected with the gospel—spreading it wherever he went;
- a leader—breathing life in everyone he met;
- a finisher—striving, enduring to reach the end a winner.

25
Paul on Trial

WHEN FESTUS TOOK over from Felix, he went to Jerusalem to become better acquainted with the people he was to govern. There he encountered the chief priests and Jewish leaders, who presented their charges against Paul (Acts 25: 1-2).

The Jews were doggedly determined to kill Paul. For two years they had been seething over their failure in previous attempts. So they tried another ploy. "They urgently requested Festus, as a. favor to them, to have Paul transferred to Jerusalem, for they were preparing an ambush to kill him along the way" (Acts 25:3).

Even today the enemies of the gospel remain undaunted in their purpose. They keep at it and do not give up easily. All too often they put Christians to shame. As a result, we are prone to quit. However, we should not be so easily deterred, for we have many promises in the word of God that should keep us praying, witnessing, loving, and reaching out in compassion to the lost.

Sowing in Tears
God has promised that our efforts for him will not be in vain

(see 1 Corinthians 15:58). The psalmist wrote, "Those who sow in tears will reap with songs of joy. He who goes out weeping, carrying seed to sow, will return with songs of joy, carrying sheaves with him" (Psalm 126:5-6).

This principle proved true in Jesus' ministry. He was a man of sorrows, but he persevered in his ministry to everyone around him. He wept over Jerusalem. He preached the word constantly. Paul was also filled with love and compassion: another marvelous example of the power of compassionate perseverance.

When things seem tough, pray without ceasing. That's the road to an assured victory. We may become weary, but we should always remember God's promise:

> He gives strength to the weary and increases the power of the weak. Even youths grow tired and weary, and young men stumble and fall; but those who hope in the Lord will renew their strength. They will soar on wings like eagles; they will run and not grow weary, they will walk and not be faint (Isaiah 40:29-31).

Dave Kraft, a friend who served with The Navigators in Sweden, told me about a Christian woman who had been praying for years for her children's conversion. Her daughter had married a young, successful businessman in Stockholm, Sweden, and the couple had a large, luxurious home and everything money could buy.

A friend offered the businessman a stack of discarded religious records. The businessman took some even though he was totally unfamiliar with religious music. One evening, after his children were in bed, he poured himself a drink and sat down to listen to his new record collection. He was intrigued. He liked the music and played the records night after night.

One night he dreamt that his phone rang while he was sleeping. In his dream he got up, answered the phone, and heard a voice on the other end of the line say one word before hanging up: "Decide." For seven nights he had the same dream. Each time he had followed the same routine. He went down to his basement, poured himself a drink, listened to his religious records, and went to bed. Always the dream was the same—a phone call and a voice saying, "Decide."

After a week the dream did not recur. A day or so later he was listening to his records again after having a little too much to drink. He called his mother-in-law—the Christian woman who had been faithfully praying for him and his wife for years—and told her about his dream. He asked her if she knew what it meant.

"Yes," she said. "Jesus is telling you to decide to invite him into your life to be your Savior and Lord." Immediately he hung up the phone, prayed, and invited Jesus into his life. He told no one what he had done.

Some weeks later Dave and Susan Kraft visited the businessman's home. As the evening progressed, Dave gave his testimony about how he had received Christ and asked the man if he had ever done that. To everyone's surprise, he answered positively and told his story. Dave was amazed. The man pointed over to his bar and said, "See, you can tell it has not been used for some time. I have stopped drinking." When he was alone with Dave he mentioned his concern for his wife, who was not yet a Christian.

Soon after their first meeting, however, through the Krafts' witness, the man's wife also became a Christian. God answered the persistent prayers of a mother who wouldn't give up.

As Paul again faced the schemes of the Jews, he did not despair or give up.

When the Jews asked Festus to bring Paul to Jerusalem, Festus denied their request. Why did he do that? He was new in the job, and it wouldn't have hurt to grant those important men a favor. So why did he refuse their request? Humanly speaking, there is no obvious answer. However, consider Proverbs 21:1: "The king's heart is in the hand of the Lord; he directs it like a watercourse wherever he pleases." God was guiding the events in Paul's life. He had not abandoned him. He was keeping a careful eye on the proceedings.

I went snorkeling for the first time among some coral beds off the island of Tioman in the South China Sea. As I swam back and forth over the beautiful coral and watched myriads of brightly colored tropical fish, I realized the fish were not aware that I was watching them. They kept swimming around oblivious to my observations.

My fish-watching paralleled the way God observes us on earth. We are often unaware that God in heaven is watching our every move, listening to our every word, and taking note of our every thought. The non-Christian usually doesn't think about this, and even the Christian can easily forget it. When our circumstances are bleak and hopeless, it is easy for us to become discouraged. We must remind ourselves that our God will never leave us or forsake us.

I was riding in a Volkswagen bus through the narrow, crowded streets of the Moslem section of a city in South Asia. The driver suddenly looked back over his shoulder and told my wife and me, "If we hit anyone, run for it. If we don't, the crowd will kill us." We were inching our way through a crowd of thousands. My first thought was, *How could we run to safety through such a crowd?* My second thought was, *God is watching over us. He can protect us in this situation.* So I prayed and committed the matter to him and enjoyed the sights.

When we reached our hotel safely, I was reminded of John 10:11 where Jesus said, "I am the good shepherd. The good shepherd lays down his life for the sheep." Jesus is no hired hand. He never leaves his sheep unprotected. God protected Paul. The king's heart was in the Lord's hands in Paul's day, and that is still true.

During his imprisonment Paul was protected by the omnipotent Son of God. As the story unfolds, we learn a lesson which is important for a life of discipleship.

> After spending eight or ten days with them, he [Festus] went down to Caesarea, and the next day he convened the court and ordered that Paul be brought before him. When Paul ap-

peared, the Jews who had come down from Jerusalem stood around him, bringing many serious charges against him, which they could not prove. Then Paul made his defense: "I have done nothing wrong against the law of the Jews or against the temple or against Caesar." Festus, wishing to do the Jews a favor, said to Paul, "Are you willing to go up to Jerusalem and stand trial before me there on these charges?" Paul answered: "I am now standing before Caesar's court, where I ought to be tried. I have not done any wrong to the Jews, as you yourself know very well. If, however, I am guilty of doing anything deserving death, I do not refuse to die. But if the charges brought against me by these Jews are not true, no one has the right to hand me over to them. I appeal to Caesar!" After Festus had conferred with his council, he declared: "You have appealed to Caesar. To Caesar you will go!" (Acts 25:6-12).

As a Christian, Paul was still under civil authority, and willing to stand trial. We must learn from his example. As Christians we should be especially careful to obey the law and bear a good testimony. We are subject to authority. We should be thankful for the way God has ordained obedience to the law within society. Paul himself wrote, "Everyone must submit himself to the governing authorities, for there is no authority except that which God has established. The authorities that exist have been established by God" (Romans 13:1). Paul applied this principle in Caesarea.

Another great principle emerges from the conversation between Festus and Agrippa in Acts 25:13-21. Consider Acts 25:16 in particular: "I told them that it is not the Roman custom to hand over any man before he has faced his accusers and has had an opportunity to defend himself against their charges." This principle should also govern our conduct. Never prejudge a person or an issue before you have obtained all of the facts. Whenever we have a question about a brother's conduct, we should never depend on second-hand evidence, no matter how reliable the source may seem to be.

Festus had been given information about Paul by the

highest religious body in the country, but he did not act upon that information. He insisted that the accused man have an opportunity to tell his story before his accusers. All too often we judge someone merely on another's word.

Jesus clearly taught us how to approach such an issue. "If your brother sins against you, go and show him his fault, just between the two of you. If he listens to you, you have won your brother over" (Matthew 18:15).

When Agrippa heard what Festus said, he asked to see Paul. So Festus arranged a meeting, and on the day of the hearing Agrippa and Bernice arrived with a great display of power and importance.

While I was visiting a country in Southeast Asia, the Crown Prince arrived at the hotel. He received a splendid welcome. In the restaurant, where breakfast was normally served in forty-five minutes, he was waited on immediately. People stood around him ready to light his cigarettes or to laugh at his jokes. When he left for the next town, a red carpet was run out to the waiting helicopter. The ceremony and pomp given to earthly rulers contrasts starkly with the manner in which the Son of God humbly entered this world, lived in it, and died in it.

Once again the scene was set for Paul to give a clear witness for Christ, only this time he would be addressing a king. Again we recall the Lord's promise: Paul was God's "chosen instrument to carry my name before the Gentiles and their kings and before the people of Israel" (Acts 9:15).

SUMMARY:

God took care of Paul. Paul displayed the hope and confidence of a true disciple: ultimately *God* is in charge. Paul—
- rested in the protection of Almighty God;
- persevered against determined opposition;
- totally submitted to the civic authorities on earth.

26
Paul's Testimony

A CASUAL OBSERVER of the early church might have concluded that the apostles were the greatest criminals alive. At one time Peter was imprisoned with sixteen guards assigned to ensure he didn't escape again. Paul was once escorted from Jerusalem by an armed guard of two hundred foot soldiers with seventy horsemen and the officers in charge of them. However, these men were not criminals; they were the leaders of a group which had turned the world upside down. Acts 26 reveals one of the secrets for Paul's great influence in this world.

When Agrippa gave him permission to speak, Paul said, "King Agrippa, I consider myself fortunate to stand before you today as I make my defense against all the accusations of the Jews" (Acts 26:2). Paul considered himself fortunate to be where he was, and glad to speak to Agrippa. He had been commissioned by Christ to spread the gospel far and wide, yet for the past two years he had languished in chains, unable to get on with the task that Christ had burned into his soul. He could have become a bitter man, complaining constantly. Instead, he was a happy man. He was pleased to be able to bear witness to his faith in Christ. He was glad to preach the gospel to such a gathering—King Agrippa and Bernice, the high-ranking officers, the leaders of the city, and Festus.

Paul was happy because he was sure Agrippa would understand what he was talking about. As Paul told Agrippa, "You are well acquainted with all the Jewish customs and controversies. Therefore, I beg you to listen to me patiently" (Acts 26:3). Paul's happiness did not depend upon his personal comfort, but upon his ability to get on with his work. He was a man on a mission with a marvelous opportunity to take one more step toward fulfilling his divine commission.

This is one of the reasons why there is so little joy in the world today. For most people, life has no meaning; nothing motivates them, nothing burns in their souls. For most people pleasure is only temporary. It comes and goes.

Flying from Los Angeles to Honolulu, Hawaii, I was studying the Bible and ran out of notepaper. A flight attendant found me some more paper, but after a couple of hours, I ran out of paper again. So I asked another flight attendant for some more paper. "I have a notebook you can use, but you've got to tell me what you are going to use it for," she said.

I smiled and said, "I am studying the miracles of Jesus."

"Are you a Christian?" she asked, beaming with excitement.

When I told her I was, she told me she had been born again four weeks earlier. Then she shared her testimony. "I can hardly wait for Sunday to come," she said, "because my brother wants to become a Christian and we are going to a church in Los Angeles where the pastor will speak about what becoming a Christian involves."

I was thrilled by her excitement for her new life. As I looked around the plane I thought about those two hundred people heading for one of the most beautiful cities in the world. They would stay in luxury hotels, enjoy the sun and surf on Waikiki beach, eat gourmet meals, and see many of the sights for which Hawaii is famous. Although the young flight attendant might have planned on many of those things also, they were not uppermost in her mind. Her happiness stemmed from her relationship with Christ, and her excitement revolved around her eagerness to see her brother become a Christian.

I know the pastor of a spiritually powerful church in Southeast Asia. A missionary from the West, he has served overseas for many years. Once his daughter became sick and a doctor mistakenly prescribed an incorrect amount of drugs. The overdose erased the girl's mind. Today, sadly, she is able to see and hear but remains mentally unconscious. That accident could have made her parents bitter and resulted in their departure from the country they work in. But they are still there, joyfully serving the Lord and having a powerful ministry.

Humanly speaking, that pastor should be an angry, disillusioned individual. But he is not. In spite of the heartbreak he and his wife have suffered, they carry on with radiant spirits. Their joy does not come from their circumstances; it comes from God. This is also what we see in Paul's life. His experience with whippings, prisons, hunger, close encounters with death, and angry mobs were all taken in stride. He went through such experiences with a joyful, positive spirit.

After his introduction to Agrippa, Paul then spoke about his background.

> The Jews all know the way I have lived ever since I was a child, from the beginning of my life in my own country, and also in Jerusalem. They have known me for a long time and can testify, if they are willing, that according to the strictest sect of our religion, I lived as a Pharisee. And now it is because of my hope in what God has promised our fathers that I am on trial today. This is the promise our twelve tribes are hoping to see fulfilled as they earnestly serve God day and night. O king, it is because of this hope that the Jews are accusing me. Why should any of you consider it incredible that God raises the dead? (Acts 26:4-8).

Basically, Paul spoke about two things: a hope and a promise. His hope in the resurrection of the dead, and the promise of salvation were the basis of all his preaching (see Acts 13:26-39). It is surprising that Paul was harassed for preaching exactly what the Jews believed.

Next he described his own activities as a persecutor.

> I too was convinced that I ought to do all that was possible to oppose the name of Jesus of Nazareth. And that is just what I did in Jerusalem. On the authority of the chief priests I put many of the saints in prison, and when they were put to death, I cast my vote against them. Many a time I went from one synagogue to another to have them punished, and I tried to force them to blaspheme. In my obsession against them, I even went to foreign cities to persecute them. On one of these journeys I was going to Damascus with the authority and commission of the chief priests" (Acts 26:9-12).

Paul had always been a man under authority with a specific commission. His authority and commission once came from the chief priests. When he stood before Agrippa, he was still a man under authority with a commission, but now he was under the authority of Jesus Christ to fulfill his commission. Paul told the king how the change happened.

> About noon, O king, as I was on the road, I saw a light from heaven, brighter than the sun, blazing around me and my companions. We all fell to the ground, and I heard a voice saying to me in Aramaic, "Saul, Saul, why do you persecute me? It is hard for you to kick against the goads." Then I asked, "Who are you, Lord?" "I am Jesus, whom you are persecuting," the Lord replied. "Now get up and stand on your feet. I have appeared to you to appoint you as a servant and as a witness of what you have seen of me and what I will show you. I will rescue you from your own people and from the Gentiles. I am sending you to open their eyes and turn them from darkness to light, and from the power of Satan to God, so that they may receive forgiveness of sins and a place among those who are sanctified by faith in me" (Acts 26:13-18).

As we read these words it is obvious that we do not witness simply to show God our gratitude for the salvation he has given us. We have no choice: we are saved to witness. Jesus Christ is worthy of the praise of every tongue in the universe. Like Paul, we have each been given a particular mission to fulfill. Not all of us will be missionaries like Paul, who traveled around the Mediterranean with the good news. But we can all be missionaries to the family next door, to our friends, and to our relatives.

Paul then told Agrippa how he had responded to Christ.

So then, King Agrippa, I was not disobedient to the vision from heaven. First to those in Damascus, then to those in Jerusalem and in all Judea, and to the Gentiles also, I preached that they should repent and turn to God and prove their repentance by their deeds. That is why the Jews seized me in the temple courts and tried to kill me. But I have had God's help to this very day, and so I stand here and testify to small and great alike. I am saying nothing beyond what the prophets and Moses said would happen—that the Christ would suffer and, as the first to rise from the dead, would proclaim light to his own people and to the Gentiles (Acts 26:19-23).

Paul did not want to disobey the Lord. He did not want to fight with God. Anyone who tries that is in for trouble. The sports fans remember the "Thriller in Manila," the fight between Ali and Frazier which first went one way, then another. The outcome was in doubt until the very end. But there is no doubt when someone is fighting with God. The person who picks a fight with God is sure to lose.

I heard about three men who lived in a lonely, remote part of the world. They were fanatical in their opposition to the gospel. They hated Christ and everything connected with the Christian faith. One of them had a powerful shortwave radio, and one day he heard a gospel program which captured his attention. He told his two friends about the program and they too listened out of curiosity. For more than a year they continued to listen to the gospel program.

Slowly but surely, their minds and hearts were transformed by the Spirit of God. Eventually they turned to the Lord Jesus Christ in faith and repentance. They ultimately concluded they should be baptized, so they set off to find the pastor of a church some miles away. When they arrived at his front door, they announced they wanted to be baptized. At first the pastor was afraid it was some kind of trick. He knew he could be jailed or even put to death if he had won the men over from their religion. But the Holy Spirit confirmed their testimony and they were baptized. They had fought with God, and God won.

As you study Acts 26 and examine Paul's bold testimony, you might ask, "Is it easy to witness? Is it easy to obey God?" I don't find either obedience or witnessing easy. Were those things easy for Paul? I don't think so, for he told Agrippa that after preaching about repentance "the Jews seized me in the temple courts and tried to kill me" (Acts 26:21). Preaching the gospel was not easy for Paul, but since his message was so crucial, Paul was compelled to pay the price.

Paul explained to Agrippa that his message rested on two foundations—repentance and faith on our part, and the death and resurrection of Christ on God's part. God has provided everything needed for our full and free salvation. Our responsibility is to repent and believe. Those were the twin threads in all of Paul's evangelistic efforts.

Paul said the followers of Christ are the true followers of Moses and the prophets. Peter also spoke about this to Cornelius: "All the prophets testify about him that everyone who believes in him receives forgiveness of sins through his name" (Acts 10:43). Paul said the message of Moses and the prophets was "that the Christ would suffer and, as the first to rise from the dead, would proclaim light to his own people and to the Gentiles" (Acts 26:23). This was the message Paul constantly gave everyone, small and great alike, all over the world—first in Jerusalem, and throughout Judea, and then among the Gentiles as well.

Here is the single greatest reason for Paul's remarkable influence in the world: he was never sidetracked from the God-given goal he pursued. The world could be falling apart around him with riots and turmoil, or he might be encountering opposition of all kinds, but he kept witnessing faithfully and methodically.

I was reminded of Paul during a visit to Sofia, Bulgaria. On May 24th, when we left our hotel, we discovered the entire city had gathered to celebrate Education Day. There was a giant parade. Huge pictures of Marx, Lenin, Engels, and numerous local officials were everywhere. Buildings were decorated with colorful banners. Street lamps were adorned with streamers and flowers. There were no cars to be seen for many blocks, only parade vehicles. There were marchers, dancers, farmers, workers, gymnasts, musicians, children waving pine branches, flags, pompoms, and streamers. Sofia was completely transformed into a carnival scene. Nothing looked normal.

Well, almost nothing. I glanced at a traffic light on the corner and watched it faithfully changing from green to amber to red to green to amber to red. All morning long, while the wild scene whirled about it, the street light kept on with its job of controlling the flow of traffic. *That is a perfect picture of the faithfulness of the apostle Paul,* I thought to myself. No matter if the whole world was in disarray, Paul kept on with his work.

Paul concluded his remarks to Agrippa by reminding the king that the events he spoke about were true and had been publicly observed by thousands of people. He also reminded Agrippa that everything he preached had been prophesied by the Jewish prophets of the Old Testament. When Paul finished his testimony, Festus and Agrippa both concluded that Paul was innocent of any crime. "Agrippa said to Festus, 'This man could have been set free, if he had not appealed to Caesar'" (Acts 26:32).

Throughout his testimony Paul addressed his remarks to King Agrippa. But at the conclusion he looked around the room and extended his invitation to all those there by saying,

"I pray God that not only you but all who are listening to me today may become what I am, except for these chains" (Acts 26:29). Paul excluded no one: his message was for everybody.

SUMMARY:

With an attitude of joy, Paul faithfully and fervently pursued his one mission in life: to reach one more person with the message of Jesus Christ—a message which includes—
- the hope of the resurrection;
- the promise of salvation;
- turning from the rule of Satan to the rule of God through faith in Jesus Christ.

27
How to Find God's Will

LUKE OPENS ACTS 27 by stating, "It was decided that we would sail for Italy" (Acts 27:1). Who decided that Paul and some other prisoners should sail for Italy? Although various men made arrangements for the voyage, the decision was really made by God. He had decided to send Paul to Rome (see Acts 23:11). Paul had a settled assurance, based on what God told him, that he would testify in Rome. Paul was confident this was God's will.

When I talk with Christians in various parts of the world, the subject of how to determine God's will always comes up. How do you discover God's will for your life?

First, we must recognize that God is far more interested in revealing his will to us than we are concerned about seeking it. He is far more interested in leading us than we are willing to be led. He wants to guide and direct his children and has promised to do that. We can rest in that assurance. God says, "I will instruct you and teach you in the way you should go; I will counsel you and watch over you" (Psalm 32:8). We can count on his guidance. But through what means does he guide us?

Circumstances

One obvious means of guidance in Acts 27 is the simple unfolding of circumstances. God made a promise to Paul and then step by step he arranged the circumstances which accomplished his will. So Paul boarded a ship bound for Rome.

God can guide us through circumstances by either opening or closing doors. In the summer of 1978 I had planned a series of evangelistic thrusts in Beirut, Lebanon, and Amman, Jordan. When I applied for a Lebanese visa in London, I was told I would have to wait many weeks because an outbreak of war in Lebanon had resulted in a tightening of the regulations. My schedule made it impossible for me to wait long, so Lebanon was closed to me. The man arranging my visit to Amman was in London, so I called him to discuss the arrangements. He told me the University in Amman had closed, so it would be better for me to postpone my meetings there. Then I talked with another friend who was considering inviting me to visit Cairo, Egypt to assist in his ministry. However, he proposed a visit at another time—when it could be combined with my travels to Beirut and Amman. As I put all of those facts together, it was obvious God had closed the doors and redirected my journey. I thanked him and accepted those circumstances as evidence of his will.

God's Word

Another way in which God reveals his will is through his word. A missionary to French students told me how he had felt called by God to minister in France. When he shared this with his friends, they discouraged him by saying French students were taken up with philosophical questions and other intellectual pursuits and not at all responsive to the gospel. But he continued to pray and seek the Lord's will.

One day God clearly spoke to him through the Bible. He was given a deep assurance by the Holy Spirit that he should serve in France. The passage he was reading contained a promise for a fruitful ministry. He learned to speak French and went to work.

After his first year he held a week-long conference for the converts. Thirty students attended. After his second year he held another conference and eighty-four students came. I was the speaker for the conference after his third year and one hundred and thirty eager, growing Christians came. God has blessed that missionary's outreach. As we discussed the reason for his fruitfulness, he quickly turned to the passage of Scripture God had given him and gave all the glory to God.

Godly Counsel

Another means the Lord has often used in my life to confirm his will is the counsel of godly men. Some years ago I became very discouraged. Nothing was going well, and I was thinking about leaving the work I was doing. I prayed about this for weeks but nothing seemed clear. I had almost decided to leave when I called an old friend, Rev. Ivan Olson, to discuss it with him. We talked for a long time. He shared some of his own experiences and encouraged me not to give up. As I review the years since then, I'm grateful for his wise counsel. God has frequently used the advice of godly counselors to show me his will.

Prayer

Prayer is a fourth means that God uses when we seek his will. While we were visiting Bombay, India, my son Randy had a severe stomach ache. It lasted two weeks, and we were quite concerned. He became very weak and lost a lot of weight. After continuing our jouney to Istanbul, Turkey, we visited a doctor who diagnosed a mild case of cholera and prescribed some medicine. He thought the illness would clear up in a few days. But it didn't. Instead, Randy got worse. By the time we reached Bucharest, Romania, I was thinking about canceling the rest of our six-month preaching tour to return home. One morning Virginia, Randy, and I had a lengthy time of prayer together and asked the Lord to show us what to do.

We located a medical clinic and set out. On our way we passed the American Embassy and decided to see if anyone there could help us. The Marine on duty referred us to the embassy nurse. She looked at the medicine Randy had, listened to our description of his illness, and took charge. She gave him a shot, prescribed some different medicine, and by the next day he had recovered. God led us to that nurse in answer to our prayers.

Whenever you want to determine God's will, use these four means: circumstances, godly counsel, the word of God, and prayer. Even as Paul was on his way to be tried in Rome, he was at peace because he knew he was in God's will. God had arranged all of his circumstances and assured him of his presence and guidance. Paul was on board a ship, sailing to his trial before Caesar, but he didn't forget his mission.

In Acts 27:2 Luke takes special notice of one of Paul's companions, Aristarchus. "We boarded a ship from Adramyttium about to sail for ports along the coast of the province of Asia, and we put out to sea. Aristarchus, a Macedonian from Thessalonica, was with us." Aristarchus was one of those who traveled with Paul (see Acts 20:4), and he was imprisoned with Paul in Rome (see Colossians 4:10).

Why did Aristarchus travel with Paul? He was one of those chosen by God to learn from the apostle. We have already observed Paul's method of training. He usually had a group of men with him wherever he went, just as Jesus was accompanied by the Twelve. No matter what else was happening, Paul was always sharing the new life in Christ with another individual. He was constantly seeking to introduce non-Christians to Christ, or to encourage and build up those who were already Christians. Even on his way to Rome, Paul never lost sight of the need to train men.

Experiencing God's Will
When Paul's ship left for Rome, Luke also noticed the special treatment the officer in charge gave Paul. "The next day we landed at Sidon; and Julius, in kindness to Paul, allowed him to go to his friends so they might provide for his needs" (Acts 27:3). We can only speculate why Julius did that, but it's pos-

sible he was among those who heard Paul give his testimony before Agrippa. Later, however, when Paul advised against making the journey (see Acts 27:10-11), the centurion did not take Paul's advice. There are many people like this. They respect men and women of God, but don't heed their counsel.

Both Paul and the master of the ship were experienced men of the sea. Paul had been shipwrecked three times. Both men were well aware of the dangers of the voyage. But they looked at it from different perspectives. The ship's master was personally involved. He wanted to deliver the cargo and be paid. Paul was thinking of the passengers' lives.

When you launch out on the sea of life, godly, unbiased counsel is valuable. It is also rare. All too often counsel is given solely with a view to benefiting the counselor. I have seen a pastor ask a young couple to leave a job and move to the city where his church is located to tie into his program. Such advice may be given more for the pastor's benefit than for the couple's sake. I have also seen a campus worker counsel a student to wait around after graduation and join in the campus ministry, not for the student's benefit, but for the good of the worker's program. Our first concern must be for the individual and his or her welfare and development.

Unfortunately, the centurion followed the ship master's advice, and soon those traveling with Paul realized they had set off in dangerous conditions.

> Before very long, a wind of hurricane force, called the "North-easter,' swept down from the island. The ship was caught by the storm and could not head into the wind: so we gave way to it and were driven along. . . . We took such a violent battering from the storm that the next day they began to throw the cargo overboard. On the third day, they threw the ship's tackle overboard with their own hands. When neither sun nor stars appeared for many days and the storm continued raging, we finally gave up all hope of being saved (Acts 27:14-15, 18-20).

When all on board realized their lives were threatened,

they began throwing their worldly goods overboard. People will gladly sacrifice material possessions to save their own lives. But discipleship involves a willingness to sacrifice personal belongings to save others. A life of discipleship calls for sacrificial giving so the gospel may be taken to those who live in darkness.

Although many of the passengers feared the worst, God never abandoned his servant. Paul reminded the crew that he had advised them not to leave Crete, and added that God had told him everyone would be kept safe. "Last night an angel of the God whose I am and whom I serve stood beside me and said, 'Do not be afraid, Paul. You must stand trial before Caesar; and God has graciously given you the lives of all who sail with you.' So keep up your courage, men, for I have faith in God that it will happen just as he told me. Nevertheless, we must run aground on some island" (Acts 27:23-26). Paul knew he belonged to God—"whose I am and whom I serve."

As the storm raged, Paul never lost his faith. God had spoken. He knew all would be well so he encouraged his companions not to lose hope. Paul knew he was safer on a storm-tossed sea, while living in the will of God, than if he was resting comfortably at home, living disobediently outside the will of God. When a Christian is where God wants him to be, he is safe in the Lord.

We must never rely on anything for our encouragement and safety except the Lord. If he places us in an environment that would be deadly for others, it will not be so for us. The power and assurance of his presence and guidance is always with us. God has said, "Never will I leave you; never will I forsake you" (Hebrews 13:5).

To demonstrate his faith, Paul ate some food.

Just before dawn Paul urged them all to eat. "For the last fourteen days," he said, "you have been in constant suspense and have gone without food—you haven't eaten anything. Now I urge you to take some food. You need it to survive. Not one of you will lose a single hair from his head." After he said this, he took some bread and gave thanks to God in front of them all. Then he broke it and began to eat. They were all encouraged and ate some food themselves. Altogether there were 276 of us on board. When they had eaten as much as they wanted, they lightened the ship by throwing the grain into the sea (Acts 27:33-38).

The marks of discipleship are portrayed in Paul's life time and time again. During the storm off Malta it was Paul who transmitted courage and hope to his fellow travelers. Luke reports the despair everyone felt: "We finally gave up all hope of being saved" (Acts 27:20). Apparently Luke included himself and other believers like Aristarchus. But one passenger never lost hope, and more importantly, he shared his hope with the others. It did not take a crowd, a simple majority, or even a small committee to turn the tide of despair. One man who believed and acted on his faith was all God needed. That is often the case.

When God wanted to deliver his people from bondage in Egypt, he selected Moses. When he wanted to save the human race from extinction, he called on one man—Noah. When he wanted to win a battle, he used one young man—David, a shepherd boy who defeated Goliath. But remember this: it is not the individual who is important, but God who wins the victory (see 2 Samuel 23:10). God simply needs a man or woman whose life is clean and useable. We are not the ones who do the work of God—only God can do that—we are merely channels, so our lives must be useable!

When I arrived in Oslo, Norway, I was met by two young men—Bjorn and Olov—who drove me to a camp where I would be speaking. On our way we stopped for dinner at a restaurant. When I ordered a soft drink Bjorn asked if I had ever tasted Norwegian water. He said it would be refreshing, pure and crystal clear. I could hardly wait to try some, and it was just as tasty as he described.

When we arrived at the old-fashioned mansion where I was to stay I quickly prepared for a night's rest. The next morning the thought of soaking in a hot tub of crystal-clear Norwegian water was delightful. I could hardly wait to fill the bath. But when I turned on the water I could hardly believe my eyes. The water was dark brown. I emptied the tub and tried again, but it only got worse. My hopes were dashed. The water was not the problem—the pipes were. They were filled with rust which contaminated the water. If we are to be fit for our Master's use, we must live lives that are clean and holy so we do not contaminate the message of Christ or keep the Holy Spirit from flowing through our lives.

When daylight came after everyone had eaten, the ship began to break up, and the centurion "ordered those who could swim to jump overboard first and get to land. The rest were to get there on planks or on pieces of the ship. In this way everyone reached land in safety" (Acts 27:43-44). God kept his promise. He never fails; his promises are always sure.

SUMMARY:

Even when things looked grim to others, Paul knew he was safe in God's will because—
- God had told him of his plan;
- God arranged all the circumstances;
- God assured him of his presence;
- God kept his promises as Paul acted according to his will.

28
Proclaiming the Kingdom of God

ACTS 28 SHOWS us that God provides abundantly! I don't think anyone traveling with Paul anticipated the warm welcome they received when they finally struggled ashore on Malta. All of them, including Paul, would have been satisfied just to feel the solid earth under their feet once again.

But God often does much more than we ever expect. Luke records that when they reached the island, the natives were unusually hospitable. "Once safely on shore, we found out that the island was called Malta. The islanders showed us unusual kindness. They built a fire and welcomed us all because it was raining and cold" (Acts 28:1-2). Who hoped for such a welcome? Do you think Paul or Luke or Aristarchus prayed for it? I don't think any of them did, but this incident shows us how God can take care of us.

Bob Taussig, a friend of mine, is a veterinarian. He was sent to Nigeria to teach at the University of Zaria. Bob and his wife, Mary, prayed that God would give them a personal ministry among the students during their time in Nigeria. God did far more than they ever expected.

Students lined up outside Bob's office seeking spiritual

help. When the Christian leaders in Nigeria planned a follow-up program after the Lausanne Congress on World Evangelization, they invited Bob to teach a workshop on how to help new Christians grow. Bob's ministry broadened significantly. God also gave him a marvelous opportunity to minister to the Fulani people, a nomadic tribe who had never before been reached with the gospel.

We must ask ourselves some direct questions: "Am I satisfied to settle for less than the best that God has for me? Am I eager to place myself at his disposal to be used wherever, whenever, and however he wants?" There are still nearly three billion people in the world who have never heard the gospel. Has God given you a skill or profession that would make you welcome in parts of the world where missionaries cannot enter? Open your life to God. Tell him you are available. As a result of a few simple inquiries you might find yourself setting off for a ministry in a needy land. Direct your prayers to God—"to him who is able to do immeasurably more than all we ask or imagine, according to his power that is at work within us" (Ephesians 3:20).

When Paul arrived on the island, he continued to display the character of a committed disciple. "Paul gathered a pile of brushwood and . . . put it on the fire"(Acts 28:3). I'm sure he was just as wet and tired as the others. But Paul's servant spirit would not let him rest. It was second nature for him to be on the lookout for ways of serving his fellow man. He followed the Lord of heaven who had freely humbled himself to become the servant of all.

When Paul placed the wood on the fire, a viper fastened itself to his hand. The response of the residents of the island to that incident is interesting. "When the islanders saw the snake hanging from his hand, they said to each other, 'This man must be a murderer; for though he escaped from the sea, Justice has not allowed him to live.' But Paul shook the snake off into the fire and suffered no ill effects. The people expected him to swell up or suddenly fall over dead, but after waiting a long time and seeing nothing unusual happen to him, they changed their minds and said he was a god" (Acts 28:4-6). In one breath they proclaimed him a murderer, and in the next they said he was a god.

Man will fail us with his fickle nature. One moment he shouts "He is a murderer!" the next, "He is a god!" One minute, "Hosannah!" the next, "Crucify him!" But if we place our confidence in God we will never be disappointed.

After relating the incident with the viper, Luke introduces us to "Publius, the chief official of the island" (Acts 28:7). Publius practiced a virtue that is fast disappearing in our world—hospitality. Many Third World nations put western countries to shame in this regard. But Christians must remember that hospitality is frequently taught in the Bible. Paul taught the Romans to "share with God's people who are in need. Practice hospitality" (Romans 12:13).

Paul instructed Timothy and Titus that hospitality is one of the requirements of leadership (see 1 Timothy 3:1-2 and Titus 1:8). Peter wrote that Christians should "offer hospitality to one another without grumbling" (1 Peter 4:9).

God did not overlook Publius' hospitality. He used Paul to heal his father and others on Malta who were diseased. The people showed their gratitude by supplying Paul and his companions with provisions for their journey. Paul's kindness to the islanders was reciprocated. Love begets love. Kindness begets kindness.

After resuming their journey, Paul and those traveling with him arrived in Italy. Luke describes their arrival in Rome: "The brothers there had heard that we were coming, and they traveled as far as the Forum of Appius and the Three Taverns to meet us. At the sight of these men Paul thanked God and was encouraged. When we got to Rome, Paul was allowed to live by himself, with a soldier to guard him" (Acts 28:15-16).

This happy scene reminds us that we need each other. We cannot go it alone in the Christian life. God never intended that we should. He placed us in a body. When we give ourselves to knowing God in a deeper way, by living in obedience to his word, in love and fellowship with our brothers and sisters in Christ, we experience the fullness of the Christian life. The Christian life and our growth in discipleship is not easy or a natural occurrence. Growing in our knowledge of God calls for commitment and discipline. Obeying the word of God calls for self-denial. Likewise, living in fellowship with our brothers and sisters in Christ requires a servant heart, patience, and accepting one another in love.

Three days after arriving in Rome, Paul called together the leaders of the Jews.

> My brothers, although I have done nothing against our people or against the customs of our ancestors, I was arrested in Jerusalem and handed over to the Romans. They examined me and wanted to release me, because I was not guilty of any crime deserving death. But when the Jews objected, I was compelled to appeal to Caesar—not that I had any charge to bring against my own people. For this reason I have asked to see you and talk with you. It is because of the hope of Israel that I am bound with this chain (Acts 28:17-20).

They replied, "We want to hear what your views are, for we know that people everywhere are talking against this sect" (Acts 28:22). The leaders' reply is a vivid testimony to the power of the gospel. It was the topic of conversation everywhere.

This is still true today. Wherever you go in the world you will find people discussing Jesus Christ. My wife and I were dining in the Cafe des Armures, the oldest cafe in Geneva, Switzerland. The cafe was crowded with its usual cosmopolitan clientele. On our right there was a table of eight Swiss businessmen. On our left was a stately-looking elderly couple. Next to them was a large group of young men and women clad in blue jeans and T-shirts. Along one wall there was a group of musicians and artists. In the center of the room sat a young English lady and her escort. They were talking loudly enough for us to overhear their conversation.

"Have you heard that in America there are many people called Evangelicals who believe the Bible?"

Her escort seemed startled and exclaimed, "No! Really?" "Yes," she said, "I've heard it's quite popular."

The clatter of dishes and the buzz of conversations in French swirling around us drowned out much of their conversation, but occasionally words like *Calvin, fundamentalist,* and *glorify God,* drifted our way. I was intrigued. There we were in a popular restaurant in Geneva near two Europeans who were discussing the Christian faith.

While my wife and I were traveling in Yugoslavia, we met a couple from Latin America. The woman soon discovered that Virginia was a Christian and asked if she could talk with her about her faith.

While flying from Sydney to Melbourne in Australia, I observed a portly, well-dressed businessman who was engrossed in a book. When the stewardess offered him a snack, he waved her away without looking up. I caught a glimpse of the book he was reading—*Born Again,* an account of the conversion of Charles Colson, one of those implicated in the Watergate scandal.

Never in my thirty years of witnessing for Christ have I found it easier to discuss the claims of Christ than it is today. The contemporary search for truth and reality is causing many to consider the Savior.

The Jewish leaders in Rome arranged for a meeting with Paul. "They arranged to meet Paul on a certain day, and came in even larger numbers to the place where he was staying. From morning till evening he explained and declared to them the kingdom of God and tried to convince them about Jesus from the Law of Moses and from the Prophets. Some were convinced by what he said, but others would not believe" (Acts 28:23-24).

For Paul, this was not a briefing session but an evangelistic opportunity. He persuaded them; he tried to convince them to place their faith in Jesus Christ. He was not there to pass on religious information. He wanted to start them on the road to heaven. He opened the word of God—both the Law and the Prophets—to them. He was in no hurry. The session lasted all day. He preached as long as they listened. Some believed, and some did not.

As witnesses for Christ, what can we do to help more people accept the gospel? I think there are four laws of harvesting which the Holy Spirit can use.

Prepare the soil. Whenever my wife gives her testimony, she pays tribute to her mother, who prayed faithfully for her. Although she did not know how to share the gospel personally with Virginia, she prayed.

Plant the seed. Unless the seed is sown, there will be no harvest. Quite often I am asked where God is working in our world. "Wherever his people are witnessing," is my answer. Unless we witness, there will be little fruit. Seed must be properly planted. Some is scattered on the earth's surface. Some is planted quite shallow, while other seed must be buried deep in the soil. However, to plant the seed of the word of God, there is always one important prerequisite: we must make the gospel clear. Present the gospel in an understandable manner.

Cultivate the crop. Naturally, many people do not turn to Christ in repentance and faith on their first hearing. We must continue our communication with them. Befriend them. Live the Christian life joyfully before them. Answer their questions if you can. Keep in touch socially and spiritually.

Reap the harvest. Give the person an opportunity to respond. Show them how to receive Christ and help them to do it. Today there are tens of thousands of people who are eager to get into step with God. If someone simply showed them how, they would respond immediately. Your next-door neighbor may well be one of those individuals.

For two years Paul ministered the gospel in Rome. "For two whole years Paul stayed there in his own rented house and welcomed all who came to see him. Boldly and without hindrance he preached the kingdom of God and taught about the Lord Jesus Christ" (Acts 28:30-31). Here we are reminded of Paul's two-fold ministry: preaching the gospel and teaching the converts. He wrote the Colossians, "We proclaim him, admonishing and teaching everyone with all wisdom, so that we may present everyone perfect in Christ. To this end I labor, struggling with all his energy, which so powerfully works in me" (Colossians 1:28-29).

Paul never swerved from his evangelistic efforts. A zeal for evangelism burned constantly in his spirit. He was convinced of the lostness of anyone without Christ. He was convinced of the power of the gospel.

On the other hand, Paul was also committed to helping each convert grow to full maturity in Christ so the convert, in turn, would take his place in the ranks of the evangelists and teachers. Paul's vision for multiplication of laborers burned brightly in his heart and mind. The last verse in the book of Acts shows Paul boldly continuing his ministry.

Many men lose their zeal toward the end of their lives. Their spiritual vision becomes blurred and they spend their last years in decline. But not Paul. As long as he had breath he kept at the job the Lord had given him. He was convinced the world could be reached—not by a select few, but by masses of laymen trained to be laborers for Christ. He applied himself to that task to the very end.

The doctrine of the kingdom is a liberating truth that greatly widens our horizons. All believers are members of God's kingdom, a kingdom that takes a variety of forms and structures on earth. It is exhilarating to think of the day when we will all meet around the throne of God. There will be men and women from every tongue, tribe, people, and nation. All barriers will be removed; everything that divides us will be gone. We will truly be one in the Lord.

SUMMARY:

So ends the Acts of the Apostles, a book filled with challenge, instruction, hope, and encouragement. May the lessons of this book so grip our lives that we in turn will take our places among those who turned the world upside down. Like them, may we become disciples who are—

- committed to the Lordship of Jesus Christ;
- reliant on the power of God;
- guided by the Holy Spirit;
- absorbed in evangelizing the lost;
- devoted to building the saved;

that in everything God might be further glorified through us.

As we have observed in our study of Acts, the first century believers were urgently involved in the task of taking the gospel throughout the world in the power of the Holy Spirit. As the apostles gave themselves to witnessing for Christ, establishing believers, and training laborers and leaders, God blessed their ministry. Men like Peter and John modeled a commitment to prayer, flexibility, compassion, and a loving witness. Some, like Stephen, were martyred and died proclaiming the gospel of Christ's love. The missionary partnership of Paul and Barnabas exemplified the teamwork that characterized the life and witness of the growing community of believers.

Although the young church experienced fierce persecution, the believers overcame discouragement, built a tough faith, and maintained a sacrificial lifestyle. While they experienced some disagreements over methods and doctrine, they preserved the fundamentals of the faith and persevered in God's work.

As the church advanced with the gospel, laymen and women were trained to witness, equipped with a message, committed to the vision of spreading the gospel throughout the world, and humbly yielded themselves to God's will for their lives.

If we would have the same impact today, we too must see things as Jesus does, have a missionary mentality, and use all of our available resources in the furtherance of the Great Commission.

"Therefore, since we are surrounded by such a great cloud of witnesses, let us throw off everything that hinders and the sin that so easily entangles, and let us run with perseverance the race marked out for us. Let us fix our eyes on Jesus, the author and perfecter of our faith"
(Hebrews 12:1-2).